WHY YOUR MAN CHEATS... WITH ME!

SECRETS MEN PAY TO TELL A DOMINATRIX

ARADIA RAIN

Why Your Man Cheats… with ME!

Secrets Men Pay to Tell a Dominatrix™

DEWY DAZE
PUBLISHING

DISCLAIMER & DISCLOSURE

Privacy and Narrative Truth

This book contains stories and scenarios inspired by real-life experiences, observations, and encounters. Names, identifying details, and specific circumstances have been changed or fictionalized to protect the privacy of individuals and honor confidentiality. These accounts are intended to convey emotional truth and thematic insight, rather than serve as exact documentation of real events. Any resemblance to actual persons, living or dead, or actual events is purely coincidental. In many instances, characters and scenarios are **composites** of multiple experiences, crafted to represent archetypes rather than specific individuals.

Consent and Legality

All fictionalized sessions and session stories described or referenced in this book involve consenting adults and are conducted in a manner that prioritizes physical, emotional, and psychological safety. These fantasy elements are used for emotional exploration. This work is not to be confused with illegal activity; it is a professional framework of lawful and consensual adult-only behavior. BDSM practices demand communication, consent, and mutual respect.

Mature Content Warning

The content explores adult themes, including sexuality, BDSM, power dynamics, infidelity, and emotional complexities. It is intended for mature audiences who are comfortable exploring sensitive and sometimes challenging topics. This material discusses consensual BDSM activities, including forms of consensual torture, which are intended for informed, consenting adults only. All activities described should be approached with mutual respect, clear communication, and adherence to safe, sane, and consensual (SSC) practices.

Professional Boundaries

This book is designed to inform, provoke thought, and foster understanding. It is not a substitute for professional guidance, counseling, therapy, or legal advice. It is not intended to provide specific training, mentoring, or advice. The content is based on the author's personal experiences and opinions and should not be considered a directive or instruction for any course of action or play experience.

Assumption of Risk

Any actions you take based on the information in this book are strictly at your own risk. Participation in any activities, exercises, or strategies discussed in this book is entirely voluntary. The author and publisher disclaim any responsibility or liability for any damages, losses, or negative consequences arising from the use or misuse of the information contained herein.

Personal Discretion

Readers are encouraged to approach the material with an open mind and personal discretion. If you find any subject matter triggering or uncomfortable, please seek appropriate support. The author and publisher make no representations regarding the accuracy or suitability of the information for any specific individual.

By reading this book, you acknowledge that you have read, understood, and accepted the terms of this disclaimer.

UNLOCK YOUR CURIOSITIES

DEDICATION

I dedicate this book to my son.
May you explore the world honestly and freely.
You are and will always be my greatest gift.
I love you… evermore.

"In my world, men pay to tell the secrets they can't tell you:
what it feels like to be vulnerable without consequence."
— The Professional Dominatrix

INVITATION

Cheaters don't just cheat. They often premeditate. They are driven by the search for something more than secrecy. When these men are finally ready to act, they come to me: The Professional Dominatrix.

Welcome to my space, where power is honored, boundaries are sacred, and trust is everything. Whether clients cheat or don't, honesty and transparency are required.

This book is for anyone who has ever been drawn to explore, or who has ever wondered, suspected, or been hurt. It's here to give language to the questions that stay with us. Whether you are curious, seeking to understand someone you love, or interested in observing my intimate spaces, I invite you into a place where desire meets control.

Please know: I'm not your enemy. I'm your evidence.

When?
Where?
Why?
How?
And what he says about you!

Sure, you might have your assumptions about me. Maybe you think I'm a bitch, a man-stealer, an enabler, an abuser, a little unhinged, or just a common whore. I get it! Those labels come easily when a woman steps into taboo territory.

But what if this isn't just about me? What if it's about you, too? Before forming an opinion, consider what your partner may already have decided.

Don't hate the player: the woman he invited into his secret world. Hate the games that made space for me, betrayals born from a lack of respect, honesty, transparency, and communication.

I ask myself: *Am I the betrayer? Am I betraying these men who have entrusted their secrets to me by telling you everything?* I am not. I am, however, an experienced, compassionate professional dedicated to helping bridge gaps within human connections.

Over the years, many men have shared something with me: they wish I could help explain their needs, desires, and fantasies to their significant others. This book is one possible answer to that request, an attempt to put words to what has been hidden and offer understanding to those who deserve the truth.

The hard truth: Not all of my clients are cheaters, but about 90% of my male clients are in committed relationships they believe to be monogamous. While consensual non-monogamy exists, many visit a Professional Dominatrix without their partners' knowledge or consent.

What you're about to read isn't just about desire or betrayal. I'm examining the quiet complexities of human relationships, and the truths most people are too afraid to say out loud.

With over two decades of experience as a Dominatrix, I'm ready to share what I've learned: the facts behind why men cheat on their partners with me, their true motivations, and the private confessions they can't or won't share. I'll tell you, in their own words, what they say to me and the things they say about you.

As the keeper of secrets, I'll open the Dungeon door to the worlds they slip into. These are worlds where desires, needs, and fantasies are fulfilled: BDSM, Kink, Fetish, and more. Through these consensual encounters, our sessions reveal far more than physical gratification; they expose deeper emotional longings, unspoken vulnerabilities, and the craving for connection and authenticity that so many relationships quietly lack.

Throughout these pages, I reflect on the values I've seen tested the most: respect, honesty, transparency, accountability, and trust, alongside the essential skills of effective communication and active listening. These aren't lofty ideals; they're foundational tools. Without them, relationships collapse like homes built on cracked foundations.

I'm in a rare position to show you what most never see. My approach is bold, raw, and unapologetically real. I don't shy away from emotional depth because truth matters more than comfort. Especially when the cost of silence is too great. Honesty stirs things up, but if that's what it takes to help people see clearly and understand what's possibly being buried, then let's go there.

This book's perspective may feel intense and that intensity is purposeful. It's designed to inspire insight and reflection. My goal isn't to enable cheating, but to expose the psychological disconnections that lead people to seek intimacy outside their relationships. It challenges the stigma that silences honest conversations about need, emotional honesty, and desires. I hope to encourage you to think and question. Ultimately, I hope to help you see the signs, find your voice, uncover the truth, and, above all, protect your soul.

I'm not a therapist, psychologist, or doctor. That said, I am well-acquainted with the unspoken truths men reveal and don't reveal when they think no one is listening. I'm certainly not here to steal, fuck, or fall in love with your man. I've simply been the fortunate recipient of valuable, vulnerable insight from men brave enough to explore themselves in my world.

I will help you gain a deeper understanding of who the Dominatrix really is and why he chooses me to give him a *good old-fashioned spanking*. Behind every act of control lies a search for truth, and behind every confession, a desire to be known.

You're about to become the "silent observer" inside my fantasy session stories, where I'll take you deep into his kinky imagination.

Imagine this: the sharp intake of his breath as he confronts himself behind dishonest facades. The scent of a woman lingers in the air, music conducting the pace, while the dim glow of candlelight casts his shadow against a blackened brick wall. A first, nervous laugh from a man who has finally succumbed to his urges.

This is where secrets aren't hinted at. They're exposed. Where sensation and truth share the same skin.

I know that what I'm about to share **can** be difficult to read. Whether it stirs up strong emotions or simply challenges what you thought you knew, I ask only that you stay open. The fact that your man might be my submissive, subby boy, slut, little bitch, or fetish fiend—begging at my feet—could potentially disappoint, disgust, or anger you. You may also experience feelings of inadequacy, concern, curiosity, insecurities, judgment, sadness, confusion, humor, excitement, or a big WTF!

I want to pull you out of the dark and into a world of clarity, understanding, and reality. Knowledge brings awareness, and awareness often leads us to the edge of discomfort, where growth begins. From there, we gain new perspectives, deeper understanding, and the ability to relate, trust, and build more open and transparent relationships. We need compassion and empathy to turn insight into connection. We also need the truth.

For those of you turning these pages, I'm right here with you. I'm not just telling you a story; I am supporting and standing beside you in it. As you read, think of me as a voice in the room that refuses to let you settle for less than you deserve.

Use my book as a gateway to start your own journey of effective communication and unlock the truth inside your relationships. Keep in mind, what you are about to read blends real experiences with storytelling to protect privacy while revealing deeper truths.

You'll notice I may circle back from time to time. That's intentional. Sometimes we need to hear the truth from a few different angles before it really lands.

Yes, women cheat too! While this book is written about the cheating man, some patterns and insights may also resonate with women who have cheated. My primary focus, however, is on men stepping outside their relationships with a Professional Dominatrix.

In the twilight of truth, caged secrets are set free!

It is time for you to find out why your partner *could be* cheating on YOU.

With ME.

Here's your key to the Dungeon:

There is a massive difference between
sharing a secret and *confessing* one.

Paying for the privilege creates a contract:

"I give you this truth, you hold it, but
you cannot use it against me."

That is the "without consequence" part.
For many men, this is the only place they feel
safe being honest and transparent.

You have now officially become "The Fly on the Wall." 

RAINA MARKS

Raina Marks has never doubted her man. Not even for a second.

Trust, loyalty, and a mutual rhythm forged over years were the cornerstones of their marriage. She knew him, or at least she thought she did.

It started out as an ordinary afternoon. She ducked into a cozy little corner bookstore for a bit of quiet browsing and maybe a new romance novel to devour over wine later that night. But fate had other plans.

A bold, black title stopped her in her tracks.

"Why Your Man Cheats… with ME! *Secrets Men Pay to Tell a Dominatrix"*

It hit her like a slap wrapped in silk. She stared at it, almost laughing, almost offended, but more than anything… intrigued.

She flipped the book over to read the back, trying to keep her face neutral as her heart started picking up speed. Each line of the summary cut a little deeper than the last, pressing against something raw and unacknowledged: *like the way he now takes his phone into the bathroom every time he showers.* She could feel the questions rising, uninvited and unrelenting.

Wait, who are these men? Are they normal? Married? Happy? Are they the kind who tuck their kids in at night and sneak off to secret hotel rooms the next day? Is my husband one of them? Of course not! My husband isn't that guy. He's never been that guy.

And yet, she was still standing there. Still holding the book. Still feeling the twist in her chest.

Great. Exactly what I needed the day before he jets off on a last-minute overnight trip to New York.

She looked back down at the cover. The title seemed to speak straight to her, as if the woman who wrote it were daring her to look deeper.

Curiosity is a risk. But I'm already holding the shovel. And if this man I call my husband is cheating on me, you'd best believe I'll be using it to dig a six-foot hole in our backyard.

Without hesitation, she headed straight for the counter. *I'm buying the damn book!*

It's not her usual Sunday morning read, but with her man heading out of town, having the house to herself feels like the perfect time to dive into the new book.

Raina affectionately kisses her husband goodbye at the door. Her arms embrace around his body for one more squeeze. "Have a safe trip. Text me when you get there. Love you!"

Closing the door, she leans against the streaked oak for a second too long. The silence settles around her shoulders like a shawl, familiar, but heavier than usual. *He's a really good man.* But even her most confident thoughts come with an aftertaste. *Cheat. Would he?*

Hating that this thought has dared to cross her mind, she frowns. *He has been spending extra time alone in his office lately:* the soft click of the door locking behind him echoing in her mind.

The Arizona sun, already warming up the water to a provocative 69°, entices her mood, and a poolside rendezvous is exactly what Raina needs.

She slips into a cheeky black one-piece, the seamless bathing suit that supports her 5'6" frame in all the right places. Tying her long brown hair into a messy bun, she adds her sun-shielding crown and covers herself with a black sarong. With her aviator sunglasses and towel in hand, she heads out to the pool.

Pausing once more before heading outside, Raina adjusts the coffee table books by a fraction. It's a small ritual. She loves for everything to feel "just right" before she can let herself relax. Especially when she is alone. Even more so when she's about to open something she can't quite explain.

Settling into her lounge chair, she studies the cover of the book before rippling the water with a loud shriek. "What the fuck is a Dominatrix? And why would my man want one?"

Pondering, she picks at the corner of the first page of the book and sips her overly iced mocha. *Well, here we go!*

CHAPTER 1

BIGGER! BETTER! BRAINGASM!

In search of the ultimate, ULTIMATE. Bigger! Better! Braingasm… *Gasm!*

Hits your man's imagination like a tsunami of cum.

He seeks someone to guide him into a headspace that both erotically and authentically fulfills his needs and fantasies. Someone who will accept him fully and delve into the deep, dark corridors of his mind. His imagination knows no bounds, and his research has paid off. He's found a Dungeon… and a Professional Dominatrix.

I am a Mistress of sensuality, desire, and allure. Behind my beguiling cloak lies a woman of depth and complexity: an intoxicating blend of confidence, strength, and passion. Spinning my intricate web, I weave threads of awareness, compassion, honesty, and safety into a tapestry of irresistible seduction. It's a creation of grace, intention, and razor-sharp precision.

I sense the hum of his energy as he drifts closer to my space. He comes, *willingly*. My openness to hear his longings draws him deeper into my tangled web.

Every move is intentional—each glance, word, and pause designed to tempt and conquer. By offering encounters he will find hard to live without, his eagerness awakens. He finds himself grounded in my safe, sane, and harmoniously aligned realm. It is here that the space between his secrets and his urges finally closes, turning private cravings into tangible, breathless reality.

How is it possible that I… do not have to fuck, suck, or stroke off your man to fulfill his fanciful cravings? That's because it's a connection that goes beyond the physical.

In my world, consensual BDSM is built on honesty, transparency, negotiation, and trust. It thrives on active listening, compassion, bravery, and the absence of judgment. These are some of the foundations of exploration, where reverie becomes reality, shared by consenting adults.

Would you know he's here with me? Would you even suspect he's cheating? Probably not.

I watch hundreds of men come and go, each seeking escape. A revolving door of repression: the married, the single, and the in-between. Strangers and familiar faces alike, all pleading for what I offer: a fleeting moment to hold onto, until their minds begin cranking the wheel of desires once more.

I am a reader of the unspoken. The witness. The rewriter of fantasy. Their impulses become my next adventure, and I savor being the Dominant director.

The mind. The imagination. Crucial. Demanding. Enticing. Desire begins in the mind. It's there where I churn their senses. Sensually crafting interludes, wickedly plucking at whims, and mysteriously weaving them into thought. I fuck a man's mind, good and hard. With pleasure.

My clients are free to speak about every fantasy and desire that stirs within. With enthusiasm, I reassure my new playthings, they are no longer confined to a dreamy state of make-believe. I am here!

No two men are the same. Each exists on a dynamic scale of mental, physical, and emotional needs. My goal is to manipulate that scale with mastery, determining the next steps to satisfy him within the boundless dimensions of eroticism.

Is an intense *Braingasm* really that powerful? Can a safe space, paired with honest communication and understanding, unlock a man's secrets? Can their minds, heart, and desires—psychological, emotional, erotic—lead them to deeper pleasure and release?

The answer is yes. Nearly every single time.

These are the realities that get them to my private domain and usually stop them from leaving. Ultimately, they're what open up their wallets.

And, just like that, I am pulling out my bag of tricks.

They know it's go time, and they are ready to **pay to play**!

Whether you believe BDSM, Kink, and Fetish are right or wrong, one fact remains clear: they have always been and will continue to be powerful forces that draw people in. It is elemental and deeply human, regardless of judgment.

If you get rid of the crawly infestations, I disappear. However, if you don't address the infestation problems, the wandering critters will get trapped in my threads of satisfaction.

Spiders don't feed inside empty webs.

REFLECTION: RAINA MARKS

Letting the words settle in, Raina rests the book face down on her stomach. *The Dominatrix doesn't seem to just ask the questions; she uncovers the answers and peels them straight off the bone. Yikes!*

What have I gotten myself into? This doesn't feel like it's going to be a casual read. This feels like trespassing into something sacred or even a bit dangerously intense.

She adjusts herself, her mind now swirling with fascination, resistance, and anticipation. *No surprise. I've seen the lengths some men will go to keep secrets from their partners. I hate when things are hidden!*

Rising up and out of the chair, she heads to the kitchen. Feeling quiet, but charged, she pulls out the perfect ingredients and begins preparing a charcuterie platter. As she ponders the intricacies of her thoughts, her eyes trace the contours of the spread. She finds herself meticulously aligning the peppered salami and tucking the grapes into perfect little clusters. It's as if by creating a flawless, artful landscape on a ceramic plate, she could somehow organize the chaos unfolding in her mind.

Is my man trapped in her threads of satisfaction? Have I been effectively communicating with him?

She opens a drawer and grabs a small silver cheese knife. *Have we ever really talked about his fantasies? What about mine? What are my fantasies? Do I even know?*

The questions hit harder than expected. Not just because of what they are, but because she realizes how long they've gone unspoken.

With her charcuterie masterpiece balanced on one palm and a tall glass of sparkling water in the other, she returns poolside.

Exhaling while she reclines, the sun warms her skin and her mind swirls with chatter. *Pay to Play!* A harsh exhalation bursts from her. "I cannot!"

Angry at the thought: *I swear, if my husband is one of these cheating bastards, I am going to lose my shit! I don't need everything I ever believed in to collapse. And what's the deal with the pricey gifts he's been giving me lately?*

A few choice words come to mind, but Raina is instantly distracted.

Looking into the living room window, she revisits past memories. Behind the glass, nothing seems hidden within those walls that hold a thousand tiny moments. Their mutual agreements on their interior design, holiday gatherings, long talks into the night, and the many promises made between two people very much in love.

The space holds their story. But not the whole truth.

This is like stepping through the keyhole into a world many people won't talk about. And now I'm here, stuck between judgment and curiosity, unable to look away. Let's see what secrets the Dungeon door is about to reveal next…

Heart pounding and adrenaline rushing, the words spill out of her mouth. "This isn't a gossip rag, it's a psychological autopsy. Give it to me, girl! Tell me everything. I need to know the truth."

CHAPTER 2

THE MECHANIC
INTERVIEW PART 2

Wait, hold up!

Do you think this is just a BDSM sex game? Or could it be more?

What if these acts are psychological tools that reach into the core of our existence, rather than being mere moments of mindless indulgence?

I interviewed the following man to tell me more about his kinky evolution, where they came from, and his years of experience inside the worlds of BDSM, Kink, and Fetish.

"The Mechanic"—he likes it racy, and I experience a moment with my client I did not see coming.

Here is what he had to say.

The Interview: The Mechanic – Part 2: The Ending

I watched as his face became flushed. Slightly intolerant of his growing emotional discomfort, his body began to shift. The hands of a mechanic, folding into themselves. Quickly, I reached out my hand to grab the emotions that he was kneading into his palms. His leg bounced nervously, and I wondered if I was about to have a runner.

Why are you still scheduling sessions with me after all these years?

"I have a lot of issues to deal with. Sometimes these challenges cause me a lot of pain. Coming to you is my escape. I can step away from my problems when I'm with you."

Why do you feel this pain?

"I have had a lot of relationships. These relationships have caused me a lot of pain, and I have found it very difficult to get over them. My marriage ended because I found my wife in bed with my best friend. I was devastated and heartbroken. I have tried really hard to forget about what she did to me, but I can't. I don't think the pain is ever going to fully go away. Not just because of the cheating, but for so many reasons."

What does our time together do for you?

"You help me with the problems and pain I feel. Because I have a wall up, I am not able to fall in love with women that easily. Before the heartbreak, I could fall in love quickly. I can have great sex with women. When I am with them, I still feel the pain. I can't put down my wall. When I come to see you, all my problems feel like they go away. You understand me. I can talk to you. The minute I shut the door behind me; my pain goes away."

Tears began to fill his eyes as he uncomfortably tried to restrain the first teardrop. His vulnerability exposed a side of him that I hadn't previously fully uncovered.

I see you are getting emotional. Do you want to go on?

"I don't know about you, but men don't have someone to go to. We don't have anywhere to go. There is nowhere. No one. We don't have anyone we can talk to about all this stuff. I even tried going to a therapist, and that didn't help. You help me. You're the reason I can have moments where I release my pain."

As we sat there, he continued to talk about the pressures of being a man and what his life was like growing up. As an adopted boy, he grew up in a religious household. He was raised on old-school traditions and values. His adopted parents put a lot of pressure on him to become successful and to continue his religious path. He openly verbalized how he often feels guilty for engaging in his fetishistic ways that clearly go against his family's values. It is apparent that he is torn between satisfying his needs and doing what he was taught is morally correct.

Now an older man, he's frustrated. He wants a partner who shares his values and accepts his kink. He feels defeated by a modern dating world that typically expects high-end dinners and "fancy coffees" but has no room for a man with financial limitations and a complex inner life.

It was getting late, and it was time to stop the interview. However, I had one more question for him.

If you could add any other information to our interview today, what would you say?

"A lot of men think about suicide. If they are unable to find the right outlet, that is when death might be their answer."

His voice changed. The words gripped me. My own tears let him know he wasn't alone. I had to ask:

Have you thought about suicide?

"Yes!"

Honestly, I didn't expect to hear that from him. I took a deep breath, centered myself, and said the only thing that felt true:

"I would rather my man cheat on me with a Professional Dominatrix than hold a gun to his head."

What does it mean to be human? To have compassion for the parts of us that aren't always "socially acceptable"?

- Pain vs. Healing
- Sanity vs. Insanity
- Alone vs. Supported
- Life vs. Death

The importance of mental support cannot be overstated. Battling with everyday challenges is tough, and having a strong support system is essential for promoting overall wellness. We function best when we honor *every* part of who we are, even the parts that scare us. You don't need to understand BDSM to feel the power of human longing. We all want to be seen. We all want to belong.

Supportive connections carry us through the weight of everyday challenges. My goal has always been to offer a sanctuary, a place where the truth can be spoken without judgment. I don't want my clients to feel unseen or alone.

Standing behind that Dungeon door, I am reverent. Because in those moments of vulnerability, we aren't just doing a "session." We are two people sharing something much deeper than a physically charged encounter. We are choosing the weight of being known. It's the one thing money can't command, but it's one thing they find with me.

See Chapter 27: **The Mechanic Continued — The Interview, Part 1: "Let's Start at the Beginning!"** for the full interview.

If you or someone you know is struggling with thoughts of suicide, help is available. In the U.S., call or text the Suicide & Crisis Lifeline at **988** *for free, confidential support 24/7.*

REFLECTION: RAINA MARKS

Does my man feel alone? Do we have a safe space where we can be honest with each other, the kind of unfiltered honesty that reaches beneath the surface?

I know everyone has something they're carrying. We never truly know what the person next to us is going through. Life can be very challenging for so many reasons. It breaks my heart to think how many people suffer silently, trapped inside their minds.

The thought of suicide flitted through her brain, and she shuddered at the idea.

Disturbing, but realistic. I personally know several men who bottle up their emotions and keep secrets. They keep everything inside until they eventually explode. It is not far-fetched to believe that countless people struggle with thoughts like these in silence or act on them in devastating ways.

I would feel horrible if my husband were wrestling with something I knew nothing about. Would he tell me on his own, or be honest if I asked? I hope he isn't too proud and guarded to speak up.

A chill penetrates her skin, and it has nothing to do with the breeze. *I have always assumed he was satisfied because our sex life is active, what I would consider normal. I find it interesting that I equate romance, frequent sex, and affection with a healthy sexy life. Maybe it is healthy, but now I'm thinking there could be more he is not telling me.*

Reading this makes me reconsider everything I thought I knew. Every look, every gesture, and every move he makes? I want the information, but part of me wonders if this is too much. What if my man is a cheater or wants to cheat? Then what? I don't need to worry about that right now; he has not given me reason to be suspicious. But…

There is a quiet ache inside her. Not quite fear, not quite unease, something else. *I want to believe I would be open if he ever tried to tell me his secrets. But could I truly listen without judgment? I don't know! I'm not in the moment, so who knows.*

Taking a deep breath, she opened the book again. *I may be unsettled by what I read, but I'm willing to endure feeling uneasy for the sake of deeper clarity.*

Her curiosity had already been piqued, and now she was committed. Raina stared at the next page, which felt like staring into the abyss.

CHAPTER 3

WHY HE CHEATS: UNCOVERING THE CHEAT CODE

Is it "really" even cheating if he steps out of the relationship with a Professional Dominatrix?

Cheating: *The act of being dishonest in a committed relationship to gain self-gratification. This can involve emotional, kinky, or sexual engagement with someone outside the relationship without the knowledge or consent of one's partner. It is a betrayal of trust that disregards agreed-upon boundaries and undermines the integrity of the relationship.*

Some people see what I do as "enabling" the cheater. Others may see it as a form of therapy, fantasy time, or a safe release. The truth may lie somewhere in between—in the shadows, the silence, and what's left unsaid.

In my world, a session with a Dominatrix isn't an affair; it's a confidential transaction. It's an experience with clear boundaries, no emotional strings, and a fantasy with an end time. To some men, it feels like a private, controlled escape, not a betrayal.

The breach isn't just the act. It's the secrecy, the lie by omission, and the energy and truth he is giving to someone else instead of you.

Cheating isn't one-size-fits-all. It's a complex, multifaceted issue that varies from relationship to relationship. The only definition that truly matters is the one you and your partner agree on.

It's crucial to understand these nuances:

- **Physical Cheating:** This is what many people think of first—sex outside the relationship. We're talking kissing, touching, oral, penetration, or any kind of physical intimacy meant to satisfy or turn someone on.

- **Emotional Cheating:** This is about where you're giving your heart—that part of the brain we like to call "the soul." It's the late-night texts when you're vulnerable, the secrets you share, and the dreams you confide in someone else instead of the person you're supposed to be building a life with. You might not be crossing a physical line, but if you're turning to someone else for the comfort and connection that should belong to your partner, that's where the real betrayal starts.

- **Digital/Online Cheating:** Sliding into DMs. Sexting. Sending nudes. Watching cam girls. Keeping secret profiles. You don't have to meet in person to violate trust.

- **Pornography & Kink Spaces:** Some see porn, cam shows, or dropping cash on a Dominatrix as a solo adventure. Others see it as total betrayal. The real rule? Whatever you and your partner agree on. Honesty is the only policy that keeps things from blowing up.

- **Micro-cheating:** "Emotional little nibbles." Flirty texts, lingering eye contact, or suddenly becoming an "open book" with a stranger. And let's not forget the classic "Who, me? I'm totally single," when you're definitely not.

People are always trying to figure themselves out. This journey of self-discovery is a lifelong process of questioning and re-evaluating. But imagine if there were someone who could help you uncover these answers and guide you toward fulfilling your deepest desires.

The cheater steps outside to satisfy mental, emotional, and physical needs. He cheats with a Dominatrix because he's found someone with whom he can be completely transparent. Someone who doesn't judge him.

Before most men cross lines, before they schedule a session or knock on the Dungeon door, something stirs beneath the surface. They silence themselves. From a young age, many men are taught to tuck away their emotions. Vulnerability feels risky, pain feels weak, and desire feels dangerous. Speaking their truth often invites mockery, dismissal, or a breakup. In many cases, it isn't strangers they fear most. It's the women in their lives.

Too many men have been burned after opening up, their honesty weaponized in arguments or used as proof that something is "wrong" with them. They retreat into themselves to protect what they feel most deeply. They compartmentalize, protecting their egos while longing for a sense of safety they rarely experience. With me, they can let go.

People cling to secrets not just to protect themselves, but to avoid the agony of old wounds being exposed all over again. Cheating begins long before the act, when fear and silence push out honesty. Men don't always hide things out of malice; sometimes, it's simply a way of surviving internally. When the temptation gets too strong, secrecy can make giving in feel like the only way out.

Of course, not every cheater is searching for relief. Some are just selfish, cruel, entitled men who do what they want and don't care who gets hurt. Period.

By the time a man reaches his desperation point, the fantasy has often already taken hold. Obsessive thoughts loop endlessly. Maybe it starts with porn, a niche forum, or a kinky magazine. Curiosity builds until he finds ME. The fantasy transforms from imagination to reality: one message, one appointment, one *yes* away.

In my space, he is free to explore safely and openly. There are no traps, no strings, and no guilt. Some come once and move on; others return to build a connection of trust and exploration. The power dynamic may be my offering, but the choice is always theirs.

This freedom and honesty can highlight what's missing elsewhere. Inside the relationship, the emotional cheating may have already happened. Betrayal begins when the intimacy fractures, when he hides instead of communicating, and when he stops bringing his full self to the table but performs as if nothing's changed. He has built an inner world you are no longer invited into.

Most men aren't proud of being cheaters. Many fully understand that stepping outside the relationship without consent is wrong. Importantly, many of my clients have told me they would love nothing more than to include *you* in their fantasy playtime. They dream of you holding the reins. They often love the sexual experiences they have with their partners, but it isn't always enough.

So, why do they come to cheat in my world?

Some of my clients want more than their partners are willing or able to give. Others claim they don't enjoy intimacy with their partners at all, viewing all acts as a chore. Then there are the men who suffocate in shame, choosing deceit because they lack the courage to be transparent. And finally, there's the narcissistic prick who doesn't give a fuck about anyone but himself. However, 99.9% believe pursuing other options is the only path to personal fulfillment.

It's unfortunate that societal and internalized barriers get in the way of what could be powerful, connective experiences. These men are searching for that elusive "something," but they are blocked by fear, shame, or indifference. Inevitably, they give up and they give in.

They give up fighting for fidelity because they don't see a way to effectively communicate their kinky needs without being embarrassed or shunned. In some cases, they *have* tried to communicate, only to be met with complete disgust. These reactions dissolve the hope of ever including their partner in their "something more."

Other partners agree to fulfill fantasies, only to pull the "just kidding" clause. When the play never transpires or abruptly stops without explanation, the man becomes resentful. He retreats back into his mind, draws the blinds of secrecy, and opts to outsource your position.

Or, he loves his partner, but she simply isn't part of his kinky fantasy world.

Let me reiterate: there are also men who are callous, self-serving jerks. Nothing phases them. They give in, driven by a relentless need to satisfy urges they cannot ignore. Justifying their actions becomes second nature. They follow through with the hunt because they see no alternative, unwilling to live without experiencing their inner hungers. Intimate commitments fade, and they look the other way.

This exemplifies how powerful the mind can be when a man becomes consumed by desire.

They act! They are on the move like prowlers—eager, desperate, ravenous. They surrender the wrestling match of shame and fear and bring it face down on the Dungeon floor. They overcome like sexual warriors, swinging their fleshy swords as if they are on their way to conquer **World War Climax**.

Once they get a taste of what I offer, the escape becomes a necessary part of their lives.

And here's what I believe: When human beings open up, it's not weakness. It's bravery. Typically, people are not asking to be fixed; they are asking to be honored. Regardless of the circumstances.

Individuals need to be courageous enough to ask the difficult questions if they want to uncover the truths their partners are guarding. Without this dialogue, men may mislead or outright lie. They will keep you in the dark, offering just enough information to hook you. **To be blunt: you might ask and they might still lie, but at least they know you're paying attention and reading between the lines.**

I think most women want to ask the right questions, but they might not know the language or how to react when the answers surprise them. They might also fear uncovering something they can't unsee. The silence isn't always indifference; sometimes, it's just not knowing how to find the words to reach him.

Whether it's day one or day twenty-one, ask the questions! I'd ask them before getting sexually or emotionally involved. I would be straightforward. I'd probe his brain until I had a clear sense of who I was dealing with. Be curious. Investigate. **Get the data!**

Examples of questions to ask men:

- Do you feel comfortable sharing more information about yourself?
- Can you tell me what a relationship with you looks like for the other person?
- What does a healthy relationship look like to you?
- Can you define love for me?
- When was your last relationship? How long?
- What's something many people don't know about you?
- What are your non-negotiables in a relationship?
- What does intimacy mean to you emotionally, mentally, and physically?
- Do you believe you know how to effectively communicate?
- Have you ever been 100% transparent and honest with past partners about your sexual needs and desires?
- What's something you are really passionate about, and why?
- Are you romantic? Can I get an example?
- How do you handle stress and conflict?

- Have you ever had your heart broken?
- Don't you think it is only fair that you tell me upfront exactly who you are sexually?
- How do you typically define your sexuality or who you are attracted to?
- Have you ever been attracted to the same sex or does attraction feel fluid for you?
- Have you had sexual relations or sex with the opposite sex?
- Have you fantasized about being with another man?
- Have you had sexual relations of any kind with a man?
- What do you think about when you masturbate?
- How often do you masturbate?
- Do you have a specific scenario you think about every time you masturbate?
- Are you more introverted or extroverted?
- Do social norms affect you sexually?
- Have you ever told a woman your sexual fantasies and been rejected?
- What types of communication forms work best for you?
- How many times a week do you typically like to have sex?
- Have you ever tried BDSM?
- If you haven't tried BDSM, would you like to try any kinky activities?
- Are you kinky? If yes, what do you like?
- Do you have any fetishes? Have you ever had a fetish?
- Did you have something happen to you in your childhood that you fantasize about now as an adult?
- When you research on the computer, what type of sexual topics do you investigate?
- Have you ever cheated on your partner?
- Have you ever been cheated on?
- How do you define cheating?
- Do you consider emotional cheating to be truly cheating?
- What defines cheating on a partner on social media?

- Have you ever been with a prostitute?
- Would you pay a prostitute for sex? Or anyone for sexual gratification?
- Do you frequently go to strip clubs?
- How often do you watch pornographic material?
- What is your favorite type of pornography to watch?
- Do you watch pornography on your phone? Where?
- Have you watched pornography with past lovers?
- What dating apps do you use?
- Have you ever used a dating app?
- Do you use dating apps to get sex?
- Are you addicted to sex?
- Do you have any sexually transmitted diseases?
- Have you ever had a sexually transmitted disease?
- Will you get tested for sexually transmitted diseases before we have sex?
- Have you ever visited a Professional Dominatrix?
- Do you think it would be cheating if you went for a session with a Professional Dominatrix?
- What's the wildest sex you have ever experienced?
- Are you into anal sex or play? On yourself or with a partner?
- What are your favorite sex positions?
- Do you play with sex toys? On yourself or others?
- Do you want to have threesomes, or have you had threesomes?
- Are you in any way into sharing your partner with others? Swinging?
- What are your bedroom secrets?
- What gets you the most sexually aroused?
- Tell me a couple of your fantasies.
- Are you into polyamory?
- Have you ever lied to a partner about your sexual desires?
- Have you ever faked an orgasm?
- Are you on any medications for erectile dysfunction? Have you ever taken any of these pills just for fun?

- Are you embarrassed or too shy to admit your sexual fantasies or desires?
- Would you ever cheat on your partner *just* to satisfy your sexual needs?
- If I can't satisfy your sexual needs and fantasies, what does this look like for me in the relationship with you?

Questions help you piece together the mind of your "potential partner" or "potential cheater." Open the dialogue and create a safe space to get to the bottom of who these men represent themselves to be. Dare to go there!

But first, ask yourself the same questions. You can't ask what you're not willing to answer yourself.

When you avoid these necessary conversations, you're not just skipping over awkward moments, you're putting yourself, your potential relationships, and any current partnerships at risk of failure.

Accountability has no gender. Avoid it, and the consequences will speak for themselves.

Don't be surprised when your man becomes one of my men.

REFLECTION: RAINA MARKS

Luckily, it's early spring in Scottsdale, and the cement around the pool hasn't yet warmed to its usual blistering temperature.

Pacing back and forth, Raina can't help but wonder: *Would I know if my husband is cheating? Well, I have a few questions I would like to ask him.*

Let me think clearly. She rewinds the reel of their last five years together. *I think we've overcome our challenges. Sure, there've been what I'd call typical adjustments, but every couple goes through changes or hard times. Right?*

Our sex life hasn't crashed. We don't need a calendar to schedule our frisky escapades. We have our weekly rituals, mornings where we are together, weekend getaways and a lot of date nights.

Even with emotional highs and lows, we support each other the best we can. We show up, for sure! But is all of that enough? Maybe it's enough for him. Maybe not. But is it enough for me?

Her mind alters, not in self-blame, but in awareness. *I understand the whole bottling-up maneuver. As a people-pleaser, I tend to overextend, putting others first. My introverted nature holds me back from being fully transparent, especially when insecurities creep in. I make excuses. My ex-boyfriend used to call me passive-aggressive. But I wasn't trying to be passive, I was trying to protect myself. I was avoiding conflict with a man who didn't understand that his behavior was emotionally hurtful.*

Back then, I often felt alone: constantly tolerating someone else's issues and needs. I don't feel that same loneliness with my husband... but I do feel like I hold myself back sometimes. Like I sacrifice my thoughts and desires just to avoid appearing needy or annoying. Sometimes, the eggshells I walk on are unbearably crunchy. One thing I know for sure: I don't want to keep sacrificing my voice just to keep the peace.

Raina grabs the book and sits down at the deep end of the pool. *Reading about why these men cheat is making me feel strange.*

I hope my husband isn't one of those men who finds normalcy in keeping his secrets to himself. I don't want to miss the signs. What if I've blown things off or he feels I have made myself unapproachable? What if he's been trying to tell me something all along and I haven't been listening? What if I'm already part of one of his fantasies and don't even know it?

Making a big splash, she kicks the water and lets out a screech. "Oh boy!"

Leaving wet shadows on the cement, Raina grabs her towel and dashes into the house. Nearly taking the hinges off the doorframe, she flings open the closet in the master bedroom and begins to count. "1, 2, 3, 4, 5, 6, 7… 13." Thirteen pairs of leather pants.

How did I not notice this before? Is he trying to tell me something?

She runs her hand over the buttery leather. *I've only bought two of these beauties. The other eleven? All gifts, from him.*

Suddenly, it's not about the pants. It's about intention. *Is there a hidden message here, or am I just spiraling?*

She takes a step back. Then forward. Picks up a pair and examines the stitching. *And I haven't even counted the hide skirts, jackets, and bustiers.*

It's not disgust she feels; it's disorientation. *Interesting. I'm going to have to get to the bottom of this.*

What does it say? Is she surprised, or is she wondering why she has never asked the questions? *That's what unsettles me most. Not the pants. Not the number. Not even the possibility that he wants something I haven't offered. It's the silence. His, maybe. But also… mine.*

I've never asked what lives in the corners of his mind. Never dug deeper than what he's chosen to show. Maybe I thought he'd tell me if there was something worth knowing. But men don't always work that way, do they? Or do we?

I wonder if my husband has held anything back from me? Afraid I'd dismiss it? Laugh? Tease him? Use it against him? I don't think I would. But maybe he doesn't know that. Maybe I've never shown him that part of me, the part that welcomes his truth without needing to fix it, challenge it, or make it smaller.

And while she's wondering what if he's hiding anything. *It's not my fault that some men are like this. I didn't teach the men in my past relationships to be emotionally unavailable. I didn't train them to stay quiet or to hide who they are. That came from somewhere else, long before me.*

It's exhausting trying to reach someone who's shut down or refuses to be honest. To love someone who retreats when things get too real. To guess what they're feeling instead of being told. To feel something brewing and hear, "I'm fine." Or, nothing at all! No, I might not be responsible for the silence they inherited. But I have paid the price for it.

I've walked away from conversations with a pit in my stomach, unsure if I pushed too hard or not hard enough. I've blamed myself for the distance in my relationship. I've been tolerant and given grace. And even then, I still hit a wall.

I have tried. And maybe that's what hurts the most... realizing how much I've given in the past, without ever fully getting the truth in return.

Maneuvering her way back through the kitchen, she grabs another drink from the fridge and heads back outside.

Cozying into her lounge chair, the breeze whistles through the well-manicured landscape around the pool. Raina takes in the beauty of the home she and her husband created and takes a deep breath.

CHAPTER 4

FANTASY SESSION STORY
THE NEWBIE

This chapter presents a fantasy session story involving consenting adults only. All scenarios are fictionalized composites inspired by themes from my professional practice, and identifying details have been altered to protect privacy. The story explores adult BDSM dynamics, trust, and power exchange within a safe, consensual, and controlled environment.

Character Development: *A man in his early 50s. He is married and is visiting a Dungeon for the first time.*

This man is hungry at 1:00 pm, but not for lunch.

I could tell that he was nervous, as most of them show me through the many ways their body language speaks. A slight look of concern discolors a face surrounded by his short, blonde hair. I see his mind scattered, and I can tell he is wondering whether coming here was the right choice.

I always love the feeling of swallowing my wicked laugh in these moments, letting it resonate throughout my soul, before I command his narrow frame to have a seat. It is in this moment that I begin to stare deeply into him, making the tension intensify. His overall demeanor is telling me everything I need to know. What fun it is to prey upon his quivers as he settles into my couch.

"What would you like to do today?" I ask. I see my basic question sends his unseasoned mind down a spinning drain of sticky embarrassment and shyness. The word "perfect" enters my mind. *I see I have one of them!*

I persist with more questions until he succumbs to the answers. Shifting his hands over his crotch area, he admits that he has never done this before and has always fantasized about receiving a hard spanking from a Dominant woman.

The words begin to flow, and he starts to describe a fantasy he repeatedly has about being humiliated for having a small penis, spanked, controlled, and made to feel small by a woman such as myself. As the conversation proceeds, we discuss his overall health, medications, sinuses, boundaries, limitations, a safe word, and if he has eaten or drunk anything today. Mental and physical safety is a main priority!

"Are you finding it difficult to make eye contact with me?" I whisper. I stand up and hover over him. "Or is it this red slinky dress and heels I am wearing that have your attention? Let us go! You can take care of the tribute at the desk!"

Desperate already, he swiftly follows me through the black velvet curtain. As he pays, I take my bag to gather the needed session supplies. I grab specific whips, ropes, clips, a blindfold, crops, feathers, and restraints, and I place them inside. After paying, he stands there, watching me slowly place the last of my playful items inside.

I make every moment count. It is in the buildup of anticipation that the desire grows.

Off we go!

There are several themed playrooms from which he can choose, but today I have chosen a favorite of mine: The Obsidian. I command him to walk in front of me through the front door of the room. Making a sharp left, I point my finger at a narrow hallway. Before he reaches the end, I tell him he will step to the right side and get out of my way. Black walls and red leather accents welcome us as I push open the door. I stand back and hold it open for him to enter. As he passes by me, I continue to watch every expression that he cannot help but expose.

Gently, I push the door shut and purposely graze his shoulder while passing by. I make sure to remind him that I am really here, and he is about to get exactly what he asked for today. I toss my bag of tricks onto the bondage table. My commands keep coming, and I tell him to lay out all the equipment on the table in an organized fashion. Piece by piece, I watch as he nervously looks at each item and places it on the leathery contraption. I start the music, and the hypnotic sounds weave hints of lyrical intentions to sculpt the scene.

"Remove your shoes and socks and kick them under the table," I command.

I walk up slowly behind him, placing my hands around his waist. Finding the button of his jeans, I grip firmly with my long red nails and begin to pull. I take advantage of his heavy breathing and lean in. "I am not going to fuck you, but I am going to fuck the shit out of your mind!"

His pants hit the floor. Grabbing the back of his neck, I swing him around and place my knee between his legs. I drag my leg down his inner thigh. I begin to hold the lower part of his body prisoner by pressing the sole of my heel firmly down onto the crotch area of his pants. His pants make the perfect temporary restraint system around each ankle, and he is mine!

My touch begins to speak, and I am looking for him to give me the answers. He does. He wants more. Every part of him is begging me for more.

His shirt, warm with desire from his uncontrollable excitement, falls perfectly into my hands while I take it off his body. Tiny scratches begin to surface like welted conclusions from the sharp, protruding blades of my ten fingers.

I grab the blindfold off the table and cover his eyes. I command him to raise his right foot, then his left. With his pants out of the way, he stands before me with only one more article of clothing. My excitement starts with tantalizing his flesh. Teasing the inside of his briefs with my fingers, I make him wonder how far I will go. I know he is thinking: *if only she would reach down farther and circle the rim of my cock.* Keep wishing!

I pick up the riding crop from the table and smack the leather on the bondage table, giving him an idea of what is to come. I love the way the crop sounds when I firmly make contact with the leathery beast of a slab. Startled, he twitches, and I suspect he is afraid.

Success!

Pulling him away from the bondage table, I place him into the nearby bondage swing. Spreading his legs, each foot gets placed into a harness, and each wrist is bound with restraints and clamped to hanging side chains on the chair. I make my way back to the bondage table and grab a red-oiled leather flogger. In this moment, I prefer oiled leather to increase the intensity of the sting when the falls of the flogger connect with his flesh.

His only choice is to feel my wrath. It is a dance. It is a vibration that connects us as we fall deeper into the state of Dominant and submissive headspaces, elevating our playtime and allowing the maximum level of pleasurable benefits.

Standing in front of him, the words calmly begin to leave my mouth. "I think you are pathetic. As I am sure you have noticed, I have not yet removed your briefs. I did not need to take them off to have an idea of how small your penis appears to be. I have no desire to see that puny nub. No wonder you are here and must pay for my services. I cannot imagine anyone else giving you or your cock the time of day!"

The flogger gently makes contact with his inner left thigh. Then on the right thigh. Now harder. And harder. "I am only giving you what you deserve for failing your lovers. I know you are not a pleasurable fuck. I am sure there is someone out there who would thank me for my efforts."

He cries out. "Yes, Mistress, yes! You are not wrong!"

Him calling me Mistress shows me he has done his homework. But he has not passed the exam. I did not give him permission to speak, and now I must punish him further. A light slap to his dick shall suffice. "I love a whimper; I think I want another one! Start counting out loud to ten."

With every passing number comes another slap and another whimper. "Ten came too quickly. Count out ten more!" Walking to the back of the swing, I gently slap his cock five more times with the flogger. My face, now close to his, tilts gently to meet his cheek.

Asking him, "Do you know why your two-inch nub received multiple slaps?"

"I'm not sure, Mistress!" he proclaims.

Whispering in his ear, "Because you must have permission to speak to me."

My hands begin to caress his neck and down his chest. My breath makes contact on his cheek as I move my lips in close to his. I tease him and tell him exactly what he will never be able to have. I begin to remove the restraints and command him to carefully exit the bondage swing.

Off with the blindfold. "Now it is time for your spanking." I remove most of the remaining equipment from the bondage table. I decide to keep out a leather paddle, a feather tickler, and a pair of spiky, black leather vampire gloves.

After sitting on the table and placing a large towel over my lap, I call him over. "Turn around and put your back towards me. Take off your briefs and cover your little nub with them. After your nub is covered, turn back around and come to me."

I command him to climb up on the table to lie across my lap. "Do not drop those briefs. If I end up seeing that disappointing thing you call your dick, I will kick you right out of this room. Immediately!"

Following my rules, he gets up on the table and presents his ass to me. I command him to drape his body across my lap. After a series of hand spankings, I move on to the leather paddle.

Intermittently, I kindly offer a tickle with my feathers across the entirety of his body. I feel his warm bottom beneath my hand, the temperature rising with every swat of my paddle. The redness begins to envelop his bottom, and I do not hesitate to give him more. It is the perfect time for me to use my vampire gloves, laced with protruding spikes, on his sensitive bottom. The lightest touch is enough to make him squirm with sensations.

I am done with him, and off my lap he goes. I send him and his briefs-covered nub to the back corner to face the wall.

After retrieving a surprise, I drop a white foam cup at his feet. "I am contemplating whether I will allow you to touch your useless dick. Hmmm. Decisions, decisions!"

I walk over, grab his watch, and bring it back to show him the time. "Looks like your time is up!"

I command him to move away from the wall and tell him to pick up the foam cup. Pulling the cup from his hands, I walk, cup in hand, over to my purse. My laughter sonorously penetrates the room. The bold, black lines on the cup from my Sharpie will send a humiliating reminder with him out the door.

Back at the wall, I command him to watch while I so generously write him a sweet note on the cup: "Little Dick! Pathetic. Useless. Failure. You get what you deserve!"

"Speak and show me your respects!" I order.

"Thank you, Mistress!" he whimpers.

Looking seriously at him: "That is better!"

"See what happens when your dick is not worth anything? Later today, you will find a private place to milk that nub into this cup and release your semen. I want you to read my written words as you stroke. Let it be a reminder of what a disappointment you have been to me."

Turning away from him: "You may freely speak. Now, get dressed and get out of here!"

A serenade of profuse gratitude flows over me in his presence. I close the door behind him and begin to clean up after the session.

REFLECTION: RAINA MARKS

I will never look at another foam cup the same way!

Raina has had her first taste of being a "Fly on the Wall" during a fantasy scenario.

Ugh. Eek! Just—no. Absolutely not. I wonder if this guy actually followed through with what the Mistress asked of him when he got home… poor wife. Probably welcomed him with a kiss, none the wiser.

Is it possible for this woman to have this much power over these men? If so, I might need a few lessons!

She tosses her sunhat. *I find it interesting that this newbie took the chance and is risking everything because he is a curious man. He is testing boundaries like it is a game. And now, he is a cheater!*

I just don't understand why anyone would want to carry this much deceit around like dead weight. It is not only wrong, but exhausting: to compartmentalize your whole life into two different realities.

Is that part of the thrill? Living two different lives? She shakes her head. *No, that is not thrilling. That is cowardice disguised as a fantasy.*

Oh, goodie! Now we get to find out when, where, and how these scheming rats cheat!

WHEN? WHERE? HOW? HIS CHEAT MAP

Finding a Professional Dominatrix to fulfill his wishes isn't difficult. You'd never suspect that the pleasure specialist is right under your nose.

Whether we are a professional or amateur, it's as easy as a quick search, a visit to specialized websites, or even mainstream platforms. Social media, dating apps, and dedicated kink communities have made it more accessible, visible, and normalized. This is true even if it's still not always socially or legally accepted everywhere.

In my experience, 95% of men who walk through the Dungeon door are visiting me to step behind the passageway of hidden pleasures. They are here to have the experience. They are ready to spend their money and enter into a play session.

Session/Sessions/Sessioned/Sessioning: *A mutually agreed-upon exchange, measured in time, defined by intention, and compensated accordingly. Within its boundaries, limits are respected, fantasies explored, and roles embraced.*

The other 5% of men aren't visiting my space to just jump into anything physical. They're here to talk. To ask questions. To share a piece of their fantasy or open up about something that's lived inside them for many years.

Yet, 99% of the time, after the initial conversation, those same men reach into their wallets and pay the tribute. Something inside them has already been activated and the excitement has them by the balls. It's time to fulfill their fantasies.

When?

When exactly is he with me instead of you? He cheats in the morning. He cheats in the middle of the day. He cheats at night. He finds the time inside his busy schedule to squeeze in a session.

Where?

Men seek out a Professional Dominatrix at a commercial or private Dungeon, studio, lounge, house, hotel, kink party, or club.

But how?

Let me give you all the details!

Commercial Dungeons and private studios, lounges, or clubs are located throughout most major cities. Having a variety of sanctuaries to choose from makes it convenient for men to schedule an appointment with a Dominatrix. Finding a *domain of pain and pleasure* is as easy as opening a magazine, newspaper, or searching the internet. Most commercial or private spaces have websites where people can learn more about the play space.

In other cases, he may find a Professional or Non-professional Dominatrix who conducts sessions out of her home, hotel, or private play space. These Dominatrices may or may not have a website, but often advertise themselves on kinky websites, social media platforms, parties, clubs, magazines, or newspapers.

A commercial Dungeon is open to the public (men and women) during select business hours and welcomes walk-ins. They typically have a lot of private rooms for playtime. Men choose to visit a commercial facility due to its convenience, availability, flexibility, and the wider selection of women to choose from.

Commercial spaces typically have several women on hand to accommodate the needs of clients. Biographies, complete with pictures of the ladies and detailed explanations of their services, are posted on the Dungeon's website for clients to review.

Once a man has found a location that offers services to meet his requested needs, he may arrange a meet-and-greet with the lady of his choice. He can request this with a phone call, email, or by walking into the commercial space during regular business hours. Clients are typically vetted by phone, email, or in person.

After being chosen, the selected woman will have a conversation with the man prior to the session. They will discuss his fantasies and the Dominant will decide to engage in a session or not. The rules will be covered, and all safe, sane, and consensual aspects of the session will be addressed and negotiated. If he wants a cameo with other ladies in the house, it's usually arranged before the session, but he can also request it during the scene.

Private Dungeons, on the other hand, are not open to the public and do not typically welcome walk-ins. They are less flexible and require the man or woman to schedule a session by email or by directly calling the Head Mistress. On their website, clients can view biographies of the available women, with photos and detailed service descriptions. Men often choose a private play space for its complete privacy or because it's where the Mistress of their choice works. These play spaces have been known to offer more services (Golden Showers, Scat Play, Anal Play, Sex, Medical Play, Piercing/Cutting, etc.) than commercial Dungeons.

Commercial Dungeons typically have several rooms to choose from, each with different themes. Common design options include chambers, medieval-style rooms, medical rooms, vaults, boudoirs, classrooms, hospitals, Victorian-themed rooms, office-themed or domestic kink settings, and more.

Private play spaces typically include the same well-equipped spaces, but usually differ in the number of themed rooms they offer. Sometimes, it may just be a simple living room, one Dungeon themed room, or bedroom area used for play.

The Architecture of the Dungeon: A Psychological Inventory

A well-equipped BDSM playroom is a theater of intention. Every furnishing and implement is designed to facilitate a specific psychological process, moving a man away from his "real world" identity and into a state of total presence or total surrender.

Zone I: Furnishings for Physical & Mental Anchoring

These larger pieces provide the framework for the session. They take away mobility to heighten anticipation.

- **St. Andrew's Cross (X-Cross):** A wall-mounted frame for standing bondage that spreads the body into a vulnerable "X."
- **Bondage Table, Bench, or Spanking Bench:** Padded surfaces (some angled) designed for securing the body in various positions, ideal for impact or display.

- **Bondage Chair:** Fitted with cuffs and D-rings to restrict a client's movement while seated.
- **Stocks / Pillories:** Devices for securing the neck, wrists, or ankles, often used for humiliation or exposure.
- **Suspension & Gravity:** Rope suspension rigs, ceiling hooks, slings, and sex swings allow for partial or full suspension, removing the grounding force of the floor.
- **Confinement:** Cages and jail cells create a sense of total containment, perfect for power exchange or pet play.
- **Theatrical Props:** Desks, chairs, and even coffins. A desk may seem ordinary, but here it is a throne for the Dominant or a restraint station for the client.
- **Positioning Aids:** Liberator-style wedges and ramps used to support the body at specific, reachable angles.

Zone II: Implements of Sensation & Impact

These tools move the mind out of the "logical" and into the "physical."

- **The Sting & The Thud:** Floggers (rubber, leather, or suede), paddles (wood, rubber, leather), riding crops, canes (rattan or acrylic), and whips (single or multi-tail).
- **The Sound of Submission:** The slapper creates a loud cracking sound that amplifies psychological intensity upon contact.
- **Sensory Depth:** Wartenberg wheels (pinwheels) for prickly sensation, vampire/spiky gloves for stud-embedded touch, and feathers or dusters for light teasing.
- **Extreme Sensation:** Ice for temperature shock and low-temperature candle wax for controlled dripping.
- **The Intricate & Specific:** CBT and Nipple Play tools including weights, stretchers, clamps, and clips.

Zone III: Restraint, Silence, & Sensory Control

These items are the "quiet" tools that amplify the internal experience by limiting the external world.

- **Physical Ties:** Leather cuffs, handcuffs, hand mitts, and rope (ranging from basic ties to intricate Shibari/Kinbaku).
- **Separation:** Spreader bars to keep limbs apart, ensuring constant exposure.
- **Sensory Deprivation:** Blindfolds to heighten anticipation, and hoods or gas masks to isolate the client in their own breath and thoughts.
- **Total Immersion:** Straitjackets for full-body immobility and leather/latex body bags for total enclosure.
- **The Silence:** Mouth gags (Ball gags for speech restriction or spider gags to keep the mouth locked open) used for oral scenes or degradation.

Zone IV: Transformation & Feminization

This is where the "Husband" or "Businessman" is completely replaced. This kit allows for the complete shedding of the masculine ego.

- **The Foundation:** Lace panties, padded bras with inserts, thigh-high stockings, and garter belts.
- **The Wardrobe:** Slip dresses, nightgowns, skirts, feminine blouses, and the structural intensity of corsets and waist cinchers.
- **The Aesthetics:** Wigs, makeup kits (lipstick, mascara, eyeliner, powder, blush), jewelry (pearls, chokers, clip-on earrings), and perfume.

- **The Stance:** High heels in larger sizes that challenge balance and posture.
- **The Archetype:** Sissy maid outfits and costumes, often accented with bows and bells.
- **Symbols of Ownership:** Collars and leashes (made of leather, fabric, or chain) used to lead, direct, and symbolically command.

Zone V: The Atmosphere & The Aftermath

The environment is tuned to support the psychological shift, while the "Aftercare" ensures the ethics of the space.

- **Atmosphere:** Full-length mirrors for exposure, Lighting controls (red, purple, dimmers, candles), and sound systems for ambient soundscapes.
- **Privacy:** Curtains, drapes, and dividers for theatricality.
- **Organization:** Storage/display walls to neatly hang masks and tools.
- **Hygiene & Aftercare:** A critical station containing antiseptic wipes, gloves, first aid kits, clean towels, blankets, water, and snacks to ground the client after the storm of the session.
- **Miscellaneous Tools:** Padlocks and keys, ribbon, silk scarves, duct tape, zip ties, and leather harnesses. And more.

Tributes and Donations

Prior to the session, the client typically doesn't sign a waiver, and no contracts are involved.

The client can pay tribute by cash or credit card. The credit card charge listed on a statement typically sounds more discreet than the Dungeon's real name. You might want to check for "Consulting

Services," "Property Management," or "Health & Wellness" on those statements. The truth is often wrapped in a boring label. Privacy is protected.

Excessive amounts of money are spent by men every year to fulfill their needs. Whether your man visits a commercial or private space, I can guarantee he's paying out a substantial chunk of money per visit.

Donations or tributes vary depending on the services, state, Mistress, commercial rates, and private Dungeon rates. I can't provide exact amounts donated for these services, but I can say that they range from a low of $100 to several thousand dollars per visit.

In a commercial Dungeon, donations start at the first half hour. Men can schedule an appointment for 30 minutes, 45 minutes, 1 hour, or more. At the end of a session, a client can extend his time with the play partner.

Private Dungeons typically begin by the hour. It is common for a client to schedule a two-hour appointment. Sessions can be booked for hours, a full day, a week, or up to several weeks, etc. Some men pay monthly fees for regular ongoing services.

Phone and video sessions are also available, typically starting at 30 minutes and lasting for hours. Donations typically start at $75.00 to $150.00 per hour, though some professionals charge less, while others charge significantly more.

Men are willing to "pay to play" at any cost when desperation takes hold of their will. The uncontrollable urge to splurge gives a whole new meaning to pleasure spending. Or, in some cases, sin-spending!

Financial Servant

If your man is a financial servant, tens of thousands of dollars could be slipping right into the hands of a Dominatrix. These men are out there, and trust me, they love to hand out their money. Whether it's lavish gifts, extravagant experiences, or *cold hard cash*, they have no problem giving it all to the Mistress who commands their devotion.

Is your man's "hobby" or "investment" actually a tribute? Follow the money, and you'll often find the Mistress.

Gifts and Tips

If a man wishes to adorn his Mistress with gifts and tips, the amount of money can quickly add up to thousands of dollars. Shoes are among the most common gifts a client will buy for his Mistress. Really expensive shoes! Cash, clothing, perfume, jewelry, play toys, electronics, and food are also popular offerings brought in by clients. And so much more!

When is all this happening?

The Daybreak Enthusiast

The affluent businessman looking to steal a moment of pleasure before heading into the demands of his day. He is looking for that quick A.M. "fix" to energize and charge his mind. I am the fuel to kick-start his day amidst the whirlwind of his professional endeavors. Horny, desperate, and raring to go!

This enthusiast is wide-eyed and eagerly bursts through the door. He gets down on his knees and is ready to be verbally Dominated and controlled. He tends to reserve the same Dominatrix and typically becomes a regular client.

These clients usually schedule a session before they head off to work. Most of the time, the session lasts for 30 minutes or less, and they visit me one to three times per week. Under normal circumstances, they will stick to their usual fantasy and do not change their session preferences. Most of these men are in committed relationships.

My well-to-do businessman embodies a blend of professionalism and financial success. He is usually generous beyond the session tribute and offers a tip.

Time is ticking, and he has his eye on the clock. He takes one last breath to fortify his spirit before plunging into the potential challenges that lie ahead. Grinning from ear to ear, he swiftly makes his way out the door.

The Afternoon Delight

They are like snakes slithering through time until they find an empty moment to strike. These men are drawn irresistibly to my doorstep. Seeking refuge during their lunch break, between meetings, or right after work, they enter my space, finding refuge from the demands of their day. Relishing the moments, they are excited to relinquish control and submerge themselves in the escape. Together, we communicate and plan a session around what will make them feel better.

"Mr. Midday Pleasure" can be anyone, and the majority of them are in relationships. These men come from all walks of life—a factory worker, businessman, doctor, lawyer, teacher, entrepreneur, truck driver, out-of-state visitor, retired guy, tech man, artist, and more. They prefer to see their regular Dominatrix, but if their Mistress is unavailable, they'll usually session with another Mistress or Switch (plays both Dominant and submissive roles).

For these clients, scheduling looks very different. It's common for him to either call ahead to schedule his session or to walk in unannounced. Sessions usually last anywhere from 30 minutes to 2 hours, and his visits could be weekly, biweekly, or monthly.

In my experience, about 95% of these clients avoid weekend sessions. They struggle to explain to their partners where they're going on a Saturday afternoon. The fear of being caught, followed, or questioned keeps them on edge.

Unlike the Daybreak Enthusiast, these men don't cling to one specific fantasy. Their desires change depending on their mood, and our time together reflects that ever-changing nature.

The Night Crawler

Making his way in the night, his anticipation eagerly seeks out a nocturnal symphony. The moonlit hours are successful in drawing out his urges. His cravings for intimacy and connection serenade his soul as he embraces the darkness.

Merging a tapestry of thoughts, he debates and contemplates. Often, he is the mysterious caller, whispering in the ear of the desk lady. He has questions and, at times, wants to titillate her ear with his naughty thoughts, only to find himself on the receiving end of a phone being hung up. His game is quickly over.

Then there's the forsaken soul, lonely and often introverted. Stealthily, he approaches the establishment and rings the doorbell. Entering with his head down, he closes the door behind him. Unable to make eye contact, he creeps his way up to the desk and asks to see a Dominant.

Most of these men will see any Dominatrix who is available for a session. They will session for 30 minutes to 1 hour. These clients are sporadic in how often they book sessions, and there's no way to predict if or when you'll ever see them again.

The "Regular" Night Client

He only comes out at night!

The night client sessions after hours due to his work schedule. He loves to play at night and sneaks away at any opportunity.

It is normal for him to visit the establishment weekly, biweekly, or monthly. He will schedule 30-minute to 3-hour sessions by phone or walk-in. He prefers to see his regular Dominatrix; however, he is flexible and will schedule with an available Mistress.

This client often tips outside the session donation.

Day to Night Man

"What the hell are you doing here?"

"Mr. Afternoon Delight" makes an unusual appearance for a twilight pleasure indulgence. He has made his escape and wants a night howl. He is looking to satisfy his needs after a long day and will session 30 minutes to 2 hours.

Only I am surprised, since I'm used to seeing him in the middle of the afternoon for his usual fix. Something about this unexpected timing tells me he's out of alignment.

Out-Of-Towners

These clients come from all over the world, with some being long-time regulars who have been coming for years, even decades. While some of these men are single or widowed, the majority of them are in committed relationships.

Out-of-towners visit the facility at all hours of the day, each with their own unique longings. They typically book appointments for several hours or more. Many of these men schedule their sessions weeks or even months in advance, making sure to book their time with their regular Dominatrix. However, it's not uncommon for them to squeeze in a cameo with other ladies during their visit.

The out-of-towner is often known for being generous, typically leaving a hefty tip as a gesture of appreciation for the experience.

The Looky-Loo

This man walks into the establishment with a clear goal: to see and speak with as many women on the schedule as possible. He's not necessarily interested in booking a session; rather, he craves the conversation and the experience of being in the atmosphere. He concludes his personal mission, seeking some sort of validation in the act itself.

Whether they come in at dawn, after dark, or somewhere in between, these men know what they are after. By the end of the visit, even without a session, they've eased their curiosities or unburdened their tensions. Refreshed and renewed, they leave, feeling unshackled and rejuvenated, ready to step back into their worlds.

Content Notice: *This overview contains descriptions of consensual BDSM activities, including forms of consensual pain play. It is intended for mature, informed, consenting adults. All activities described should be approached with mutual respect, clear communication, and adherence to safe, sane, and consensual practices.*

Here is an idea of what these men want and do to fulfill their BDSM, Kink, & Fetish fantasies during our playtime sessions:

The Fetishist

I hear:

"I brought a backpack full of stockings today that I want you to try on for me!"

"I am addicted to my fetish!"

"I am fixated on women smoking cigarettes. I want to be burned and used as a human ashtray!"

"Please don't wear any deodorant so I can smell your body odor. I have an armpit fetish!"

"My rubber fetish started when I was ten years old after I watched my aunt use dish gloves!"

"I love feet!"

There is a lengthy list of fetishes that men find pleasurable. In my experience, approximately 25% of my clientele have a fetish.

The Fetishist is very specific about what makes him tick. He is solely focused on his obsession and usually comes prepared to play. He provides a detailed description of what he likes about his fetish and why. Whether he has a foot, shoe, food, raincoat, clothing, or lingerie fetish, he loves to explore his kinky addiction.

Examples:

If my client has a latex fetish, he will bring a bag of rubbery items for us to wear. He loves to show off his collection and see women in the shiny material. With excitement, he will dress in full gear and wait patiently for me to try on his outfits. I model the rubber pieces for him and tease him.

The lingerie fetishist loves to slip his bare bottom into a pair of lacy panties. He is ready to provocatively explore his bottom drawer of desires. He puts on quite the fashion show and feasts his eyes on my garter belt and fishnet stockings.

Typically, the fetishist comes to the Dungeon already knowing what his fetish entails. On occasion, someone will discover a love for something new and turn that discovery into a fetish.

The Pain Slut

I hear:

"Give me a hard spanking, with no warm-up! I want to really feel the sting for being such a bad boy!"

"I want to feel the pain all over my body!"

"I love a lot of pain mixed in with my pleasure!"

"Pain makes me release all of my tensions!"

"Nothing like a hard spanking before work!"

"Mr. Pain" needs an adrenaline hit and is eager to bend over for a good spanking or whipping. Pain typically triggers the release of endorphins and adrenaline, creating a rush that feels euphoric or even pleasurable.

Whether he is a masochist or a masochistic submissive, a pain slut loves to be pushed to his limits. The experience of pain within the world of BDSM is not about harm; it is about transformation.

Participants are either seasoned players, newbies, or somewhere in between. Their tolerance can range from a level 1 to a level 10. Since the body is always changing, it is normal for pain thresholds to fluctuate. This means sessions are tailored based on the level of intensity they wish to receive that day.

In consensual BDSM, pain becomes a language of trust, vulnerability, and connection that helps reinforce deeper bonds between players. Many men experience pain as erotic, not just for the sensation itself but for the intimacy it creates.

Here is what is on the painful menu:

- Cock and Ball Torture
- Nipple Clamps and Torture
- Impact Play
- Spankings, Whippings, Canings, Floggings
- Heavy Bondage
- Hot wax
- Corporal Punishment
- And more

The euphoric rush of adrenaline increases his powers to seize the day with vigor and gusto!

The Role-Player

I hear:

"I want you to wear a suit and pretend that you are my boss. Or is it possible for you to dress up like a police officer?"

"Can we play teacher and student today?"

"I have been thinking about you since our last session, and I think I want you to play my ex-wife again."

"If only you were really my girlfriend!"

"There is no way my wife would act like my doctor!"

Whatever the role, I can step into character like an award-winning actress.

Imagination, mixed with a dose of creativity and enthusiasm, brings these fantasies to life. It is a powerful space where individuals can step outside daily boundaries and embody fantasies that explore control, vulnerability, and desire.

Whether it is the strictness of a teacher-student scenario, the girlfriend experience, or a consensual master-slave exchange, role-play allows participants to deepen their psychological connection. It is a way of exploring power through symbolic and theatrical means.

The power is in the details. I am elaborate with my role-play scenes. I love to use props, costumes, scripts, and anything else I can find to enhance the playtime experience. These scenes often heighten erotic tension and emotional intensity, providing a structured outlet for surrender. Within the safety of consent, role-play in BDSM becomes more than a performance; it is a ritual of trust, transformation, and mutual pleasure.

Example:

Me: "You are late, Mr. Lloyd! Did you bring the papers I asked you to pick up from my other office?"

Client: "Oh man, I forgot!"

Me: "As your boss, I am responsible for seeing that you are properly punished for your ignorance."

Client: "Yes Ma'am, I understand!"

Me: "I will give you three choices of punishment. One, you are fired. Two, you work the next three months on probation with no pay. Or three, take off your clothes and I will punish you my way."

Client: "I can't do the first or second option. I have no choice but to take the third."

Me: "Then strip down! I don't have all day to deal with your stupidity."

Sensory Deprivation

I hear:

"But I can't see you, Mistress!"

"I go to another place when I am with you."

"All of my senses are heightened when we play."

"Something happens to me when I can't see or hear. Especially because I am being spanked at the same time. I feel loopy!"

"I am so relaxed and feel brand new."

Sensory deprivation entices the senses and is a form of sensation play that works by reducing or eliminating stimuli. Many of my clients describe the experience as relaxing and meditative.

By eliminating one or more of their senses, I can heighten their reaction to my touch. If I want to elevate their awareness, I take away one sense at a time. Blindfolds are the most requested item for sensory play because sight is the easiest sense to remove. Clients love the anticipation of not knowing when, where, or how they are going to be touched or sensually tortured. Taking away their sight enhances every step of my stiletto. This suspense increases their excitement, giving them a deeper sense of satisfaction.

BDSM hoods are often used to block eyesight, hearing, smell, and mobility. Depending on how I want to deprive my client, there are several types of hoods from which I can choose. Other items such as body bags, tape, plastic wrap, earmuffs, and earplugs are used to restrict the senses and bring them pleasure.

Sensation Play

I hear:

"I love your touch, Mistress!"

"I am so relaxed after a session with you, Mistress."

"Can you please tickle me with the feathers, Mistress?"

"I get so excited because of the mental and physical stimulations."

Like sensory play, sensation play heightens mental, physical, and sexual pleasure through one or more of the five senses. I deliberately engage the senses to bring him pleasure by seducing his nervous system.

It's not about pain. Not yet! Anticipation rises, leaving him breathless in the uncertainty of what comes next. The mind starts to spiral long before the body is even touched, and that's the beauty of sensation play.

This is where the craft lives. I focus on timing and subtleties. I know how to build tension without words, making the skin ache for contact before I ever provide it. Cool metal dragged along a thigh, the slide of silk, the threat of heat, or the tease of my hand; each touch rewires focus and pulls him inward. It's not just sensory; it's psychological. Every flicker of feeling becomes a promise, and every pause is a question.

I often enhance one sense while depriving another to amplify his overall experience. This type of kink is highly requested and fits into almost every style of erotic play. Simultaneously, I offer mental and physical sensations that can be experienced with or without pain.

While it lives within the realm of Sensation Play, the Somatic Kink shift is more intentional. We aren't just looking for a reaction; we are looking for a release. We use the body as a map to find where the man has buried his stress, and we use sensation to dig it out.

I am the sensualist, creating a beautiful experience. My wardrobe initially invites him in, and he is visually imprisoned. My touch relaxes his soul, and I intensify the experience by adding implements that tease the flesh. The music is on and the lighting is set perfectly to begin my hypnotic adventure. I add a hint of luring smells, delicious tastes, or possibly a blindfold, ice cubes, and hot wax to complete the journey.

Precision & Calibration

I hear:

"What did you find out today?"

"You knew exactly when to give it to me harder!"

"Next time I want to use the headband!"

In my sanctuary, we move beyond the simple mechanics of kink and into the realm of wellness exploration, using the body's own signals to map the path toward a deeper, more resilient self.

Neural Play & Biofeedback takes a client to the intersection of cold technology and raw submission. By monitoring real-time data—heart rate, the rhythm of the breath, the spike of stress—I can calibrate the intensity of a scene with surgical precision. This is science-based surrender. It allows me to measure a man's response before he has the words to name it, stripping away his ability to hide.

In my Dungeon, the body is the dashboard. I use HRV monitors to track the milliseconds between heartbeats, watching for the exact moment the executive brain surrenders to primal instinct. While he is blindfolded, EEG headbands allow me to monitor brainwaves, signaling when the static of the boardroom has finally faded into the deep, rhythmic hum of subspace. Galvanic skin sensors act as a biological polygraph; these finger clips measure micro-sweat, exposing the truth of arousal before he can even identify it himself.

There are no secrets with me.

The Digital Mask

I hear:

"I love how you see everything."

"Push me even harder today!"

"Where are you taking me today Mistress?"

"I wish you could touch me!"

"One day I am coming to see you!"

My client doesn't come into the Dungeon for simple punishment; instead, he enters Virtual Reality (VR) scenes to follow my commands.

Through digital immersion, these scenes are designed to test the limits of the mind within a safe, simulated void. Whether used for long-distance dominance or as a psychological simulation for deeper play, VR allows the mind to enter the sanctuary while the body remains behind.

Through the use of an avatar, a digital shield, clients can shed their public face entirely, finding a level of anonymity that the physical world cannot provide. This is global sovereignty: the ability to maintain a commanding presence from across the world, Dominating the senses without ever touching the skin.

Specific equipment and an app reinforce my role as the Sovereign. Even when I am physically absent, my "eyes" are everywhere. I am inside his mind through the EEG data and inside his digital world through the VR stream. My client is never truly alone; he is always under my watch.

Bondage Boy

I hear:

"Tie me up, Mistress! I don't ever want to escape you."

"Nice and tight, Mistress, please!"

"I feel safe when I am bound up."

"Nothing relaxes me more than being bound down to the table. It's comforting!"

"I wish you could tie me up every day."

"Bondage Boy" wants to be tied up and controlled. Whether he is my caged prisoner, a roped-up mummy, or bound by leather restraints, there will be no escaping my trap.

There are many reasons why these men like to be bound and controlled:

- **The Power Exchange:** He loves the feeling of giving up control and having no power.
- **Security and Comfort:** The physical restriction offers him a sense of calm. This helps him manage anxiety, find relaxation, and discover his center.
- **The Escape Artist:** He wants to face the challenge of breaking through my chains, cuffs, rope, and restraints. He loves a good struggle!
- **Aesthetic Pleasure:** Visually, he finds the artistic expression of intricate rope work to be a form of beautiful, kinky art.
- **Erotic Teasing:** Many men love the idea of being bound by a beautiful woman while being erotically teased and pleasured.
- **Role-play:** Bondage serves as the foundation for many of the theatrical scenarios we create together.

Haaaa! "What time did you say you had to be home?"

You're Such a Naughty Girl!

I hear:

"May I please wear the pink tutu and ruffly panties? I love it when you put the pink sparkly lipstick on me."

"Can I be your slutty girl today, Mistress?"

"I wish I could be a girl all the time."

"I'm a dirty slut, and I need you to punish me!"

"I fantasize about other men using me as a slutty sex toy."

"I finally feel like myself!"

My naughty girl is ready for her lipstick. What color do you want today?

I say this with so much love: "What fun we have!" My cross-dressers and sissies traditionally wear clothing typically associated with the opposite gender. They are excited, willing, and beautiful.

Autogynephilia describes a man's experience of sexual or emotional arousal tied to imagining himself as female. I see that these desires are deeply personal; they go far beyond wearing panties or catching a glimpse of oneself in a dress. These moments awaken special parts of his identity where femininity becomes both a persona and a desire. Many find these experiences to be relaxing, cathartic, and a powerful way of reducing anxiety.

Whether they are experimenting through curiosity or are seasoned players, these clients genuinely love the act of embodying a woman. Autogynephilia isn't a fetish to be dismissed or a pathology to be feared. It is a raw, undeniable charge they feel when the idea of being feminine becomes intoxicating.

The fun begins with wigs, jewelry, makeup, and high heels, but it ends with learning to walk the walk. We spend time reviewing how women sit, talk, walk, and flirt. We also have deep conversations about life and their specific needs.

Often, my clients want the cross-dressing experience combined with acts of verbal or physical humiliation. Some desire forced feminization, which includes being directed to adopt feminine clothing and roles during our time together. Others prefer the experience to remain informative, gentle, and sweet, while some enjoy a combination of both styles.

In my experience, these men want to experiment with a side of themselves that society often tells them to hide. Dressing like a woman offers comfort and enables them to better manage their emotions. While many are initially nervous about expressing these secrets, they eventually find the courage to live out their fantasies in my care.

Stop your crying! *You Big Baby!*

I hear:

"I caca! Punish me, Mistress!"

"I'm just a big baby boy!"

"I want to suck on a nipple. Please!"

"I brought several diapers for you to change, Mistress."

"I want Mommy!"

You heard me right; he wants to be a baby. Off with his suit, and on with the diaper. Mommy's little baby is such a good boy. *Tickle! Tickle!*

The adult baby, also known as autonepiophilia, is a sexual and non-sexual fetish play. These men will role-play specific parts, ultimately turning him into, "Little Joey."

Some men tap into regression. This is their escape from standard adult responsibilities and realities. These cheating babies lose themselves in an infant mentality and experience an entirely different type of release. This type of play isn't about sexual stimulation alone; they find comfort in the surrender and emotional release.

I offer (GFD) Gentle Femdom scenes where I offer a nurturing, "Mommy-style" Dominance. I focus my attention on the care, praise, and "loving authority" rather than any kind of harsh punishment. The big baby loves to be nurtured and attended to, leaving himself completely dependent and vulnerable to his surroundings. These players will dress in adult baby clothing, diapers, slippers, etc., and they love to suck on their favorite pacifier. We make sure to get out their baby toys, stuffed animals, and special blanket. *Everyone needs a little cuddle!*

There are several types of scenes that these players will choose to fulfill their childish needs. Some men want the positive feeling of being emotionally comforted. The acts of being cared for spark the feelings of childhood, and they once again become enthralled in mommy's embrace.

Verbal humiliation and being talked down to are common elements in the dynamic between caregiver and baby, though they aren't always present.

Other men simply have a diaper fetish, and their obsession gives them a load of icky satisfaction.

Age Play: Part 2

I hear:

"Will you take good care of me?"

"I just want to play!"

"I don't want to feel old!"

"I feel so safe now!"

Age play is a consensual role-play where an adult adopts the mindset and behaviors of a younger age. In my sessions, this usually means the client steps into the role of a "little" while I act as the parental figure or caregiver. For these men, it is often the only profound way they have to escape the crushing weight of their adult lives.

The real draw here is the total surrender of responsibility. These men are often high achievers, CEOs, or industry leaders who spend every waking hour making difficult decisions. The opportunity to be told how to act, what to wear, and how to behave provides a sense of relief they can't find anywhere else. It is a psychological reset. It allows them to tap into a state of innocence and vulnerability that their professional lives would never permit.

The scenes we negotiate can vary. It might involve wearing diapers, using pacifiers, or receiving nursery discipline for misbehavior.

Outsiders often mistake this for a purely sexual fetish; my clients know better. For them, the non-sexual elements are the most therapeutic. The feeling of being "minded" by a firm, caring authority figure creates a bubble of security that dissolves their anxiety.

Everything in age play rests on a foundation of trust and iron-clad boundaries. Because this role requires such extreme vulnerability, I have to be hyper-attuned to the client's emotional state. Whether the scene is playful or disciplinary, the goal is always the same: providing a safe space where a man can finally shed his adult identity and find comfort in the simplicity of being small.

Food Play / Sploshing

I hear:

"I love the way the food feels all over my body. The smoothness of the pudding gliding over my skin is erotically satisfying."

"Food play is so fun!"

"I love the way food looks on a woman's ass."

"Food is messy and sexy!"

"I wish my girlfriend would smear food all over my cock."

"My ultimate dream is to smear the food all over someone else's body."

Sploshing, otherwise known as fetish food play, is a messy good time. This play can involve arousal or be entirely non-sexual; it all depends on the energy exchanged.

This experience can be a full-body seduction. It might be the drip of honey down a hipbone, a strawberry teasing parted lips, or the commanding act of feeding from a hand that doesn't ask, but only gives. It can be ritualistic, humiliating, or nurturing. It is a way of saying, "I own this moment, and you."

It is sensory overload. Taste, texture, and temperature are used to tempt and build unbearable tension. Food play welcomes various textures that hit erogenous zones, stimulating pleasure points into a delectable buffet. The slippery or sticky sensations are exciting, and these clients are addicted to seeing the food on skin rather than a plate.

Like all kink, its power lies in intention. Sometimes it is not about the food itself, but what the act of food play exposes. I have clients who seek indulgence and others who are looking for control. What remains is the question of who eats, who watches, and who is going to clean up the mess.

Whether he wants me to smash my hands into a tub of cookie dough or watch me drip sauce from my sharp fingernails, this food fetishist is hungry for satisfaction. Clients bring in various items to whet their appetites: pizza dough, cake, wet cat food, yogurt, pudding, squid, and burgers are just a few examples of this kinky cuisine.

Sploshing gives a whole new meaning to sitting down for a good meal. Bon appétit!

Pay up, Bitch!

I hear:

"Take my money! All of it! Go through all my pockets, Mistress."

"My money is yours!"

"It feels like the ultimate control when you take my money."

"Oh no! You are taking all my money!"

"Make me go to the ATM and withdraw the daily amount."

"I will pay your bills, Mistress!"

Financial Domination (Findom): *A consensual financial fetish where the "pay pig" or "money servant" willingly gives control of their money or gifts to the Dominant individual (FinDomme).*

Money servants are great for the bank account. If a Mistress is fortunate enough to obtain one of these men, lucky her.

Unfortunately, "Mr. Deep Pockets" does not come around too often. But when he does, Ka-Ching! I must say, I hope this is not your man.

The Dominant woman makes demands for various items or cash, and he must pay up. In other situations, she doesn't have to make demands; he freely showers her with money and gifts. Money servants are known to hand over thousands and sometimes tens of thousands of dollars to their Mistress. Occasionally, it is even millions.

For some men, giving money to a Dominatrix isn't just about control; it is the kink itself. Every dollar they hand over is a reminder that their value lies in serving rather than spending. It is a tangible surrender that allows them to feel owned without a single finger laid on them.

Men become money slaves because the transaction turns them on. It strips power from the wallet, their last fortress of control, and they hand it over willingly. Serving a Dominatrix financially feeds the part of them that aches to be useful, used, and emptied. Money isn't the real currency here. The focus is on what giving it up represents. For a financial submissive, handing over cash becomes a ritual of submission and a moment of pure vulnerability. That vulnerability is the fuel that drives the desire.

They crave the ache of denial, the sting of discipline, and the sharp thrill of knowing their labor funds the pleasure of the Dominatrix. Being a money slave isn't pathetic; it's purposeful. It is worship, obedience, and self-erasure, all in one swipe of the card.

Humiliation

I hear:

"I don't deserve to be here. I am such a loser! Don't let me look at you. I will never be worthy enough to be with a woman like you."

"Can you bring in other women to humiliate me too?"

"I don't know why I love to be humiliated so much."

"I feel embarrassed and ashamed when you humiliate me. I love it!"

"You have an endless amount of power over me, Mistress. I know I am nothing compared to you."

"I am a pathetic man fuck!"

"I am scum beneath your Superior Being, Mistress!"

"Don't look at me. I'm trash!"

"Can you publicly embarrass me and bring in another Mistress?"

"Can you take me outside the Dungeon and humiliate me?"

"Just kick me out when you are done with me."

Clients are often into sexual masochism, where pain and surrender become part of the pleasure. Reasserting power through verbal and physical humiliation is a common request from these men. Words are just as powerful as actions, and they crave every form of degradation.

These psychological and physical games sexually arouse and erotically excite every ounce of them. They love to be made to suffer and be embarrassed, both privately and publicly. The majority of these men find nothing more humiliating than a beautiful, Dominant woman telling them what an absolute disgrace they are to society. I provide the act of superiority, the art of owning the space, and the command of the moment.

I direct, tease, and remind them of their place while they revel in the pleasure of yielding. By lowering their status, I tap into their psychological responses and heighten every sensation. The echo of everything they are not, and everything they will never be, rings in their ears like twisted sweet nothings.

Their fantasies unfold into physical and mental excitement, often culminating in a powerful adrenaline rush. Humiliation doesn't have to be sexual in nature for a client to find deep satisfaction. What they are truly seeking is the emotional intensity released during playtime. Whether the feelings are perceived as negative or positive, he is chasing the depth of the sensation: helplessness, rejection, shame, guilt, and rage.

Whether he is being paraded on a leash, barking like a dog, or whipped with verbal lashings, the submissive is typically addicted and will be back for more. Follow that up with a swig of water from a dog bowl, and we are getting somewhere.

I dispose of him and tell him to get the fuck out. He loves it!

During and after our consensual playtime, I observe my client closely. If at any time I feel my humiliating acts are being taken too far, or if his energy is drifting to a place where I am losing his interest, I will redirect the session. It is reasonable and expected for a client to shift due to fluctuating moods. Life is constantly changing; what worked in our last session may not work in the next.

Aftercare is a necessity, and I use my best judgment in every individual case. This is always the rule, unless we have prior negotiations in place where he specifically wants to leave the session feeling completely humiliated.

Trampling

I hear:

"Walk all over me, Mistress!"

"I would love to see your stiletto pressed into my balls."

"If only you could squish my balls as hard as you could."

"If I am a good slave, will you put all of your weight on my cock?"

"Don't be gentle, Mistress!"

"Your feet look so sexy squashing my flesh."

Trampling and body weight play consist of stepping on or putting weight onto a man's body, face, or genitals. Being beneath a seductress can make these men feel fearful, submissive, or humiliated. These players often crave a sense of danger.

During these power exchange activities, many men are specific about which parts of the body they want trampled and how much pressure they want to feel. Common areas include the chest, abdomen, back, thighs, and head. Endless sensations provoke them physically, mentally, and emotionally. Feeling the loss of control, pain, and submission offers them a combination of relaxation and adrenaline.

Some men love the fantasy of being under a strong Amazon woman. They will request role-play with a character who will ultimately conquer them. Wrestling requests are common when it comes to this style of session.

It is common in these sessions for the client to have both a foot fetish and a love for trampling. In this case, they may want me to be barefoot, in stockings, or wearing specific footwear such as stilettos, sports shoes, boots, or flats.

Author's Note:

I want to make something very clear: I do not put my full, unsupported weight onto their body parts. I sit in a chair or stand while holding onto a support, giving me full control of exactly how much pressure is being placed onto my client. I proceed with caution and do not step on areas of the body that put him at risk of damage. Safety is my number one concern.

Freaky and Kinky

I hear:

"I'm so fucking horny!"

"I will do anything!"

"Make me do it, Mistress! I want to be your freaky boy!"

"Whatever you want, Mistress. I am yours!"

"I'm such a kinky freak! I love it dirty and nasty!"

"Mr. Single and Freaky" wants to do it all. If there is a game to play, he is in. The dirtier the better. These men usually have zero inhibitions and an appetite for full-on exploration. He has a wild imagination and a try-anything-once attitude. Actually, he will try it twice, just to be sure!

He walks in like he knows what he wants, but he really comes here to be told. He is alone, yes, but far from empty. These men carry whole universes of kinky ideas inside them: decades of cravings pressed into polite smiles and enthusiasm.

These clients come in with big energy. They ask tons of questions, flirt like it is second nature, and sometimes forget where they are. It is not uncommon for them to push boundaries by asking to meet outside the Dungeon or suggesting a date, a relationship, or a no-strings night out.

With enthusiasm, this freaky boy is curious, eager, and often chasing the edge of sensation, power play, or taboo.

Oochie-Coochie-Coo!

I hear:

"Don't let me free, Mistress. No matter what I say. I want you to make me laugh so hard I cry."

"Tickle torture is the best!"

"I can't breathe! Ha! Stop, Mistress, stop! Please! Ha!"

"I want a dozen women tickling me at the same time. That is my dream!"

"Tickle me until I cry, Mistress!"

"Mr. Tickles" has more than just a tickle in his pickle. These tickle fetishists are a giggly good time. They love to be bound down and tickled relentlessly during this power exchange.

Typically derived from childhood, early exposures to tickling excited these enthusiasts. This craving followed them into adulthood as they sought ways to fulfill their fantasies, eventually ending up under my control.

Being tickled activates the part of the brain that handles emotional responses. When someone laughs from tickling, it might feel funny, but it is often a natural, involuntary reaction. Simultaneously, the brain registers signals sent from the skin's sensitive nerve endings, making the experience pleasurable for the person being tickled.

The anticipation adds excitement to playtime and evokes a sense of playfulness. Men enjoy the pleasurable sensations and find that tickle torture reduces stress and tension.

My sharp fingernails take to his flesh before I decide which edgy, electrical, or wispy object I will choose next to tickle his fancy. It is my goal to zone in on those extra ticklish spots. While being tickled, these clients often request role-play scenarios and plenty of verbal teasing.

Giggle! Giggle!

Mr. Masseur Touch-A-Lot

I hear:

"I am here to make you feel good. I get pleasure out of making you feel good."

"Massaging you is the best therapy."

"I feel relaxed touching you. It's so nice!"

"Any time you need a massage, just let me know."

"You deserve a massage every day!"

"Masseur Touch-A-Lot" pays for my time and brings the oil! Most of these clients are submissive and love to serve. Their greatest pleasure is pleasing the Mistress; this is how they feel satisfied. Others claim they do not feel submissive but simply love the act of giving.

Some of these men can be very shy and too submissive to ask for what they truly desire. They offer their massage service with the hope that the session will lead into more intense BDSM activities. When I recognize this, I initiate a conversation to explore their needs and offer them a different type of experience.

Not bad at all, right? Getting paid to receive a massage. *Oooooh, right there!*

Out of Breath

I hear:

"I have no problem holding my breath for 2 minutes. Let's use the plastic bag today and the nose clip."

"Breath play takes me into a deep subspace."

"The act of being risky excites me!"

"I love the struggle when I have to hold my breath just a little bit longer."

"Nothing like a gorgeous woman taking your breath away!"

Don't hold your breath on this one! Breath play is the restriction of a person's airflow during BDSM activities. Beyond the physical sensation lies the psychological thrill of surrender and control. It is a dance on the edge of danger, and it requires clear communication, trust, and respect.

Outside of the Dungeon, erotic asphyxiation is another term used for this practice. This often occurs when a person attempts to restrict their own air supply during solitary play. Breath play can intensify sexual experiences and orgasms by creating a euphoric high, but it is not a game.

This experience is not for the faint-hearted; it is a raw, intense practice that pushes boundaries and heightens sensations. My clients want the power of giving and taking, mixed with an immense amount of trust. When you restrict someone's breath, you are playing with their very life force. That is a heavy responsibility.

Author's Note:

I am not instructing you on how to engage in breath play. Under no circumstances am I recommending, condoning, or teaching you how to conduct breath play on yourself or anyone else. Do not attempt this on your own or with an untrained play partner. One wrong move can lead to serious consequences.

Examples of breath play with a client (yoga for the kink-set!):

- Telling my play partner to hold his breath for a specific time period
- Throat constriction and choking
- Holding the head underwater
- Covering the head, mouth, and nose with various wraps, clips, plugs, plastic bags, masks, and hoods
- Smothering
- Strangulation
- Chest compression
- And more

This is going to hurt!

I hear:

"I need severe punishment, Mistress. Corporal punishment!"

"I need to be punished for my actions!"

"I need discipline in my life!"

"I love the way it hurts!"

"No mercy! Please!"

"I've been playing like this for so many years."

Corporal Punishment is a consensual form of physical discipline between adults that deliberately inflicts pain for psychological and physiological reasons. Submissive and masochistic participants find great pleasure in receiving punishment during this form of impact play. This disciplinary action heightens their awareness not only through physical sensation but through the potential for mental humiliation.

Men in BDSM are drawn to corporal punishment for various reasons. It stems from an intense power exchange, the sting of pain that releases endorphins, and the deep emotional connection that comes from pushing limits. The structure of rules and punishments adds a layer of control and catharsis. This makes every strike or restraint a complex blend of gratification and pain.

It is a consensual flow of Dominance and submission that heightens every sensation. The sharp crack of a whip or the firm grip of my hand sends shivers down their spines. I let the anticipation build and listen to their hearts race. Every nerve ending becomes alive with an intense mix of fear and desire.

In this intimate power play, the Dominant gives the orders and the submissive lets go. This creates a tension that feels both passionate and primal. These men are pleased to have found a way to achieve a hit of dopamine, and they welcome the release those endorphins provide.

I make sure they get a serious attitude adjustment through the following:

- Electric shock.
- Fixed posture placement.
- Confining to small spaces.
- Hard spankings, face smacking, kicking, choking, and whippings.
- Switch: a fresh, thin branch—like from a tree or bush—used for short-term, stingy punishment. Flexible, whippy, and usually has a raw, natural feel.

- I must mention the most requested implement, the *Rattan Cane*: crafted impact tool, made from dried rattan, a type of vine-like palm. Stronger and durable.
- And more.

Just take a moment and imagine him securely placed in my stock and pillory. He can't escape, and all that is left for him... is punishment.

Primal Play

I hear:

"Do you wrestle?"

"I'm into boxing without any mercy. Can we do that?"

"I want to be captured and fight you to get away."

"How tall and strong are you?"

"I love the thrill of the chase!"

"Pull my hair and bite me!"

"Hold me down and put your weight on me."

Through a negotiated agreement called **Consensual Non-Consent (CNC)**, we establish a sanctuary for the "forbidden." We agree that while the scenario may appear non-consensual, every moment is built on a foundation of prior permission.

The chase begins. I have him pinned to the ground, our breath coming in ragged bursts as we wrestle with a raw, frantic energy. I growl at him, making it known through every ounce of my strength that he is the loser in this power exchange.

Primal play is the theater of instinct. In these specific moments, "no" can mean yes, and the appearance of pursuit, fear, and surrender is the very air we breathe. It sheds the formal ritual to uncover something deeper: raw emotion and embodied reaction. Even when the scene feels untamed, it rests entirely on a bed of trust and shared awareness.

Tease and Denial

I hear:

"Fuck, I am so aroused! I just want to cum so badly. Please, Mistress! Please!"

"Can I touch you?"

"Please, Mistress! I'm begging you! Please!"

"Fuck!"

"What do I have to do for you to allow me the pleasure of satisfying you?"

"I can't take it, Mistress! I must release!"

No cum do, and he is escorted right to the door. Erotic sexual denial is a blast!

Tease and denial are powerful physical and psychological games. Being relentlessly provoked and then refused release drives these men to a state of erotic frenzy.

I get them excited and then intentionally prolong their arousal. By bringing a partner close to the edge of orgasm and then withholding the finish, I assert control over my submissive's body and desire. This continual state of anticipatory tension blends frustration and longing with heightened sensitivity. It turns his pleasure into a form of torment that is both intoxicating and mentally consuming.

Many men find great pleasure in being denied and believe the act will intensify their eventual orgasms. Some explain that this practice even improves their sex life at home. He returns to his partner sexually charged and eager for intimacy.

Within consensual power play, tease and denial can deepen the psychological bond and make a man more desperate than ever. When he eventually receives permission to release, that orgasm is significantly more powerful.

Drop them and bend over!

I hear:

"Have you found anything to punish me for, Mistress?"

"I feel powerless when you inspect me."

"I'm 100% owned by you!"

"What happens to me if I don't pass the inspection?"

"Are you going to torture me if you don't like what you see?"

"I tried extra hard last week to keep my body hair trimmed just how you like it, Mistress."

Inspection time! I am in a position of authority and control over the submissive. As the Dominant, I command my submissive to strip naked to be thoroughly inspected. I instruct him to hold specific poses while I examine his body, posture, grooming, and appearance. At the same time, I evaluate the submissive's state of mind and overall well-being. He may be rewarded for passing the inspection or punished for failing.

This scenario can unfold privately or be carried out in full view of others. These men often crave being objectified and humiliated, especially in the presence of other women. They take pride in their vulnerability and feel a thrill in showing off the results of their inspection while remaining completely exposed and on display.

Whinny! Woof! Meow!

I hear:

"Ride me and whip me with the crop. I will obey and be the perfect stud for you."

"Am I a handsome stallion, Mistress?"

"I wish you could shove the ponytail butt plug up my ass!"

"Do you want to hear my horse sounds, Mistress?"

"Can I be a dog next?"

"I need to be trained!"

These fantasy players are excited by the power exchange between the handler and the pet. In this form of role-play, they are groomed, trained, and controlled. I offer them discipline, structure, and fun while their subservient behaviors are observed and managed. The play can be elaborated with costuming, performances, competitions, and auctions, along with all the theatrics that define the experience.

There is consensual "forced" play that includes humiliation and "non-forced" play where partners negotiate the specific scene beforehand. Typically, sessions are scheduled in advance to allow for full preparation.

Example:

Giddy up, Ponyboy! My submissive dresses in a pony outfit that includes a mouth bit, reins, hooves, and other tack. While some miniatures prefer to wear an anal plug with a tail during their session, I refrain from anal play. This does not stop these ponies from seeking a Dominatrix who will fulfill that specific part of their fantasy, but in my stable, the focus remains elsewhere.

Will he go to the highest bidder? I decide during the scenario if I will auction off my prized pony or keep him. If he fails to please me, I will humiliate him and send him straight back to his stable.

Let's see what he can do! I command my pony to prance proudly while being led around my kinky palace. He must show me how disciplined and proud he is to be in my presence. If I am pleased, he will be asked to let out a whinny, and if I feel he is ribbon-worthy, he will win a prize!

Crushing/Pressure/Size-related Fetish

I hear:

"I brought 12 overripe tomatoes for you to crush on my chest today, Mistress. Please do it with your bare feet!"

"Will you allow insects and crush them?"

"Let's make guacamole with your feet today, Mistress."

"If I bring toy cars for you to step on and hurt your feet, will you do it, Mistress?"

"Ouch! That looks like it hurts!"

"How much do you weigh?"

In the world of Crush, the thrill is in the destruction. This fetish involves the desire to observe objects being crushed on a person's body or on the ground. Clients become excited as they watch items squirt and squish underneath my feet, hands, or latex-clad body.

The behavior is often linked to both sadistic and masochistic tendencies. Masochistic crushers identify with the object being destroyed. Excitement becomes apparent as they watch items squirt and squish underneath my feet, hands, or latex-clad body. Sadistic fetishists, on the other hand, fixate on the person doing the crushing or want to perform the act themselves. Players don't have to pick a side and can certainly embody both perspectives.

Macrophilia is a fetish centered on extreme size differences. This often involves imagining oneself with a giant or a much larger partner. It is rarely about weight; rather, it is the scale that matters to the player. This could include height, muscle, overall bulk, or simply the fantasy of feeling tiny next to someone enormous. For many, it is less about sex and more about the emotional response. Being small makes a person feel safe, overpowered, or completely surrendered.

Human obesity and other size-related fetishes can fall under this category, including fantasies about being smothered or crushed by another person. In my practice, I conduct only "soft" crushing. This involves the use of objects rather than high-risk physical weight. Please research "hard" crushing at your own risk.

Various items arouse these fetishists: fruit, specific food groups, balloons, toys, and cigarettes are just a few examples of the materials used to satisfy their hunger for destruction.

The following requests are excluded from my list of services, and I do not offer these acts of play. However, there are individuals in the profession who do offer these services:

Sex

I have heard:

"Do your services include sexual activities?" ME: "No!"

"I want to be fucked in the ass." ME: "Not going to happen!"

"Can I wear a butt plug?" ME: "No!"

"What if I just slip my dick between your thighs?" ME: "Absolutely not!"

"Can I at least have a hand job?" ME: "No!"

"How about using your feet?" ME: "No!"

The client wants to receive a handjob, footjob, blowjob, anal play, strap-on dildo play, vibrators, ttittyfuck, or sex along with his BDSM adventure.

Sex includes vaginal, anal, or oral activity that involves physical intimacy between the participants. Other forms of sexual engagement may include manual stimulation, or the use of feet, thighs, and breasts to provide pleasure. These acts involve mutual stimulation designed for both physical satisfaction and a deeper sense of connection.

Sexual acts often incorporate various forms of BDSM play. Most clients will request that these kinks be integrated directly into the sexual encounter, blending the power exchange with physical intimacy.

Cuckhold

I have heard:

"Do you have a guy you can fuck in front of me?" ME: "No!"

"I'm into watching a woman with another man." ME: "Not going to happen!"

"I can't satisfy a woman with my small dick. I like to watch a big cock fuck my woman." ME: "Can't help you with this one!"

"Do you role-play the fantasy of me being cuckhold?" ME: "Yes, we can do that!"

A client seeking a cuckold dynamic with a Professional Dominatrix wants a consensual experience focused on witnessing the Mistress engage in sexual intimacy with another man. This experience is about more than just the sexual act. At the center is a complex interplay of arousal, tension, and emotional release.

At its core, this dynamic is about surrender, power, and vulnerability. The thrill comes from watching, imagining, or knowing that someone else is taking what he cannot. The mixture of jealousy and excitement heightens every sensation, creating a space where control, trust, and longing collide. It is a level of intimacy and desire rarely felt in everyday life.

For many, cuckolding taps into a deep and often hidden need for humiliation. It brings a sharp awareness of limits, powerlessness, and one's specific place in the dynamic. Feeling exposed or "less than" can be intensely arousing because it strips away defenses and forces an encounter with raw emotion. In this space, shame and pleasure become inseparable. Guided by a Dominatrix, men can explore parts of themselves they might never confront otherwise. The process can feel both challenging and freeing.

Scat Fetish/Scatophilia/Coprophilia Poop Play/Poop Kink/Diaper Fetish

I hear:

"Nothing. I have never been asked to conduct any form of feces play."

Where's the toilet paper? Feces are the primary ingredient for this activity.

These acts involve one person smearing feces or defecating onto another person's body. It can also include watching a partner defecate onto an object or another participant. Some clients even seek to purchase feces from a play partner. These experiences can range from solo play to sessions involving multiple partners.

Scat players find pleasure in the smell, texture, and visual nature of the feces. Some participants choose to ingest it, and most find that the entire process leads to intense sexual arousal. These men often have very specific preferences; some will even ask a Dominatrix to alter her diet to control the smell and consistency of the waste.

Whether it is the warm sensation he enjoys or the taboo of the act itself, scat play serves as a way for a man to let go of deep-seated shame. For many, this is considered the ultimate form of humiliation and submission. His desire for this type of play is often a core part of his erotic identity. Sometimes, a person must explore these extremes during playtime to achieve the level of satisfaction and surrender they require. One might certainly say that this is extreme.

Golden Showers/Pee Play/Pee Fetish/Watersports/ Piss Play/Piss Kink/Urolagnia/Urophilia/Undinism

I hear:

"Can I drink your piss, Mistress?" ME: "No!"

"I love to keep the smell of urine on me all day." ME: "Still not doing it!"

"It's so humiliating to have a sexy and Dominant woman pee on me." ME: "Not happening!"

"Will you stand over me and shower me with your golden juices?" ME: "No!"

This is a popular request. A client will ask the Mistress to urinate onto his body or into his mouth. Other acts include urinating into a cup for consumption, wetting oneself, or incorporating a diaper fetish. In many cases, a submissive will ask for permission to urinate as part of a role-play scenario, turning a basic bodily function into an act of profound obedience.

These men often view this as the ultimate expression of Dominance and submission. For them, being "marked" by the Mistress creates a deep psychological connection and a feeling of being owned. Some are drawn to the taboo nature of the act, while others simply find the warmth and sensation of the liquid to be sexually stimulating. Within a power dynamic, the act of a Dominant relieving herself on a submissive reinforces their specific places in the hierarchy, stripping away the client's ego and replacing it with a sense of total surrender.

Needle Play/Play Piercing

I hear:

"Do you do pierce play?" ME: "No!"

Play piercing involves a skilled practitioner using sterile hypodermic or acupuncture needles to pierce the skin. This scenario is always negotiated prior to the act, ensuring both parties reach a clear, consensual agreement. While some engage in this for sexual pleasure, others seek the unique sensory experience and the psychological challenge of the needles.

During the session, the Mistress places and manipulates the needles to create a variety of physical sensations. Some enthusiasts seek more extreme forms of genital piercing, such as the Prince Albert. This specific piercing passes through the urethra and exits the underside of the glans. While intense, it is a highly sought-after mark of submissive endurance.

It is common for the client to experience a massive endorphin rush during the procedure. In some cases, this intense physical and mental state results in the man ejaculating without any direct sexual stimulation. The body simply reacts to the overwhelming sensory input and the release of internal chemicals.

At the end of the session, the needles are removed and proper aftercare is provided. The client must then follow a healing protocol for the small puncture sites left behind. This transition from the sharp intensity of the needles to the soothing nature of aftercare is a vital part of the trust dynamic.

Extreme Medical Play/Cutting

I hear:

"Will you be my doctor and give me an enema?" ME: "No!"

"I'm into heavy medical play and can bring in my play equipment if you like?" ME: "I don't do heavy medical play."

"If you won't do medical play, do you know someone who will?" ME: "Yes!"

Partners act out medical scenarios for physical, psychological, or power exchange purposes. The scenario is negotiated prior to the act, and both parties reach a consensual agreement that can be either sexual or non-sexual in nature.

Typically, role-play, degradation, and the thrill of forbidden thoughts draw people into this kind of play. These activities open the mind and body to new sensations and extreme levels of intensity. In some situations, medical play involves bodily fluids such as saliva, urine, blood, or semen. When players are being responsible, safety and health become the top priority. All participants must proceed with care and professional awareness.

During more extreme physical procedures, the Mistress may use a variety of tools and techniques. This can include monitoring vitals or using medical implements like catheters, disposable lancets, scalpels, staples, or bandages. Sensory play might involve ice, numbing sprays, dental tools, or breathing masks. Electrical stimulation or impact play could utilize TENS machines or other controlled devices, always avoiding the heart and ensuring no participants have underlying heart conditions. Specialty devices and bondage can include chastity, extreme restraints, prostate play, or sound sets.

Every action by the Mistress is intentional and measured. By blending control, sensation, and theatrical role-play, she creates a thrilling and immersive adventure. The experience is designed to be exciting while remaining grounded in the care and safety of everyone involved.

Branding/Bond Branding/Burning

"Will you brand me?" ME: "No!"

"It's my deepest desire to have your initials branded on me." ME: "No!"

"I swear I will let you brand me if you want to!" ME: "No!"

A person has their flesh burned to leave a permanent or temporary mark.

In a BDSM session, a client may ask the Mistress to cause him pain by extinguishing a cigarette on his flesh. This act can result in a permanent or temporary mark. He may have a specific fetish for women smoking or find the act to be an expression of superior Dominance. For many, this form of humiliation is a gateway to reaching true submission.

In other scenarios, the Dominant is asked to brand the submissive as a mark of ownership. This occurs in both professional and long-term private relationships. The client often views this as an act of complete devotion, while others find the intense level of pain to be deeply satisfying. Some participants simply find body modification to be aesthetically pleasing or sexually arousing.

There are several methods a Dominatrix may use to brand her client. Single-strike branding is the most common approach. Other specialized options include: cauterization, moxibustion, electrosurgical branding, cold branding, and micro-branding. Some practitioners also use a violet wand for micro-branding techniques.

The Residue

After reading about what I might do to your man, you may be feeling "Squick."

Squick: That visceral, "get-it-off-me" feeling that hits your gut when your reality is forced to acknowledge a fantasy that feels alien or wrong.

Welcome to the potential reality that your man could be one of these fantasy seekers. It is natural to feel surprised, amused, confused, disgusted, or even uneasy. I hope that you will gain new insight, not to change your morals, but to understand that this world exists for a reason that goes far beyond the "wrongness" you might feel right now.

I want to remind you that these BDSM activities occur between consenting adults. These are people looking to explore and fulfill their needs, desires, and fantasies. These acts are not for everyone, but many participants who dabble in a variety of BDSM experiences feel truly seen, heard, and celebrated. Many find not only deep satisfaction but also self-growth, healing, and moments of euphoric bliss. It is a journey of release, relaxation, and revelation.

Maybe your man has already asked for a slice of the kinky pie. Ask him. Find out. But be prepared: once you ask the question, you can never go back to not knowing the answer.

REFLECTION: RAINA MARKS

Gasping, Raina sits up straighter. *I am somewhat squicked out! I am falling down the rabbit hole on this one. Are you kidding me?*

She glances around, looking for something: comfort, clarity, maybe an excuse to stop reading. *What time is it? It is time for wine, right?*

The details pounding through her mind—when, where, and how—pummel her skull like a jackhammer that refuses to shut off. She needs relief: relief from the weight of what she is now feeling.

Questioning everything: *Where is my husband, really? Could he be one of those "Afternoon Delight" types? He is out of town right now, and I have no idea what he is doing. I don't trace his every step. I have no clue if he has ever seen a Professional Dominatrix… or someone else, for that matter. I keep reminding myself that I have always trusted my husband.*

She pauses, second-guessing herself. *But should I?*

The question lodges itself in her throat. *The wild array of kinky offerings is making me feel, frankly, unprepared. Some of the activities don't bother me, but most of them are a definite pass. From the sounds of it, I would not be surprised if my husband fancied some sort of kink or fetish. I have never even heard of three-quarters of this stuff. I do not think I could come up with these kinky activities in my wildest imagination.*

It is great that these acts happen between consenting adults, but I can't ignore the part that is hard to stomach: the cheating man participating in them.

The wavelengths in her brain oscillate rapidly as she absorbs new insights into the mind of a cheating man. *I want to learn more!*

Nervous. Interested. Alert.

CHAPTER 6

INTRO TO BDSM, KINK, & FETISH

"One man's normalcy can be another man's fright."

> **BDSM:** *An umbrella term that stands for Bondage and Discipline, Dominance and Submission, Sadism and Masochism. It refers to a wide range of consensual practices and power dynamics where partners explore roles, sensations, control, and fantasies. What sets BDSM apart is the emphasis on consent, trust, communication, and safety.*

These exploratory practices can include acts such as roleplay, restraint, spanking, psychological Dominance/submission, or erotic pain. It's good to recognize that sexual activity isn't always the point. For many, BDSM is not just about physical stimulation, but about emotional connection, vulnerability, and self-expression.

While I cover an overview of BDSM, Kink, and Fetish in this chapter, it's important to note that these subjects are vast and nuanced, far too expansive, broad, and complex to fully explore in just one chapter.

> **BDSM** (Bondage and Discipline, Sadism and Masochism, or Submission and Dominance).
>
> **B** in BDSM refers to Bondage: the practice of consensually tying, binding, or restraining a partner.
>
> **D** for Discipline in BDSM: the act of rules, control, and/or punishment over a submissive partner.
>
> **S** in BDSM stands for Sadism: the enjoyment of inflicting pain on your partner.
>
> **M** in BDSM stands for Masochism: the act of enjoying and receiving pain, mentally or physically, from a partner.

BDSM should be about consent between adults—always. BDSM may look intense, but it's based on clear and informed consent. Everyone involved agrees to the rules, limits, and roles ahead of time. It's a golden rule that nothing should ever be forced between play partners.

Informed consent is the basis of any BDSM dynamic. This is what keeps the mind and body in a safe, sane, and consensual space. What differentiates BDSM from abuse is the presence of consent, intention, and care. Partners check in with each other before, during, and after a scene—physically and emotionally—to make sure everyone feels supported. Negotiation, safe words, and honest communication help set boundaries so the experience is respectful and enjoyable for everyone involved.

Trust is everything. Before any play starts, partners talk openly about limits, desires, and expectations. Without trust, power exchange stops being liberating and starts becoming dangerous. Both people need to feel safe, seen, and respected, or the experience can do more harm than good.

BDSM itself is a huge spectrum. Some seek intense sensation or power; others crave emotional submission, roleplay, ritual, or the freedom of letting go. It can be deeply sexual or non-sexual, and it can be about connection, control, expression, or identity.

Kink vs. Fetish

Or is it just a preference?

- Fetish: A sexual or erotic necessity or strong psychological fixation.
- Kink: Non-normative interest that enhances pleasure but isn't essential.
- Preference: Simply an interest someone enjoys or is drawn to.

What is Kink?

Kink: *The use of non-conventional sexual practices, concepts, or fantasies. This word is also commonly used to describe BDSM. However, BDSM is one category within kink. The term refers to any sexual interest, practice, or fantasy that falls outside of what's considered "mainstream" or "vanilla" sex.*

That delicious twist on sex that makes the ordinary feel extraordinary. It's a path you take willingly because it excites you, not because you have to.

Kink can include a wide range of activities, such as:

- Roleplay
- Fetish play (feet, latex, etc.)
- Voyeurism or exhibitionism
- Sensation play (ice, wax, feathers)
- Power dynamics (Dominance/submission)
- And more

All BDSM is Kink. *But not all Kink is BDSM.*

You can be kinky without being into BDSM. They're connected, but they're not the same thing. Kink is broad and playful, sometimes experimental and sometimes subtle. It shakes up the routine and turns up the heat between people. Really, it's anything that steps outside the usual script of sex.

BDSM goes beyond the acts themselves. It's in the way power moves between people, the roles we take, the trust we give, and the control we exchange. Some are drawn to all of it; others gravitate toward one part more than the rest. There's no rulebook, no hierarchy, no "right" way to explore. What matters is what calls to you, the spark inside that whispers, *Yes… I want this!*

What is a Fetish?

Fetish: *A desire where gratification is linked to an abnormal (and sometimes obsessive) degree to a particular object, body part, clothing, etc. This can be sexual or nonsexual.*

A fetish is more than just a preference; it's a unique spark in the psyche. A deeply personal thread that ties desire to something specific, unexpected, or symbolic.

He explains, "It feels like a second skin. You feel so soft, and the rubber smells so good. This is what I love!"

His hands glide up and down my red latex catsuit. I grab his hands and place them on my bottom. "Touch here. Now move your hands slowly all over my ass."

He falls to his knees and begs me, "Please, can I touch your legs, too?"

He adjusts his cock, and his desperation is almost cute. "Go ahead, I can see my latex makes you horny."

Pleading, his voice weakens. "Can I touch you all over, Mistress? Please?"

Smirking at him, I respond, "Time will tell. For now, take your hands off me."

To someone with a fetish, it can feel like an irresistible current, a certain object, act, texture, or scenario that unlocks a sense of arousal, comfort, power, or vulnerability. It may be leather, feet, ritual, power play, or even the sound of a voice in command.

At times, the focus isn't sex at all, but identity, fantasy, or a safe space where mind and body feel fully alive. A fetish isn't something you choose, it's something most people discover. When embraced, it can open up a deeper understanding of yourself and let you explore your desires more freely. Oftentimes, the fetishist will seek out a lifestyle play partner or a Professional Dominatrix to help intensify their experiences.

Lingerie, latex, leather, clothing, panties, feet, shoes, food, hair, fingernails, smells, and body parts are just a handful of the fetishistic desires that men possess. In my experience, once a man directs his attention and becomes obsessed with a specific object, body part, or sexual fixation, they remain forever fixated.

For example, a person can become mentally and sexually aroused by their partner wearing a latex catsuit, but this does not constitute their love for the catsuit as a fetish. Some people enjoy latex for its look, feel, or fantasy appeal, without needing it for sexual arousal. In that case, it may fall under kink (a non-traditional interest or preference), style, or subcultural identity (e.g., in the fetish fashion or BDSM communities).

Fetishes are mostly sexual needs and have an emotional, psychological, or sensual charge. For example, a person experiences sexual arousal, deep excitement, or erotic attachment specifically tied to latex clothing, texture, smell, or appearance. The latex becomes a central or necessary part of their arousal or play. It's not just about fashion or style; it has become an attachment inked to their overall human system.

However, there are exceptions to this dichotomy. Many true fetishists can still mentally and physically become aroused by their partner even if their kinky object is nowhere nearby. These players can engage in ("vanilla") activities and achieve their release. I believe this is person-to-person specific, ever-changing, and reflects individual circumstances. I know, I have experienced this exact situation!

In brief:

- Kink (Focus): Behavior, activity, dynamic.
- Fetish (Focus): Centers on a specific object, material, body part, or act.
- Kink & Arousal: Boosts arousal but isn't required for it.
- Fetish & Arousal: Often needed for arousal.
- Kink & Psychology: Not always psychological.
- Fetish & Psychology: Often has deeper psychological roots.
- Kink & Social Views: Seen as fluid, cathartic, and a radical form of self-exploration.
- Fetish & Social Views: Often pathologized as a "condition," though when consensual, it is a vital—and harmless—expression of the core self.

Roles of Participants

Participants step into roles or identities that shape the nature of their play and relationships. These are not assigned based on gender or stereotypes, but chosen based on what fulfills the individual. Whether temporary for a session or established as a full-time dynamic, these roles—Dominant (they lead), submissive (they surrender), Switches (they do both)—are defined by trust and choice.

There are titles specific to the scene, and community roles are typically defined as:

- Top: The person giving sensation, control, or stimulation.
- Bottom: The person receiving it.
- Switch: Participants enjoy both Dominance and submission and may take on different roles depending on the partner or scene.
- Service Submissive / Slave: Serves the Dominant in domestic or ritualistic ways.
- Kinkster: General term for someone into Kink/BDSM.
- Fetishist: Someone who focuses on a particular object, material, or act.
- Caregiver: A nurturing Dominant in age play or emotional relationships.
- Primal (Hunter / Prey): Focused on instinctual power exchange.

BDSM Roles: Dominant

Dominant roles in BDSM come with a wide range of titles, each reflecting different dynamics, identities, or interests.

Some of the most common include:

- Domme / Dominatrice / Dominatrix / Domina: Female Dominant.
- Dominant / Dom: Male Dominant.
- Master / Mistress: Often used in more formal or structured arrangements.
- Daddy / Mommy: Caregiving roles within DDLG or age-play dynamics.
- Handler: Often seen in pet play contexts.
- Rigger: The person who ties in rope bondage.
- Sadist: Someone who enjoys inflicting consensual pain.
- Top: The one Dominating.
- Kinkster: A broad, inclusive term for anyone engaged in Kink.
- Brat Tamer: A Top who specializes in "Brats" (submissives who act out or misbehave on purpose to be put in their place.)

BDSM Roles: Identity Through Interests and Communities

Others may identify through their specific interests or communities, such as fetishists, leather or latex enthusiasts, or sex workers who incorporate BDSM into their professional roles.

BDSM Roles: Submissive

A submissive is the willing receiver. They submit themselves differently to each Dominant or play partner throughout their chosen experiences. Submissives may be commanded to take on a role that displays "action" and appears to be of a Dominant nature. However, their position as a submissive is to remain obedient to the Dominant's orders.

Submissive roles in BDSM come with a wide range of titles, each reflecting different dynamics, identities, or interests.

Some of the most common include:

- Submissive / Sub / Owned Submissive
- Slave
- Property
- Devotee
- Pet (e.g., puppy, kitten—often used in pet play)
- Little / Middle (in age play or caregiver/little relations)
- Brat (a playful, defiant submissive)
- Rope Bunny (in rope play; the one being tied)
- Masochist (enjoys receiving consensual pain)
- Toy (objectified or used in play)
- Slut / Slut Shaming Play (erotic play involving consensual humiliation)
- Baby Girl / Baby Boy (affectionate submissive role, often in DDlg play exchange)
- DDlg play is between two consenting adults
- Daddy Dominant plays the role of a caregiver to the Little Girl role of the submissive
- Or… *a special Little Bird ;)*

Slave Role

In BDSM, the term *slave* refers to someone who chooses, freely and consensually, to submit to a Dominant. This usually happens within a structured power-exchange dynamic called Master/slave, or M/s. These relationships are often deeper and more intentional than casual play. They can be long-term and, in some cases, extend into daily life, with the slave voluntarily giving up certain types of control over behavior, roles, or responsibilities.

It's important to be clear: this has nothing to do with historical or non-consensual slavery. In BDSM, the role exists because of trust, negotiation, and enthusiastic consent between adults. For those who identify as slaves, the experience can feel grounding, meaningful, empowering, or deeply intimate. These interactions can take on many forms that feel ritualistic, domestic, erotic, or spiritual, depending on the individuals involved.

The word slave carries weight and can be emotionally charged, so some people prefer alternatives like owned submissive, property, or devotee. But no matter the label, what matters most is clear communication, informed consent, and mutual respect.

For a man who carries the world on his shoulders all day, "slavery" isn't about losing his freedom, he simply wants the freedom of having no choices to make.

An Example of a Subculture

Some subcultures are more niche or imaginative, like the Furry Fandom, where people who love anthropomorphic animal characters express that interest through art, costumes (fursuit), role-play, or meetups. Most furry events are social and creative, though there are adult-only corners of the community as well. How people take part is personal and flexible, shaped by their own interests, boundaries, and the groups they connect with.

The Term "Vanilla" used in the BDSM/Kink/Fetish Communities

In these communities, the term "vanilla" is used to distinguish people who prefer more traditional sexual practices from those who explore kink. Calling someone "vanilla" signals that they enjoy conventional intimacy and don't usually engage in what others might consider unconventional or alternative sexual activities. The term is widely recognized around the world and has become a simple way to differentiate mainstream sexual preferences from more adventurous or experimental practices.

Whether you are new to BDSM or experienced, the most important thing to understand is that it's not about hurting people or being hurt. The practice is about trust, boundaries, and creating intense, meaningful experiences together.

Author's Note: Other common BDSM practices will be defined as you journey through the book, culminating in **Chapter 35: The Dungeon Dictionary** for deeper insight and terminology.

REFLECTION: RAINA MARKS

Popping up and off the lounge chair, Raina swiftly makes her way back to the kitchen. It is definitely time for wine!

She pours herself a generous glass of Prosecco, the soft fizz rising like a celebratory sigh. Lifting the glass, she nods to herself. "Well, that was helpful!"

Swirling the bubbles with a faint smirk: *I now have a better understanding of these deeper planes of kinky volitions. I have to admit, I'm finding it all oddly interesting, even if some of it feels a little bizarre.*

To each their own, I suppose. It's just too bad cheating has to be part of something that's clearly so necessary for these men: something that is obviously an important piece of their lives.

Back at the deep blue wonder, she swirls the sparkling liquid in her glass, the sun casting a prism of glistening temptation onto the rim. She takes a sip, feeling a tiny wave of satisfaction slide down her throat.

I understand that everyone wants and even needs to satisfy their needs. I get it. I do. But why does the satisfaction come at the cost of someone else's trust?

Her thoughts trail off into an imaginary rant she's not quite ready to finish. Here we go again, little fly.

Smirking. *Buzz, buzz!*

CHAPTER 7

FANTASY SESSION STORY
MUMMY MAN

This chapter presents a fantasy session story involving consenting adults only. All scenarios are fictionalized composites inspired by themes from my professional practice, and identifying details have been altered to protect privacy. The story explores adult BDSM dynamics, trust, and power exchange within a safe, consensual, and controlled environment.

Character Development: *This client is in his mid-twenties, lives in my city, and is a heavy player. He never speaks of his personal life and generally visits the Dungeon twice a year.*

The air is sharp with the distinct smell of heavy metal. Wall-to-wall steel imprisons anyone who dares to enter. Mirrored walls reflect reality whenever my prisoners are told to expose themselves. The Dungeon room confronts its intruders with a barred jail cell, a seven-foot-high metal torture chair, and a massive steel cage. At the bottom of the metal cage, the seven-foot holding tank locks and traps anyone I place inside. The cold metal top turns into a bondage table where I tie down my victims. Metal side rails feature a metal top canopy for various bondage contraptions and playful torture.

I place a blindfold, cellophane stretch wrap, breathing hose, CBT (Cock and Ball Torture) rope, leather bondage mitts, earplugs, pinwheel, safety scissors, water bottle, padlocks and keys, chain, and over 50 feet of rope onto the steel table. I have everything I need to securely mummify my kinky captive.

Bound by the hands of fate, it is time for me to lock him away in my vault of eroticism.

Commanding him: "Step into the jail cell and remove all your clothing. Neatly place all your belongings on the bench. When you are finished, turn around and face the wall, and put your wrists behind you through the bars."

Putting my hands through the cell bars, I lean in. The cold metal sends a chill down my spine, and I am ignited to take over his submission. I grab his hands and slip my fingers into his. With our hands linked together, I apply pressure and firmly squeeze: a little reminder of who oversees this two-hour adventure. Abruptly, I remove the iron restraints from the cell door and make my move.

Clink! Clank! Wrists shackled. "Now, let us talk!"

We briefly recap how he is feeling before proceeding with the session. I remind him of our safety signals: a three-finger ritual. One finger communicates that he is breathing fine and is comfortable. Two fingers communicate that he is still comfortable but needs water. Three fingers communicate that he is struggling and needs to get out of the mummification.

I review my preparations, start the music, and remove him from the cell.

Placing the blindfold over his eyes, I ask him to take deep breaths.

As he stands near the metal post, I secure one leather bondage mitt onto his left hand and moderately tie up his testicles with the CBT rope. Now it is time for me to craft his full-body rope harness.

Slowly and precisely, I begin to tailor his first layer of nylon entrapment around his body. I need his arms secured, so I lasso them down by his sides with the rope. As I tug him into me, I can feel the looming cords tighten. "Soon you will no longer be able to move. With any luck, you will still be able to breathe."

Maneuvering both ends of the rope under the others, I can see my woven mastery coming to life. The blue texture, like sapphire ribbons, embraces him with discipline and control. He is no longer his own as he descends into an intricate mind game of our power exchange.

After intricately working, my twisted strands are complete. "It only gets worse from here! Remember to stay calm and breathe slowly. I am going to give you the ultimate experience and take you into a world of sensory deprivation."

I prepare the breathing hose. Fabricating a makeshift strip of duct tape to secure the hose to his mouth will make it impossible for him to spit it out. I insert the earplugs to take away as much of his hearing as possible. Taking security precautions, I leave out his right hand for him to perform his safety signals. Starting at his feet, I carefully spiral a thick layer of cellophane over the rope harness and any exposed skin. Using a gentle hand, up and around his body I go. As his human form disappears, my mummified figure takes shape. Stopping at his neck area, I insert the breathing hose into his mouth and plug his nose with my fingers. "Breathe in and out of the hose. Are you comfortable, and are you able to breathe properly?"

Mumbling: "Yes, Mistress."

Concealed beneath the enveloping artistry, the wrap intensely covers his head like a translucent hood. He is no longer able to breathe out of his nose and must count on his mouth breathing to stay alive. Guiding him a few inches back, I tie off his rope harness to the steel pole. Next is the chain. After wrapping the chain around the pole and his body, I grab the padlocks and lock them at his ankles, and his middle and upper body areas, securing him in place.

Teasing him: "Better hope I do not lose the keys to these padlocks." The projecting hose that is coming out of his mouth begins to drip and spit onto the floor.

Unpleased: "I did not think I was going to have to punish you this quickly. However, you have already made a mess to be cleaned up. Maybe I will save this spit for you to lick up after I get you out of this cocoon."

Only he is unable to fully hear me, so I decide to punish him anyway. Covering the hose with the tip of my finger, I watch his right hand. His fingers begin to quiver, so I let go of the hose. I do not want to go too crazy on him. Yet!

Reassuring me, he signals with one finger, and I continue with my plan. Around his groin area, I cut a small square into the cellophane: a doorway to his tomb of precious jewels.

With a fiendish giggle: "What have we here, ancient artifacts?" A protruding shaft stares me down, welcoming me to play. I am even more excited to see his tied-up testicles, nice and firm. Taking out my pinwheel, I drag the spiky points against his cock and balls. Every roll of the wheel makes his body tense up. If I do not roll gently, I will make him bleed.

A hard cock makes for a perfect whipping post. I grab a riding crop from my bag and slap the shaft of his cock with a sharp sting. Pulling at the testicle rope, I do not stop slapping his cock until the rope unravels.

Thinking: *Hmmm, clothespins. Do I have any in my bag? I think so!* After finding ten clothespins, I pinch each pin all over his ball sack. I can hear through the hose that his breathing is beginning to increase rapidly.

Leaning into his ear: "You had better pace your breathing, because I am not going to stop." Even though he has not signaled two fingers, it is time to offer him a bit of water. I remove the duct tape and hose from his mouth. I bring the edge of the water bottle to his lips and give him a small sip. Watching his fingers, I see that he has put up two fingers signaling that he would like more water. Down goes the H20. "Drink up; you are going to need it!"

The clock is ticking, and his time is coming to an end. I place the breathing hose back into his mouth and seal the duct tape. Sitting back in my chair, I grab a magazine, turn up the music, and set my timer for 20 minutes. It is time to wait it out.

By surrendering control, my client can focus entirely on my touch, the anticipation, and his emotions, without distraction. These moments intensify the physical sensations and deepen trust between us, creating a powerful psychological and erotic experience.

Tick-tock. Tick-tock. The buzzer sounds, and it is time to release my prisoner from his enclosure. First, I remove the breathing tube from his mouth. Next, I take the medical scissors and cut the cellophane away from his face. Then I unlock the padlocks and remove the chain. With one long swoop of the medical scissors, I cut the cellophane up the front of his body. I remove the clothespins from his testicles, take out the earplugs, and take the blindfold off his face. For stabilization purposes, I keep his rope harness attached to the pole.

After a brief period, he reacclimatizes himself, and I take him out of the full-body rope harness.

"Free at last!" I have him sit down on a chair. After a brief discussion about the session, how he is feeling, and plenty of liquids, I command him to go back into the jail cell and get dressed. Because I love sending these men away with homework, I send him away with a few remains from our session: a bag containing the clothespins and testicle rope.

Commanding him: "Later today, when you have a moment, I want you to go into a private area. I want you to tie up your hard cock and clip all ten clothespins back onto your ball sack. Then I want you to stand in front of the mirror and masturbate your cock while whispering, "Thank you, Mistress!"

Enthusiastically responding: "Yes, Mistress! I will obey and think about our session today. Thank you, Mistress! Thank you!"

Laughing, I command him: "Now, go!"

REFLECTION: RAINA MARKS

Sip. Sip.

Raina downs a big gulp of her wine with a mixture of fascination and secondhand anxiety.

"Ugh! Mummy me-oh-my! That's intense," she mutters. *I'm glad they have that finger system in place, or that could've turned into a horror show.*

Her mind doesn't know if it should send signals to clap or to cover her eyes. *I don't really get how this Dominatrix does all this stuff. I'd be terrified that something would go wrong. Some of these BDSM games are risky. Like, really scary!*

A tiny chill trickles down her spine as she reads what's up next. "Of course," she whispers, eyes narrowing.

Raina folds one leg beneath her, pulling the towel tighter around her lap like a shield. *Do I really want to know?*

A silent moment stretches out as her thoughts swirl like the last bubbles in her glass. *It's infuriating. I'm angry for all the women who don't know what their cheating men are doing. It's like they are waiting for a blow they won't or can't see coming. Part of my brain can't help but feel paranoid.*

Please not my man. Not my man. But the mantra feels hollow. Even as she pleads with herself, a quiet admission creeps in, bitter and sharp. *There's a part of me that isn't naïve to the fact that my man might cheat.*

She exhales deeply, like a silent concession. Her frustration coils tighter in her chest: at him, at herself. *Have I brushed any possible signs under the rug? How many times did I excuse the late texts, his abrupt mood changes, and our emotional distance? I hate that I'm even asking these questions.*

And yet, here she is: left wondering.

CHAPTER 8

WHO IS THE MAN THAT CHEATS... AND OBEYS?

They're not always who you think they are. Men cheat for complex reasons, and there are no hard and fast rules.

The cheater isn't always the cliché—the bar-hopping, smooth-talking predator on a mission. More often, he's the man you'd never suspect: the "good guy," the attentive husband, the soft-spoken professional who holds the door for strangers and tucks his children in at night. He is the man who kisses his wife before heading to the office, perhaps even texting "I love you" before slipping into a secret he's been nurturing for years.

A man who cheats isn't always motivated by sex. He isn't necessarily looking for a one-night stand or even a conventional affair. What he's after is far more difficult to ask for and even harder to admit.

Behind the facade, questions he doesn't know how to voice pulsate in his brain:

- If I let go of my power, would she see me as weak or finally see me as real?
- If I asked for permission instead of taking it, would she say yes and accept me as I am?
- If I needed an escape from reality, would she open the door and guide me through it?
- If I craved an erotic connection, not just a release, would she be open enough to explore it with me?
- If I needed something different, stronger, and more electric, would she stand aside, let me have it, and still take me back?

These men typically don't want to destroy what they have; they claim to value it. Many of my clients tell me they truly love their partners. They carry the weight of their guilt, yet they are paralyzed by their unmet needs. Unfortunately, the version of the man who sits at the dinner table each night is rarely the whole story.

There is something deep inside of them that remains unexplored. When they don't feel safe or seen in their truth, they seek fulfillment in the shadows. They struggle with communication, self-control, or the suffocating fear that opening up will cost them everything. Without the tools or the courage to speak honestly, those needs find other outlets.

Somewhere along the way, life tamed them. They barely noticed when it stripped them of something wild. Now, they aren't just looking for grand gestures; they are starving from the slow, deep ache that builds when a man's needs go unmet for too long. They dream of surrendering that ache to someone who can sit with it without fear or judgment. Someone who doesn't ask them to compartmentalize, behave, or explain.

Hi, yes... it's me again. And this—this is where I step in.

As a Professional Dominatrix, I don't just listen to their secrets;

I extract them. Gently, but boldly. I am searching for the parts of themselves they don't yet understand or know how to say out loud.

With me, these men are looking to satisfy the psychological, emotional, and intimate hungers tied to power, control, and taboo fantasies. In our time together, those needs are cultivated through ritual, intention, and my consciously held presence. I lead him toward the one thing he's never been brave enough to ask for: himself.

While I categorize these men for you, keep in mind: they are fluid. A client may move between these categories effortlessly when the intensity of his need finally exceeds his restraint. It is important to note that while not every client I see is unfaithful, they all share one thing: they are here.

Disclaimer: *The individuals described in this book are consenting adults. The scenarios are based on personal experiences shared with me in a professional, consensual context. This book is intended for informational and educational purposes about adult BDSM dynamics, not as psychological or medical advice.*

Mr. Triggered

I hear:

"I was teased by a neighbor girl when I was younger and the memories stuck with me."

"I have a deep secret I have held onto all these years."

"I masturbate to a past experience!"

"I want to role-play a specific scene."

"When I was younger something happened that I never stopped thinking about."

There is a specific type of man shaped by the inevitable ways life grips his evolutionary makeup. These are the men sculpted by the primal drive to "fuck and release," but they are also caught in a modern script where temptations are a buffet of tantalizing morsels, constantly within reach.

Yet, for this man, the hunger isn't just about the present; it's about the echo of the past.

I'm talking about the experiences that were confusing or emotionally charged in childhood, moments that resurface in adulthood as symbolic elements in fantasy, now viewed through a fully adult lens. These men carry psychological patterns formed long ago that dictate how they understand themselves today. They arrive at my door with a mix of fascination and hesitation, finally ready to examine the parts of their identity they've spent a lifetime suppressing or secretly fantasizing about.

These individuals aren't driven by mindless impulse; they are guided by a deep, thoughtful curiosity. Certain memories or recurring themes feel compelling not because they demand reckless action, but because of the emotional intensity locked inside them. Within the sanctuary of a consensual, structured session, these reflections can be explored safely and with sharp intention.

We have to acknowledge the outside world: media, social circles, and cultural expectations all play a role in shaping what we find exciting or taboo. But inside my walls, that noise fades. Exploration remains grounded in conscious choice, trust, and clearly defined boundaries.

In my experience, these "adult players" aren't looking for a thrill, they're looking for clarity. They find emotional release by finally walking down the mental pathways they've been told were off-limits.

When these clients come to me, most aren't asking to relive the past; they are asking to understand themselves in the present. Others, however, are finally ready to step *into* the past—to touch the parts of themselves that have lived only in the shadows of their imagination for decades.

Role-play draws its power not from imitation, but from transformation. Together, we take what was once confusing or unresolved and we explore it boldly, safely, and consciously.

Mr. Clarity Hunter

I hear:

"I can't stop thinking about why I want to feel powerless and humiliated in front of a Dominant woman."

"I am constantly fantasizing about a powerful woman talking down to me."

"I try not to masturbate to these thoughts, but I can't stop. Is something wrong with me?"

"I have always been interested in BDSM, but I want to understand more."

"Do I have psychological problems?"

"It excites me to think about being tied up. But why do I think this way?"

"Can you help me gain clarity as to why I want to lose control of myself?"

"Mr. Clarity Hunter" is deep in his head. Desperate to make sense of the swirling thoughts and unspoken fantasies that have haunted him for years, he arrives with a thousand questions. Uncertain, but curious, he leans into the space we create together, and he is hungry for answers. It's not uncommon for part of our session to be spent unraveling pieces of his life, gently teasing the threads of his desire into the light.

As the fog in his mind begins to lift, something changes. He starts to understand himself, what drives him, the cycles he falls into, and his ache for something more. With that clarity comes a newfound confidence. He asks fewer questions and begins asking for what he wants. This is where things get interesting. This is where they get real!

Clarity seekers like him often return to me, eager, and drawn to the way this space makes them feel. They get a taste of this kind of freedom, and rarely stay away for long.

Mr. Low Self-Esteem

I hear:

"I feel safer here. I can open up more!"

"I don't really deserve all this fun!"

"Do you think I'm weak?"

"I don't want to feel anything but powerless."

"I feel awkward and don't like myself too much for doing all this!"

"Coming here is easier than trying to date."

This man's low self-esteem has him broken down inside a ditch full of avoidance and lack of self-worth. He's not necessarily looking for freedom, but some kind of structure without any judgment.

In the Dungeon, he can hide from reality and keep his cheating secrets in the dark. For many of my clients, cheating feels somehow safer than telling the truth.

My client visits me to escape for a moment, to take a rest from his internal chaos full of self-loathing and constantly feeling like he is insufficient. Unfortunately, he has learned that wanting makes him weak, inconvenient, or selfish. In my presence he can be uncertain or needy without having to disappear. He often struggles with two sides of himself: the man who is approved of and the man who is quiet, ashamed, and full of secrecy. The secrecy he likes to call control!

This is where the contradiction lives and this is where his shame seeks release. Sometimes that release becomes erotic and laced with lies. Honesty would mean he would have to risk disappointment, rejection, or the possibility that his needs might change how he is loved. Usually, this man that isn't afraid of being caught, he's afraid of being known.

Now he has turned himself into a cheater. The trust in his relationship is broken and so is a part of him. He shows who he is on the inside by clinging to rules with me. He betrays, yet obeys. Unable to trust himself with his own desires, he hands that responsibility to me.

Mr. Hardwired

I hear:

"I met a woman that started Dominating me when I was twenty."

"The first time I had sex with a woman, I was her submissive!"

"I was her sex toy!"

"She tied me up and I had no idea what BDSM really meant."

"Since my first kinky encounter, I have never stopped being kinky."

Wired forever?

I have heard this explanation repeatedly. These men were introduced to BDSM and kink in their early twenties or younger by women who guided them into these worlds before they had a chance to explore their own sexual identities. That initiation left a mark, one that shaped the way they experience desire, intimacy, and trust for the rest of their lives.

Some of these men have a hard time with "vanilla" intimacy and are continuously attracted to BDSM and the familiar roles. For them, BDSM and kink became the way they came to understand pleasure, control, and surrender. It's their default pattern that has been reinforced over many years. I wouldn't really call them habits, because they have been embedded deeply into what they feel defines a big part of who they are.

For most of their adult lives, BDSM has been more than fantasy. These acts are thrilling, rewarding, and identity-affirming, but they also became layered with shame, secrecy, and doubts around self-trust.

Being guided by a more experienced partner early on can lead them to rely on others to help shape their intimate sense of self. They come to me because I recreate their early experiences or help them with that need for intimate structure. Most of these men, through their confessions to me, state they have flat out cheated, betrayed, broken boundaries, and tested loyalty. Over and over again!

Mr. Mad Man

I hear:

"I don't know what's going to happen, I'm just tired of all the drama!"

"I just need a break!"

"I cheat because I want to punish her."

"I don't feel like I get what I deserve."

"Everything is pissing me off. On top of all of it, I can't even get her to fuck me, let alone fulfill a fantasy of mine."

"The relationship is almost over anyway; I don't care anymore!"

"Fuck it, I'm horny!"

"I'm tired of not getting what I need!"

"Whatever, I'm not going to stop coming here. I can't live without this in my life!"

"You are the only person that really makes me happy, this is my escape!"

"I usually feel guilty, but not today. I can't deal with her or life anymore!"

"I feel like I can finally breathe!"

"I feel devalued by everyone!"

"If I didn't have you, I would not be able to cope with my life."

"Why can't I just like what I like?"

These men walk in like turbulent machines, ready to spray down the walls with their overly pressurized sexual hose. It's extremely common for them to pay me a visit when things aren't going well between them and their partners. The stressors of life have them playing, *"Knock, knock! Who's there at my door? Let me in!"*

Reality is slapping these men silly. They throw two shits to the wind if they are tired of life, bored, frustrated with their partner, craving excitement, needing release, or simply not getting enough sex. Anger has taken control of their minds, and they are on a quest.

They have a certain look when they enter my den. With furrowed brows and downturned lips, they walk in tense and rigid.

Their frustrations follow them like a trail of army ants, each one trying to carry the weight. They are desperate for that escape. They are not looking for forever, but they are looking for that breath between the noise.

Once inside, their signs of agitation are usually followed by a big sigh, a sigh of relief. They are momentarily free and looking forward to forgetting what brought them to me in the first place.

It's time for me to give my client a real attitude adjustment, and he's more than willing to spend his money taking my kinky course. Just like that, I've slapped him straight back into reality.

Our time together may be temporary, but it's potent. It gives him just enough to return to his reality a little steadier and a little stronger. He is able to face what waits for him with a touch more clarity, and far less fury. Even a short escape can feel like salvation when it's done right.

Mr. Lonely

I hear:

"It's so nice to be here with you. You are so beautiful. I have been looking forward to coming here today for so long. Do you think we could just talk for a little while before we get started?"

"I wish you were my girlfriend!"

"Being alone sucks!"

"I feel so much happier after I spend time with you."

"If I didn't have you, life wouldn't be worth living."

"Will you dance with me?"

The lonely man craves more than touch; he aches to be seen. Whether he's searching for connection, kinky play, affection, or simply a woman's full presence, what he's truly longing for is *belonging.*

Loneliness is a heavy, layered feeling. It moves through him as sadness, frustration, boredom... sometimes even anger. When he is in my presence, something reframes, and he is happier and more content. These feelings help him feel a little less invisible.

With great compassion, open arms, and a spark of reassurance, I welcome my lonely men into a space to share something they may not find anywhere else: presence, connection, and kindness.

I listen, not just with my ears, but with my energy. I pay attention to what they crave emotionally, mentally, and physically. I know our time together matters. Sometimes, it's not just play, and can feel more like a lifeline.

This client is running on empty and desperate for human support and contact. He needs and wants what he doesn't have in his daily life. He loves to role-play and often will request that I play his fantasy girl or an attentive and caring partner. Typically, these sessions will include BDSM activities with spankings or equipment.

With me they aren't ignored inside their loneliness and our time together becomes their one constant. Giving them something to count on and not just the thing they enjoy, but *need*. This isn't for fantasy alone, but for the emotional oxygen it gives them. I don't take that lightly. I hold that space with intention, knowing I might be the one place in their world where they can just be... touched.

Mr. Addicted

I hear:

"I'm coming back next week. This is great! I love it!"

"I watch porn non-stop! Especially BDSM related porn."

"I think about kinky stuff all the time. Sometimes I get off and I am ready to go again."

"I can't stop thinking about sex. I am horny all the time. I think I am a sex addict! LOL."

"I am a sexual person. I need sex!"

"Sex is great. I wish I could cum all day long!"

"It's just sexual gratification!"

"I'm a sex addict! Coming to the Dungeon is just one way I fulfill my needs."

"I feel out of control with my sexual desires!"

"I will do anything to satisfy myself!"

"I need more than just sex!"

My sexually addicted clients live on the edge of hunger, driven by an insatiable need for sex, porn, strip clubs, BDSM, fantasy, or kink. It's not just desire, it's compulsion.

Compulsive sexual behaviors don't appear out of nowhere, they're felt deep in the mind and body. Once dopamine surges, it can feel like a switch has flipped. For many of these men, the hunt begins, and they seek the next rush as if survival depends on it.

When they come to the Dungeon, they're not just chasing pleasure; they're craving release. Any stimulation will do, as long as it delivers that intoxicating rush. The release becomes an escape hatch, a way to dissolve stress, anxiety, or the chaos they are experiencing that day. Or a way to feed their addiction!

Their thoughts revolve constantly around intimate gratification. These men always have a reason, an excuse, or a rehearsed justification. Their BDSM interests are wide and untamed, always seeking out that next thrill and high.

When are they here with me? Any time of day is the "right" time for these men, and nothing stops them. Once they taste the freedom of exploring their desires without judgment and the ease of my availability, they keep coming back.

Mr. Substance Abuser

I hear:

Crickets.

Typically, they are quiet and do not expose themselves with words.

If you think you are unsure of what your man is doing,

I guarantee you, the drug-seeking man has no idea what he is doing most of the time, either. This guy ultimately has no regard for you or himself. The substance abuser's behavior is unpredictable, impulsive, reckless, and often driven by poor decision-making.

Druggie clients are like hollow trunks. You can try to fill them with substance, but you are barking up an empty tree.

Some of these clients are difficult to detect right out of the gate, and others reek of their substance abuse. Others try to mask it, but I can feel it. The moment I detect someone is under the influence, I shut it down, and they're escorted out immediately.

I had a client years back who came in for a session. It was not obvious that he was under the influence until we were in the private room together. He was excited to show me the perfect lines of cocaine he had railed out on the bondage swing seat. I exited the room and had him removed.

For months, this client made ongoing efforts to regain my trust. He would call the Dungeon repeatedly, trying to speak with me. He made numerous attempts to schedule a session together, but had no success for months. After six months, I agreed to have a sit-down conversation with him. We discussed the events that took place in the last session, my rules, and the fantasy he was looking to fulfill. It appeared that he was not under the influence, and I agreed to move forward with the session the following Tuesday.

Carrying Prada, La Perla, and Gucci bags, he rained money as he walked through the door. Money fell from his pockets, and like a chipmunk, I gathered up the greenery and shoved it back into his pocket. He was clueless! I remember him trying to hand me the cash out of his stuffed pockets. He was offering up his credit cards to me like pieces of gum. I rejected his advances and kept putting the credit cards and cash back into his wallet.

I moved forward with the session. I commanded him to remove his clothing, I checked through the rest of his pockets, and I found no signs of drugs or alcohol. Even though he seemed sober during our initial meetup, I could tell, once we settled in, that he was not 100% in his right mind. I had an important decision to make. Instead of sending him back out on the street, I decided to go forward with the session. In this situation, I wanted to observe his state of mind further, and felt that it was a safer decision for the client to rest out what appeared to be an aftermath of a morning alcohol venture.

Our session time was set for two hours. Only I did not follow his exact fantasy plan and used my discretion to better reflect his condition. The two of us dressed in La Perla nighties, and I had him lie down on the bondage table. We spoke of many things, drank a lot of water, listened to music, and I tickled his ear with slutty girl rhymes. Dressing like a rich little slut was his forte, and dirty words aroused his mind. After the two hours were over, I had him dress and gather his belongings. I made sure that all his money and credit cards went right out the door with him. Except for all the beautiful designer swag that I was graciously gifted.

Several months later, he came back in for another session. Only this time, he was 100% sober.

The Dungeon room was dark and still. We sat side-by-side on the black cushioned bench. He explained to me that one month prior, he was released from a rehabilitation center for being an addict. With his eyes looking straight into mine, he began to thank me. I listened and felt a high level of compassion warm up my body.

Telling me. "Most women would have taken advantage of me. They would have taken my money and my credit cards without hesitation. Thank you for not doing that to me, and thank you for being patient with me. I came here today, not to session, but to tell you how grateful I am that you gave me a chance to see you again that day. It meant a lot to me!"

He got up and left. That was the last time I saw this client. He died of an overdose shortly after I saw him.

Mr. Masochist

The **"M"** in BDSM stands for **M**asochist.

I hear:

"I love pain!"

"I love where my head goes when I feel the pain!"

"It hurts so good!"

"I can take a lot of pain, so don't hold back!"

"I get such a high from all the endorphins that are released during our session."

"I need to give up control!"

"The pain helps me relieve my stress and anxiety."

"I find the pain sexually arousing!"

Here's an example of a masochistic session with a repeat client:

"I have this fantasy that keeps playing over and over in my mind. I find myself religiously masturbating to these specific images. I am going to let you in on a little secret of mine. I don't just visualize the fantasy while I masturbate; I use a paddle on my ass at the same time. I love to think about being verbally humiliated by a Dominant woman, and I like feeling the physical pain.

Here is what I would like us to do. I am going to lie down on the floor on my side. I want you to tower over me and verbally humiliate me. Use the whipping cane on my ass and don't stop! Do it hard! Keep whipping me and tell me things like, 'I am a worthless piece of shit.' Tell me I need to be punished, and I deserve what I get. If I do a good job, you will bring in your girlfriend to smother my face with her soft cotton panties. Make her sit on my face for a long time so I can smell her pussy through her cotton dreamcatchers."

The masochistic man derives sexual gratification from humiliation, self-denial, and emotional or physical pain. He can be masochistic, submissive, or a combination of both. The submissive side is obedient, passive, and ready to conform. The masochistic side takes pleasure in pain.

Other men can be defined as a sadomasochistic player. The sadist in him generates pleasure, especially sexual gratification, by inflicting pain or humiliation on himself or others.

These clients often struggle to feel physical pleasure unless their minds and bodies are pushed to the edge. For them, pleasure and pain can happen at the same time, wired together in the brain's dopamine and opioid systems. When these systems fire, the masochist can experience a deep, erotic release. The relief that comes from pain adds to their pleasure, leaving them both euphoric and empowered.

Here are some of the things I've noticed and heard from these men during our sessions:

- The exchange of power is deeply satisfying; letting go can bring relief, even peace.
- Some are drawn to toxic or abusive dynamics, craving the intensity of sadness, anger, humiliation, and shame.
- Many struggle to say no, so I have to be careful and responsible during play.
- They're driven by motivation and the thrill of the chase, always testing limits.
- Positive pain play often lifts their emotional state and can even dull the perception of pain.
- They try hard to please me, sometimes sacrificing themselves; their sense of unworthiness fuels a rush of elation, and it's my job to keep that balanced.
- They crave drama and theatricality; I design scenes to deliver the strongest dopamine hit.
- They're addicted not just to stimulation, but to the achievement of it.
- Many say they "love pain," or at least need it to process something deeper.

Many cheat because acting out their pleasure/pain fantasies on their own is no longer enough. They want to play in real time, with a real person, and *will* find a play partner. If your man is a masochist, the hunt to get his painful fix may be critical and he's on a mission.

Success! "Mr. Hungry for More Pain" has finally found someone to satisfy his needs. That tempting taste that he wants more of and can't wait to feel again. Other men have played in the past, are seasoned players, and are desperate for another turn. They love finding someone else to join them inside their masochistic games.

Having masochistic interests doesn't mean someone has a disorder. What matters is how it affects their life, not the interest itself. Many men explore these desires safely and without disruption. Simply enjoying or fantasizing about masochistic acts doesn't make someone "disordered." This only becomes a problem if it causes serious distress or interferes with daily life.

Each masochist has unique preferences and motivations, but all activities must be consensual, negotiated, and safe. It's common for masochistic clients to request spankings, whippings, nipple clamps, ball-busting, testicle weights, cock squashing, choking, smacking, food play, intense bondage, and more. Extremists may ask for piercing play, cutting play, or medical play. Some even request defecation and urination from a Mistress.

I play with men who are extreme masochists, seasoned players with high pain tolerance. Some are masochistic but not submissive, seeking only the physical pain that triggers them mentally and physically. They crave the endorphin rush, which immerses them in a deep, euphoric headspace or subspace. Many of these players describe feeling like their minds are in a cloud for days after our session. They explain how seeing the redness or bruises on their skin can transport them right back into this headspace. They often use this state of mind and session memories to masturbate or to fuck you at home. *So, I've been told!*

Whether it's drugs, alcohol, gambling, arguing, perfectionism, or even the rush of an orgasm, all these things can spark that euphoric feeling just like pain play. But it's not all about indulgence and escape. If you're into exercise, meditation, giving back, or learning, you can still experience that same mental, emotional, and physical high. Your endorphins start flowing, and just like the masochist, you can surrender to the natural mood boosters of your body. Happiness and joy get a little lift, all thanks to endocannabinoids, those brain chemicals that send you soaring into euphoria.

So, in a way, you and the masochist have more in common than you might think. Here's to that blissful state of euphoria!

Mr. Curiosity

I hear:

"I have always been curious about visiting a Dungeon and often fantasize about being controlled by a Dominant woman."

"What exactly goes on here at the Dungeon?"

"Really? Can I do that?"

"This is exciting. I want to tell you everything I fantasize about."

"I had no idea I could fulfill my fantasies like this with someone like you."

"Am I really even cheating? I'm just curious!"

Whether he is a potential *Newbie* or a *Looky-Loo*, these clients are curiously investigating their possibilities. They have repeatedly relived their fantasies inside their minds, and they can no longer resist the curiosity. And now, they are open to cheating.

These clients walk a path paved by curiosity, one that leads them straight to my Dungeon. Compelled by thoughts they've tried to ignore, they finally surrender to the pull of their desires. Here, in this space I've carefully crafted, they're free to ask the questions they've never dared to voice and explore the fantasies they've only whispered to themselves in the dark. They're often surprised by the breadth of experiences I offer and the services they didn't know existed. Once that surprise settles, excitement takes over. You can see it in their eyes: the realization that they've found what they've been searching for all this time.

Typically, these men ask a lot of questions in the beginning and want to start with the basics of BDSM play. Their kinkiness is often broad, undefined, and tangled in layers of curiosity. Cautiously at first, they all seem to share an open mind and a willingness to explore. They want to dip a toe in, not dive headfirst, unsure of how deep their cravings truly run.

Soon after our initial encounter, *after the walls of hesitation begin to crack,* he reaches for his wallet. With trembling excitement and nervous anticipation, he opens his pocketbook and takes the kinky leap of faith straight into the session. From fantasy to flesh, the journey begins.

The first few sessions together are usually more instructional and simplified. Steadily, we add more playful activities as time goes on. "Mr. Curiosity" becomes more transparent, losing his inhibitions more and more with every visit. Often, they become regular clients, but it is not unusual for them to be a one-hit wonder and disappear.

Mr. In Control

I hear:

"I have a fantasy I want to share with you. Even though I am a Dominant man, being in control all the time can be daunting. I am tired of being in control all the time. I want to be in a safe space where I can lose control."

"Please, Mistress, take the lead!"

"I am in control all day long, and I need to surrender myself to you!"

"Just tell me what to do, please! I am exhausted and tired of running the show. I need a break!"

"In my mind, I no longer want to be the man!"

"Coming here helps me break my routine! I need some excitement!"

"Mr. In Control" no longer wishes to be in control. He wants to be out of control.

These men are Dominant in most—if not all—aspects of their lives, and they come to me seeking to be set free. Often burned out by the weight of the world, they crave something few understand: a rebalancing of power. They don't want to think anymore. They don't want to lead. What they desire is relief, an escape from the relentless mental, emotional, and physical pressures of life.

A man who is always in control finds himself at the forefront of constant responsibility, at work, at home, and in his social world. That constant demand to perform, decide, fix, and lead wears him down. So, he comes to me to cope. When he surrenders, he's able to find peace. I take the reins, reducing his burdens and offering him the space to breathe, decompress, and reset.

Others come with more exploratory intentions, curious about their psychological wiring. Maybe they want to know what it feels like to be submissive. Maybe they've fantasized for years about a true power exchange. Inside the safety of my space, we explore this together, uncovering sides of him that rarely see the light of day. The novelty of alternating control is more than intriguing; it becomes a gateway to growth, excitement, and self-awareness.

Some want to understand submission as a concept, to observe how I command a scene with confidence, purpose, and clarity. It opens their minds to personal growth and deeper self-reflection. Watching me lead teaches them something about their own leadership, emotional intelligence, and the nuanced art of communication.

Inside the Dungeon, he becomes another man. The once unshakable Dominant finds himself melting into a submissive or relaxed headspace, finally free from the grind of external expectations. He is ready to receive my commands. He is eager to obey. These men curious, brave, and vulnerable, are often some of the most well-behaved, open-minded, transparent, and emotionally connected clients I see.

I have also noticed that once they surrender and lose themselves inside this "out-of-control" world, they often find something they didn't expect: healing. These sessions offer them the mental, emotional, and physical balance they've been craving, and that balance keeps them coming back for more.

Mr. CBT and His Sidekick Mr. Ballbuster

I hear:

"Tie up my balls, Mistress! Do you have those big weights you can dangle down from my testicles?"

"Is my cock big enough for that ball harness?"

"I feel so weird that I want you to do this to me!"

"Do other men like CBT?"

"Use the pinwheel and weights today, Mistress!"

"Kick me hard, Mistress! Right in the balls!"

"I want to get down on my knees and have you launch me as far as you can with your foot, kicking straight into my testicles."

Cock and Ball Torture (CBT): *The consensual act of inflicting pain and constriction directly to the male genitals.*

Ball-busting (BB): *The consensual act of inflicting pain and constriction to the cock and testicle areas. These men love to be kicked, kneed, slapped, or punched in the genitals. Both acts are requested BDSM activities, and most clients will incorporate these activities into their overall playtime experience.*

This is not for the faint of heart. Consensual *Cock and Ball Torture* and *Ball Busting* are not just for kinky enthusiasts.

Are these men wired differently? A lot of men will do anything to have increased pleasure when it comes to their sexual arousal. Pain and constriction are applied to the male genitals by the Dominant. Toys and devices are used during the play experience and make the genitals more accessible. Some men love the sensations of having extra-sensitive genitalia. Cock and Ball torture gives them just that!

The bigger the better! When the cock and testicles endure any type of restraint or torture, they become more sensitive and larger. With every touch of the hand or slap of the riding crop, their sensitivity to pleasure begins to increase. Men have explained that their orgasms can be stronger, and they find CBT to release an enormous amount of tension.

Men who are into cock and ball torture are consensually here for the pain and pleasure. They love the erotic humiliation and control, and they want to please the Mistress. They love being at the mercy of a Dominant woman. Feeling powerless and hopeless heightens the pleasures.

If they are simply into pain without the power exchange component, this form of pleasure torture brings them great release, relaxation, and sexual pleasure. They do not necessarily need to play the role of a submissive to find the acts satisfying.

Here is a list of painful activities these players will ask for:

- A good lasso tied snug around their ball sack or down the shaft of the cock
- Weights and other supplies strung down from their testicles
- Trampling: A firm cock and/or ball squish under my boot
- Cock and/or ball harnesses
- Chastity devices
- Bondage
- Testicles pulled by rope or chain
- Wax play
- Squeezing, kicking, electrostimulation, genital spanking, tickle torture
- Medical play
- Piercings
- Verbal erotic humiliation
- And more

Mr. Nipply Nip

I hear:

"I want the heavy nipple clamps today, Mistress! Can you squeeze them extra hard?"

"Pinch them harder, Mistress! Please."

"My nipples must be linked to my erogenous zone. Having them pinched gets me so horny!"

"I can't cum unless my nipples are being pinched."

"It's my zone! My sexual zone of pleasures."

"Slap my erect nipples!"

> **Nipple Torture (NT):** *Physical pleasure and/or pain applied to the nipples of a play participant through various techniques and devices.*

Approximately 40% of my clientele love nipple stimulation. The nipples are an erogenous zone where they love to heighten their erotic stimulation.

Men, like women, can experience enhanced sexual arousal through stimulation of the nipples. A lot of men have a connection between their nipples and their cocks, enhancing their intimate gratification. Some men have even expressed that they are able to reach climax more quickly if their nipples are tweaked with pain or pleasure.

To arouse his nipples, I usually stimulate and warm them up before any act of play. Typically, arousal of the nipple affords me a better grip on the areola, making it easier to apply nipple equipment. These men love it when I look them directly in the eyes and increase the pain in their pointy little nips. It is extra special when I talk dirty and remove the clamps or other devices, letting the blood flow rush back into their nipples and releasing oxytocin (a hormone that is associated with having an orgasm). Bring on the sensitivity!

Nipple play can involve everything from nipple clamps,

clothespins, and rubber bands to pinching, slapping, scratching, flicking, whipping, or even potato chip clamps. It might include ice play, hot wax, feathers, weights, brushing, tickling, or other various BDSM rituals.

Safety comes first, and all necessary precautions are taken. Soothing and aftercare are part of the experience and are necessary for most clients.

Whether it's sexy talk or something a little rougher, it's all about exploring what heightens sensation and what deepens the connection.

Mr. Extreme Thrill Seeker

I hear:

"It's so wrong for me to be here! I can't believe I do the things I do!"

"I'm such a bad boy. Punish me!"

"I can't help it! I'm just a bad man!"

"Make it intense and disgusting. I want excitement!"

"I like it risky!"

"Do you think I can change my ways, Mistress?"

"I want it extreme!"

This rule-breaker finds excitement in being a bad boy. He gets a thrill out of what is exciting and even taboo. He has no reservations about taking a risk, and the adrenaline rush turns excites him. He loves saying "yes" to forbidden acts that are otherwise against the rules.

Taboo fantasies are those secret desires that live just beyond the margins of what society deems "appropriate." They're not necessarily about doing something wrong, but about imagining the forbidden. Often layered in curiosity, rebellion, and raw vulnerability, these fantasies give people a safe mental space to explore power, shame, control, or surrender.

The sexual thrill seeker cheats not always because he's unhappy, but because he's insatiable. The moment something feels "off limits," it becomes irresistible. Sometimes it's less about love or loyalty and more about the heat, the chase, and the forbidden thrill that delivers the dopamine rush.

Inside the taboo fantasy, lies a shortcut to stimulation, and a dicey stand at the edge he's always after. That edge makes him feel powerful and alive. It represents: freedom, release, or even a kind of healing. It's a way to step outside the polished version of himself and reach a deeper truth, something primal and real.

In a safe, consensual space, taboo fantasies can offer more than just arousal; they can offer liberation. This fuels him. This client thrives on variety and surprise, always ready to push a little further, and taste something new.

As an example. My regular client shows up for his monthly spanking. Even though he is in a relationship, he requests to leave with red paddle marks on his bottom. He explains to me how he loves the risk of keeping this secret from his wife. Having to be on high alert and knowing he will have to figure out a way to hide his *apple bottom* from her excites him. The risk he takes prolongs the experience he had with me, and he can get a greater return on his kinky investment.

Mr. Subby Boy

I hear:
    "Hello Mistress! May I come in? What can I do for you today?"
    "Do you need anything? I am here to serve you!"
    "You look lovely today! I am excited to see you, Mistress!"
    "I was born to serve!"
    "I try to serve my wife, but she just doesn't get it."
    "I have always been submissive."
    "I'm shy. I feel comfortable telling you about myself, though."

Tell the subby boy what to do, and he'll most likely do it. He makes a great service boy, too!

"Remove all your clothing except for your boxers. Take your position and kneel on the red rug. Make sure to have your palms facing up and your chin down. I expect you to refrain from making eye contact with me today. For starters, you will act as my coffee table. I need to finish my lunch. After I enjoy my meal, you will rub my hands and feet. You will then lick my dishes clean and be on your way out of my sight. I have important things to do today, and I can't be overextending myself here with you."

Kneeling. "Yes, Mistress!"

These clients come to the Dungeon seeking more than just play; they come to surrender. They crave the presence of a woman who not only understands their submissive ways but also knows exactly how to handle them.

Power exchange isn't just a want; it's a *need*. Whether it's role-play, restraint, or ritualized service, their deepest satisfaction comes from pleasing their Mistress. To serve is their pleasure. When they kneel in my presence, it's not out of weakness, it's devotion. They long for someone who can read between the lines of their fantasies and guide them confidently through their submissive world, one command at a time.

Often activated in childhood, some submissive men report recalling games with peers that later became linked to sexual arousal in their imaginations. Over time, these fantasies shaped their thoughts, and certain role-playing scenarios, like "sheriff and prisoner," became recurring elements of their adult sexual interests.

I have known a lot of these subby men to hold Dominant positions in their professional careers. However, in their personal lives, they have deep-rooted desires to be solely submissive. Many are naturally submissive and tend to be shy, quiet, and/or introverted. They desire emotional attention, love to hear that they are a "Good Boy!", and will do 99% of what they are asked to do.

Other submissive men uncover their leanings through personal exploration or through the seductive nudge of someone who opens the door to the lifestyle. Once they step into that submissive space, it clicks. They often say, "I feel most like myself when I'm submitting to a woman." More than kink, what matters is alignment. They simply may have been born this way. They don't feel a loss of control through their surrender, but they do feel a sense of return to who they truly are.

I understand the commands these submissive cheaters wish to hear whilst kneeling at my feet. I give them what they need, and they take care of me like a good little servants.

Mr. Fetishist

I hear:

"After I put on these lacey panties, can I smell your armpits, Mistress? The smell makes my dick so hard, and I want you to see how hard I am in these panties."

"I love feet. Can I suck on your toes, Mistress?"

"I love the feel of rubber. It turns me on!"

"High heels are so sexy! I constantly dream of them trampling me."

"Do you think I am weird for having a smell fetish?"

Fetishistic desires and fantasies often stem from prior experiences that created strong mental associations. When a man links his arousal to a non-sexual object—like a rubber dress—his mind can become sexually stimulated without the need for direct sexual activity. This psychological and physical response creates a sense of pleasure or excitement, often without traditional sexual interaction.

In my experience, many adult clients trace aspects of their fetishistic desires back to childhood. A particular memory or sensory impression from youth can become a fixation in their imagination, eventually evolving into a powerful adult sexual interest. For these men, their fetish is not something they can simply ignore, it becomes an integral part of their sexual identity, often turning into an intense and sometimes compulsive fixation.

Sessioning with a Dominatrix allows the fetishist to fully indulge in his ultimate fantasy. He is ready to reveal his obsessions and addictions, and he wants his Mistress to join in on the play. The fetishist wants to play dress up with me, dabble in their kink, and be seen by someone who doesn't judge him. He finds satisfaction in no longer having to play alone with his fetish; food, high-heeled shoes, foul smells, feet, body parts, or that one irresistible piece of lingerie.

Seeking out others who understand or share these fixations gives them the freedom to either explore the fantasy or release the weight of guilt and shame. Having a play partner who offers acceptance in what is often a solitary and misunderstood world brings them excitement, relief, and validation. With me, their secrets are no longer hidden in the dark—*they're celebrated.*

Mr. Cheaper to Keep Her!

I hear:

"I don't give a shit about my wife. The marriage was over a long time ago!"

"If I divorce her, she will take me for everything I've got!"

"It's cheaper to keep her! This is why I cheat!"

"I would divorce her if I could. But I can't because of the kids."

"Divorce isn't an option. I just do what I must do!"

"I come to you because it's safe. I don't want to blow up my marriage or get caught cheating."

"I have a lot to lose. With you, I feel a sense of safety, and I am willing to take the risk."

"The passion is gone in my relationship."

"It's hard to hack you, so I feel comfortable knowing you aren't on some dating site."

"I don't think we are in love with each other anymore."

"Sometimes I think my wife is cheating on me too!"

"It's a loveless, sexless marriage!"

"Sex is a boring chore with my wife."

"Seeing you has become something I have normalized in my life."

Some of these men straight-up tell me, "It's cheaper to keep her." And they mean it. Staying in the marriage keeps the house, the image, the bank account, and the kids… all in place.

Divorce is often messy, expensive, and disruptive. But emotionally, many of these cheaters have already left. They've checked out, tuned out, and turned off long ago. Cheating, to them, isn't some big moral crisis because it has become a quiet rebellion. It's their way to reclaim something they feel they've lost.

Most of these men don't flinch with guilt. Remorse? Rarely. Cheating has become part of their rhythm, normalized and almost routine. The only thing they're really afraid of is getting caught and facing any possible consequences.

Booking time with me isn't just some wild indulgence; it becomes a necessary becomes a necessary resuscitation. They are desperate for the stimulation and the pulse of something *real* to pull them out of the dullness. They will do almost anything to numb the ache from feeling stuck.

They'll speak about change, talk about counting down the days, but until that day comes, this is a part of their fix. Inside the Dungeon, they find what they need: discretion, intensity, and freedom.

Our time comes with no strings and no emotional mess to disrupt their home life. For many, this *is* the medicine, just a simple transaction. A way for them to hit the ignore button on reality.

REFLECTION: RAINA MARKS

"Mr. Cheaper to Keep Her" makes me want to throw up! What an asshole! To think there are possibly thousands or even millions of women out in the world who are being exposed to this type of male mentality. This is a massive disappointment, and women deserve to be told the truth. These men are selfish pricks and are stealing time away from everyone involved in the relationship. And of course, this cheating man is most likely going to continue with his deceptive ways and leave his woman in the dark. Appalling!

Mr. Serial Cheater

I hear:

"It's not cheating! Just because my woman doesn't like kink doesn't mean I should have to suffer. I should be able to get what I want!"

"I don't think I have ever been faithful. It's just not who I am!"

"Whatever, I'm not going to get caught cheating!"

"I wish I could stop cheating, but I can't!"

"I am always looking for excitement!"

"I have cheated on every woman I have ever been with."

Once a cheater, always a cheater? For "Mr. Serial Cheater," absolutely.

These men are always in pursuit, finding ways to slip around emotionally or physically. Whether driven by a lack of empathy, commitment issues, or just plain restlessness, they are endlessly chasing their next fix. They crave stimulation—emotional, sexual, forbidden—and they'll do whatever it takes to feel a pulse, even if they have to burn their world down just to see the sparks.

Here's the thing: they don't hide it from me. They come to me with zero shame, fully aware of their debris. No apologies. I am their moral vacation—the only space where the "Good guy" persona can finally be dropped. They don't want forgiveness; they just want to be satisfied… again and again.

Many of my clients have confessed their need for new experiences, the rush that comes with stepping outside the lines. Some will tell me they love their partners, but the pull for someone else's attention is a hunger they refuse to starve. Others admit they're addicted to the adrenaline, uncomfortable with vulnerability, or grappling with attachment issues that make "home" feel like a cage.

Then there are those men who feel unworthy of their partner's love. Without realizing it, they begin to sabotage the relationship. For them, cheating isn't just a betrayal; it's a preemptive strike. They act on the belief that they don't deserve what they have, so they destroy it before it has the chance to leave them. They carry a heavy weight of self-doubt and a paralyzing fear of intimacy, using the act of cheating to protect themselves from ever being truly seen.

Serial cheaters are always in search of the "new," craving the high that comes with variety. Their BDSM sessions reflect this restlessness; they are eager to switch up playtime activities, constantly chasing the next escape. In my space, their internal chaos finds a rhythm. They don't have to deserve anything here, they just have to endure it.

Mr. Religion

I hear:

"I fantasize about blasphemy. I know it's wrong, but for some reason, it really gets me sexually aroused."

"I'm going to hell for this!"

"As a minister, I feel so ashamed of myself!" (Said with laughter.)

"Make me wear panties in church, Mistress!"

"I need full discretion!"

"I wore panties today under my pants, while giving my sermon in church."

The religious cheater has devotion to God or faith, but that doesn't keep him from walking through the door.

Despite calling himself a man of faith, he's more than willing to set aside his religious principles for the sake of intimate satisfaction and the indulgence of his sinful impulses. Some will casually joke about their shameful actions, laughing it off as though it's no big deal. I don't really witness any guilt over what they're doing. Others, though, remain silent, as if not speaking about it makes it less real. For all of them, the Dungeon becomes a place where their faith and their fantasies collide.

These cheaters want a mix of BDSM play activities. Everything they want goes against the grain of their religious beliefs and societal norms. Every now and then, a client will insist on being punished for what he calls his "sinful" behaviors.

Would it even be punishment? No, for them, it's more of a deeper, deviant satisfaction. A release found in indulging their most forbidden attractions. These irreverent men tend to be repeat clients and stick to their usual session requests. They return time and time again for the gratifying "shame on you" of what society and their God deems unacceptable.

In the end, they find a twisted kind of freedom in their blasphemous indulgences, a freedom that defies every rule they've sworn to follow.

Mr. Can't See Her That Way

I hear:

"She's a mom to my kid. I just can't ask her to do these things."
"No way! She won't understand the things I want to do."
"She's a great wife, but I don't see her playing these games."
"I don't want to gross her out. I don't think she can handle it!"
"We don't talk about kinky stuff."
There's a specific kind of man who walks through my Dungeon

door, and this man worships his wife, adores his children, and still... cheats.

Many men don't consciously choose to separate their wives from their fantasies. It's not that he's chasing another version of love. The woman he has chosen as his partner is seen as *pure* in his eyes. This woman, the mother of his children holds a sacred, untouchable role in his mind. He sees her as nurturing, steady, and responsible. She's holy in the way society may romanticize womanhood after motherhood. The things that awaken his body don't belong in the same room as the woman who sings lullabies to his children.

Suddenly, the woman he once ravished in the backseat, the one he used to undress with eyes full of hunger and heat, becomes the one he protects, provides for, and keeps safe. She becomes *home* and with that title, something divine. In that sacredness, emotions get silenced. He still loves her and still wants her, though not always in the ways he used to.

He's built two separate altars: one for the woman he married, and one for the woman he lusts after. Yet, he can't bring himself to let them merge.

He compartmentalizes and doesn't know how to tell her the truth without watching her break. He's convinced that once he let her into his hidden world, she'd never understand, look at him the same, or want to touch him ever again.

He's terrified of corrupting her image in his mind and even more terrified of shattering the one she holds of him. Instead of risking rejection from the woman he respects, he seeks satisfaction from the one he feels safe being kinky with.

That's the irony. He cheats not out of thinking she's not enough, but because he thinks she's too much. *Too pure. Too loving. Too good.*

This is when he brings those parts to me. His secrets, shame, and uncontrollable desperate parts. He is able to release them behind my closed doors, in a space built for precisely this kind of truth. And then he goes home. To her!

Mr. Transaction

I hear:

"I'm just here to get what I need."

"I don't want to talk!"

"I have no interest in that!"

"Please just do these things only, and then I have to go."

"See ya!"

"Just do what I ask of you!"

"I'm not into small talk!"

"Mr. Transaction" comes in like he's ordering a meal. He is precise, detached, and has already decided what he wants to do.

Our conversations can be very limited and typically he isn't that curious about the person in front of him. This is not a shared experience for him; it's a transaction. I am a simple purchase, a service he's paying for, and like any other service, he expects it to be delivered exactly how he wants it to play out.

He appears to be deeply compartmentalized. He's split the act of Domination and submission away from its relational potential, stripped it of mutuality, and made it into a controlled environment where vulnerability is off-limits.

I feel like a lot of these men carry shame and are afraid of being seen. Other times, they are seem steeped in entitlement, believing the money in his hand earns him ownership of the moment, and by extension, the woman.

He may rattle off a list of fetishes, protocols, or "must-haves" in the scene, as if reading from a well-worn script. Or he might send a long list of instructions beforehand, detailing his desired fantasy down to the color of the latex gloves or the number of seconds he wants to be punished. What's consistent is the emotional distance. I am a vessel, a tool, and a high-end appliance built to serve a function: his arousal.

Mr. I'm Sooo Bored!

I hear:

"My wife and I don't spend that much time together anymore. I am bored with our sex life, and I miss the excitement."

"I need attention!"

"I don't want to get divorced, but I need more in my life."

"I miss the excitement of a new relationship."

"I don't get the attention I used to get, and I need attention!"

"I'm bored!"

"Life is too routine, and my wife and I don't spend time together like we used to."

"I cheat because I love the attention I get from someone new."

"Yes, I'm having sex with my wife, but the emotional excitement isn't there anymore."

"I know what I am doing is wrong, but I need more fulfillment."

"Mr. Boredom" is craving intensity, longing for something that ignites a spark inside him. His daily routine has lost its vitality, and his relationship no longer offers the physical or emotional connection he craves. Seeking a release, he looks for an outlet to escape the dullness and satisfy the yearnings that his current life just can't reach.

At first, many of these men are hesitant, unsure of taking the risk. However, as their desires begin to take control, curiosity pushes them forward. Once they decide to take the plunge, they show up ready to explore and test the waters, eager to unleash the needs they've been keeping at bay.

When in a relationship, many truly love their partners, but life has a way of draining the electricity. The weight of daily responsibilities, routines, and expectations slowly smothers the fire that once fueled their connection. Sadly, these men often don't vocalize their needs, leaving them to search for that missing pulse elsewhere.

For those who are single, dating, or recently out of a relationship, the story is much the same. Life feels hollow. The passion is gone from both their sex lives and daily routines. They need something more. They want a jolt to awaken the dormant hunger they've been missing.

In the Dungeon, they find a place to ask for exactly what they want, where the attention is all theirs. It's their chance to indulge in a safe, consensual experience that breaks the cycle and brings the intensity they crave. They are interested in a full range of BDSM services and welcome my ideas to expand their own fantasies.

Mr. Everyone Else

I hear:

"I'm just stopping by to see what goes on in a place like this."

"Do you have women's clothing and shoes that fit my size?"

"Can you dress like a teacher and punish me for being bad in class?"

"I came here today to offer you a massage."

"I love feeling the weight of your body on me. Just lie on top of me!"

"Does it gross you out that I want you to put a dead squid down my pants?"

"I brought a piece of light sandpaper with me, and I want you to rub it all over my body!"

"Can you spank me for being a bad baby and not finishing my bottle?"

"High-heeled shoes turn me on. Can you model these shoes I brought in for you?"

"Why should I limit myself in life?"

"I am taking responsibility for my kinky ways, and I am not hurting anyone!"

"I love the anticipation, excitement, and fear I feel when I don't know what you will do to me next!"

"You are so sexy and hot! I swear I will do anything to please you!"

"I can tell you love being a Dominatrix! Thank you for always making sure I have a great time!"

"This isn't a game to you, is it? You seem authentic when you Dominate me!"

"When I give up all my control to you, I feel powerless and owned!"

"I am afraid to have an affair, but I know there is full discretion here, so I feel safe."

"With you, I can be specific about what I am looking for and get it!"

"It's easier to pay for fun like this!"

"I thought I was ready for all the responsibilities a relationship brings, but I don't think I am."

"The romance is dead!"

"I just want to be seduced!"

"I need passion and eroticism in my life!"

Take every word in this chapter, strip them down, and you'll find the blueprint for the men who find their way into my world. These men are driven by desire and drowning in secrets. They are starving for something they can't or won't express to their partners, let alone a stranger on the street.

Whether my client is a crossdresser, a role-play fanatic, a pain addict, a fetishist, a bondage lover, or someone who lives for the experience of humiliation, he is really seeking one thing: permission to exist. He needs to know he can be exactly who he is without being judged, shamed, or rejected.

My clients aren't evil. They aren't broken. They are human.

In my Dungeon, I make it clear that they don't have to apologize, even for choices I might not support. I don't have to respect the betrayal to acknowledge the man standing in front of me.

REFLECTION: RAINA MARKS

Raina makes a quick stop at the bathroom, splashing water on her face like it might somehow rinse off the thoughts clawing at her mind. She changes into a neutral-toned set of linen pants and a slouchy off-the-shoulder cashmere pullover: the kind of lounge wear that lets you disappear into your own skin.

Hitting the bed, she stares up at the bedroom ceiling. *I just need a minute! Why can't these men keep their urges in check?*

As she lies back on the bed, Raina steadies her breath, closing her eyes as the weight of the book's revelations presses against her chest. *Wow! There are so many types of kinky cheating men. I'm starting to feel like there isn't a man on this planet who doesn't have some hidden desire or secret. Some fetish or something.*

Where is their willpower, their respect, their dignity? Where is their honesty, at least? Aren't there any "normal" men left? Normal: what does that even mean? What happened to monogamy? Emotional safety? Vanilla sex with a side of loyalty? Morals? Have the lines moved so far that expecting honesty now feels naïve?

With a sharp exhale, she's back on her feet, heading straight for the refrigerator. Like a woman on the verge of throwing something, she opens the doors and grabs a can of sparkling water. Pops that bitch open like a pressure valve and gives a loud shout. "Consequences!"

Not speaking about the single men, but these cheaters don't seem to care about consequences or Karma for that matter. As though the rules don't apply to them. Like the damage they cause is just collateral. Do they even think about the people who love them? I guess they have no concern for their partners or their families. It's all just a mess!

Walking past his office, temptation persuades her thoughts. *Look at this den of dark woods and power. A masculine haven, he calls his office: the place he surrenders to after a hard day. Where muffled conversations and late-night preludes linger.*

Raina falls deeper into an emotional trap that has her feeling a need for control. *I've never gone through his things before. I have always respected his space. Not once have I probed into his need for privacy. Trust me, he is a very private man.*

Acting on raw emotion and suspicion, she fears she will not be able to abstain from the heat of the moment. *Oh… why not? There's nothing stopping me. What's the harm in having an innocent look inside? I have every right.*

Touching the mahogany-glazed desk, her fingers tap at the latch of the first drawer. Contemplating whether to pull or not, she becomes dizzy with guilt. *Just one drawer. One look. A top drawer of possible reassurance or… secrets.*

Breaching his privacy, she begins to pull. Even if it hurts, even if it wrecks everything she thought she knew: she needs and wants to know.

CHAPTER 9

A STUDY IN CONTROL AND CARE: WHO IS THE DOMINATRIX?

Professional Dominatrix: *Though the title is traditionally feminine, the field includes men, non-binary, and genderfluid individuals who command the space with equal authority. The Dominatrix provides BDSM (Bondage, Discipline, Sadism, Masochism) services in a consensual, professional, and commercial context. These services are provided in exchange for compensation. They assume a Dominant role in BDSM dynamics, leading clients who crave submission, discipline, or specific fetishes. It may be performance art, power play, or just a space for people to explore their desires, safely and on their own terms.*

> **Lifestyle Dominatrix:** *A person who engages in Dominant/submissive dynamics for personal, non-commercial reasons, as part of her relationship or identity. Lifestyle Dominatrices practice Dominance in their personal relationships in their everyday lives. These consensual interactions are a part of their identity where they share their power roles with a submissive.*

There is much more that defines a Professional Dominatrix. Control and care are two sides of the same coin. To understand a Dominatrix, you have to understand that her power isn't about cruelty, it's about awareness and so much more. Every command, every touch, and every rule is crafted with intention.

What follows reflects my personal experiences within the BDSM scene, it is not a handbook about every Dominatrix. Each Dominatrix expresses herself in her own way, according to her style, values, and boundaries. While it may not be my approach, it is theirs, and I am not here to judge their choices. This includes lifestyle Dominatrices and how they navigate their non-professional world within BDSM, Kink, Fetish, and fantasy.

The Foundation: Consent and Responsibility

> **Consent:** *The foundation of everything we do. This is not a one-time agreement; it's an ongoing conversation. In my sessions, consent is fluid—spoken, unspoken, and watched closely every step of the way. Without it, there's no real power exchange, only abuse, and that is unacceptable and has no place inside any play scene.*

We are the play partners and possible secret our clients wish to engage with away from home.

For a Dominatrix, consent is the cornerstone of every interaction, shaping a space where power is exchanged safely and with mutual respect. This consent is established through clear communication, negotiated boundaries, and an ongoing awareness of a client's physical and emotional well-being.

Titles, Names, and Identity

From Mistress to Madam, the titles and names Dominatrices choose reflect their authority, identity, and the power structures they create.

Dominatrice, Domme, and Domina are other forms of the more common word Dominatrix.

Participants and clients may refer to the Dominatrix as Mistress, Lady, Madam, Goddess, Boss, Ma'am, etc., or by their official Domina name. Other nicknames may be used as well, and it is up to the Dominatrix to decide how she will be addressed.

For example, the title Mistress is typically used as an overall forefront to our professional stage names. This is also frequently used as a response when being addressed by our play partners. (E.g., "Yes, Mistress!") All Dominatrices have a stage name such as Mistress Lacy, Lady Nova, or Madam Monique. This chosen name is usually used by the Dominatrix for the duration of their professional and/or non-professional journey.

As Dominatrices, we are often the reflective listener, supporter, and life coach. We are not therapists or psychologists (though some of us may actually be or feel like we are). Sessions can be deeply cathartic, but they are not a substitute for qualified mental health care. What we offer is a space for exploration, release, and self-discovery, but it should never replace the guidance of a trained mental health practitioner.

The Dungeon: Spaces of Power and Play

Dungeons, whether commercial or private, serve as controlled environments where fantasy, education, and community thrive.

Most Dominatrices work inside commercial or private Dungeons. As previously stated, commercial spaces are open to the public and offer Dominatrices, Switches, and submissives by appointment or walk-ins. Scheduling is posted online and men can book sessions accordingly.

Private spaces are owned by individual Mistresses, submissives, or other members of the community who have the means and desire to create a controlled, intimate environment. These spaces are not open to the public, and anyone wishing to participate must contact the owner or Mistress directly to arrange a session or visit.

Many of the facilities offer special events, educational classes, and parties where professionals or the public can attend. In some cases, it's the Dominatrix herself who teaches and guides others through the art of Dominance with the same sharp intuition, discipline, and erotic intelligence she brings to every session.

The Dominatrix Mindset

The Dominatrix holds an undeniable, commanding position in the exchange between herself and her clients. This is not up for debate; it's an inherent fact.

A superior mindset, we do not claim to have. But holding a superior attitude? That we can do. Beyond the walls of our space, we are not better than anyone else, nor do we place ourselves above any other human being. The exception, of course, is when we are role-playing with a client and the scenario calls for adopting such a superior persona.

Too often, Dominance is misunderstood as aggression or emotional detachment, when in reality it demands restraint, responsibility, and care. Healthy Dominance is not cruelty. Ethical Dominance requires emotional intelligence, self-awareness, and a clear understanding of consent and boundaries. We must have the ability to hold strength and care at the same time, without confusing power with cruelty.

As professionals, we are creators—emotional, mental, and physical communicators. We are the insight, the satisfier, the therapeutic ear, and the entrusted person on the other side of the fantasy. While we remain patient, we are unwavering in our authority, guiding our actions and decisions with purpose.

Compassion and empathy are not opposites of Dominance. A Dominatrix shouldn't confuse Dominance with emotional absence. Reckless Dominance lacks empathy; intentional Dominance depends on it. Through awareness, our strength lies in our ability to read both the body and the mind. It is our responsibility to fully hear, interpret, and understand what our clients are trying to express, even when they themselves are not fully aware of it.

With confidence, we hold the space, controlling not only the environment but also the needs and safety of those in our presence. Health, safety, and the mental and emotional well-being of our clients are always our top priorities. Every play act is performed consensually, ensuring that all participants are respected and fully engaged in the experience. Our responsibility does not end when the scene does; it extends into care, integration, and emotional awareness beyond the moment.

The Many Faces of the Dominatrix

Behind the whip, Dominatrices embody diverse lives beyond their work personas.

I've known Dominatrices who are plumbers, neuroscientists, nurses, teachers, actresses, mothers, radio hosts, business owners, medical students, therapists, and more. Most are, without a doubt, highly intelligent, educated, talented, and extraordinary individuals.

If you passed us on the street, sat next to us at a PTA meeting, or found yourself in a college class with us, you would never guess that we wield whips or captivate men from all corners of the globe.

Like nearly all human beings, the Dominatrix embodies both submissive and Dominant sides. Just because we occupationally hold the position of a Dominant woman doesn't mean we are always in control. Many Dominatrices also explore their submissive roles (a submissive is obedient, passive, and conforms to the authority or will of others) or Switch roles (a Switch demonstrates both characteristics and is comfortable with submissive and Dominant roles), both professionally and personally. I've known several Dominatrices who are full-time submissives in their private lives, embracing the submissive role with their partners as part of their lifestyle.

Becoming a Professional Dominatrix

True mastery comes not from mimicry, but from mentorship, experience, and a deep commitment to the craft of consensual control.

How does one become a Professional Dominatrix?

Many begin by seeking out a local BDSM Dungeon, lounge, or studio where they can apply or undergo training. These spaces exist in nearly every state and country, and aspiring Dominatrices often begin by researching online or through magazines, flyers, and local listings to find the right place to launch their career.

For others, years of personal experience led them to adopt the title of Professional Dominatrix. These Dominatrices often open their own studios or find their place seamlessly within commercial environments.

Unfortunately, some people claim the title with barely any experience. They mimic what they see online, not realizing the depth, skill, and responsibility this work actually demands. Real Domination isn't an act. Domination is a discipline you live. It's knowing how to lead without harm, to break down walls while still holding someone safely inside. That takes far more than a corset and a crop. You don't just claim this title; you earn it through experience, guidance, and humility.

How does a Professional Dominatrix learn her craft? The BDSM world runs on trust, mentorship, and accountability. We learn from each other, guide each other, and hold each other to the highest standards of care. Beyond hands-on training, many Dominatrices expand their knowledge through online workshops, educational videos, books, and community forums dedicated to safe, consensual, and ethical BDSM practices.

Most Dungeons require new Dominatrices to receive training from an experienced specialist. However, some establishments do not mandate starting out as a submissive or undergoing formal training. In my opinion, this is irresponsible and frankly, an outrage! I strongly recommend that anyone aspiring to be a Professional Dominatrix or anyone exploring BDSM, whether professionally or not, receive proper training before engaging in playtime activities.

During my journey, I was fortunate to be mentored by a few remarkable women. Their daily comportment and expertise inspired me, and I witnessed firsthand that being a Professional Dominatrix requires not only skill but also compassion and a genuine love for the craft.

Throughout my training, we spent hours studying, observing, and practicing techniques while also learning how to master interpersonal interactions with clients. Once training was complete, my mentors tested my new skills. Fortunately, my skills proved successful, and I was added to the team, beginning my work with clients.

Style and Wardrobe: The Art of Presence

Every corset, boot, and accessory is chosen with intention, crafting an image that communicates power, seduction, and unshakable authority.

A Dominatrix's style is defined by her own diversity. Each one brings her own individual taste and unique signature to the craft.

Many of us have extensive collections of wigs, makeup, accessories, and wardrobes that allow us to tailor our appearance to specific play scenarios. Others opt for a more natural look, keeping it simple, classic, or minimalistic.

Our wardrobe isn't just about looking the part, we want to embody power, confidence, and control. Think leather, latex, and corsets that hug every curve, sharp heels that click with purpose, and accessories that speak volumes: whips, collars, and straps that aren't just for show, but a reminder of who's in charge. You can open up our closets and find items like latex, leather, lace, corsets, stockings, garter belts, lingerie, business attire, biker gear, gothic and punk styles, high heels, thigh-high boots, and more. It's a balance of seduction and authority, a carefully crafted look that leaves no room for doubt. Whether it's a fitted black dress or thigh-high boots, each piece tells you something, a story of creativity, strength, and unapologetic presence.

Activities and Specialties

From bondage play to role-specific scenarios, Dominatrices curate experiences that align with their expertise and personal boundaries.

A Dominatrix may engage in a wide range of services or choose to limit her participation to certain areas. We are never required to engage in anything that doesn't align with our comfort or moral boundaries, and it's completely acceptable to decline certain requests.

While most of us offer an extensive list of playtime activities, we also have personal "specialties." These are skills or services that require particular expertise or years of experience.

For example, *Breath Play* is a specialty involving the restriction of air to intensify erotic sensations. Those who practice it enjoy the combination of psychological and physical elements, using teasing, anticipation, and attentive control to explore and respond to their clients' desires in a safe, consensual way.

The scope of the industry is broad. Many professionals offer adult content, cam work, or other forms of erotic interaction. While some may choose to include sexual activities or intercourse in their services, others strictly maintain a boundary that excludes any form of physical intimacy.

The Aftercare Distinction: The Bridge Back to Reality

In the world of BDSM, the session doesn't end when the whip is laid down; it ends when the mind is safely returned to the "Vanilla" world. For the man who has spent the last hour as my play toy, aftercare is the vital transitional space where he sheds the submissive persona and begins to re-assemble himself. It's the transition that allows a man to go from being whipped in a Dungeon at 4:00 PM to sitting at the dinner table talking about his day at 6:00 PM.

Why Aftercare is the "De-pressurization Chamber":

- The Chemical Crash: During a session, the brain is flooded with endorphins, adrenaline, and dopamine. When the play stops, those levels can plummet (often called "Sub Drop"). Aftercare, blankets, water, sugar, and soft conversation, is the safety net that prevents a crash.
- The Identity Pivot: He cannot walk out of the Dungeon door while still feeling like my submissive. Aftercare provides the quiet minutes needed to pack those secret identities back into the dark corners of his mind so he can face his wife without flinching.
- Aftercare: Not all clients require aftercare. Some prefer to remain in the Dominant/submissive headspace they've achieved and ask me not to break character for a period of time. Others might request a harsher demeanor, wanting to maintain the intensity of the session. In these cases, aftercare may not apply, and we may remain in role, continuing the session until the client leaves.

- The Professional Pivot: It is during this time that the Dominatrix shifts from the *Commander* to the *Caretaker*. She is the one who ensures he is grounded enough to drive his car, speak to his colleagues, and kiss his partner without the "residue" of the Dungeon visible on his face.

It's the reset button that makes the double life possible.

The Rewards of the Craft

Mastering the balance of control and care is what makes this work profoundly transformative for both the client and the Mistress.

At the heart of it all, being a Professional Dominatrix isn't just about the thrill of power. It requires a deep sense of responsibility and the ability to guide someone with precision, skill, and intuition. When you can command those elements, the rewards are more than worth it.

My goal is to create an experience that is not only satisfying but safe, empowering, and deeply fulfilling. Every session is crafted with intention, attuned to a client's desires, boundaries, and emotional state. When he leaves feeling balanced and understood, fully engaged in mind, body, and spirit, I know I've done my job well. That exchange of trust, release, and connection is the true measure of success in my work.

I am the Professional Dominatrix. The Confidant. Dominant Force. Seductress. Mentor. Chameleon. Actress. Consensual Play Partner. Caretaker of the Mind. Imagination Booster. Master of my Craft.

And I am the one who is going to continue helping you have a better understanding as to why these men cannot get enough and what exactly keeps them coming back for more.

"Are you paying attention?"

REFLECTION: RAINA MARKS

Yes, Mistress, I am absolutely paying attention!

Raina tries to smother the fiery words with fabric. Tucking the book under her sweater, she asks herself: *Can't get enough of her? What does this woman have that I don't have?*

And then, like a snapback from the universe, the narrative shifts.

"As the author, let me interrupt you, dear Raina. **Nothing you don't already have and more!**"

Looking around, her words perk up. "Who said that?"

It doesn't matter. Maybe it's me, the author. Maybe it's her highest self. Maybe it's herself, layered in with every woman who's ever felt like she wasn't enough, simply because her man or someone else made her feel that way, or went looking for something… different. Not better, just different, and then has to deal with the aftermath of his fucked-up choices.

Raina lets out a slow breath. *No, I don't have the training or knowledge of BDSM play. Not that I want to play, I'm just thinking about what it would be like. I'm not exactly brimming with confidence, and I'm scared of looking like an idiot in front of my man.*

I feel like I would need more knowledge, more patience, more understanding, and definitely less judgment. And a fancy wardrobe!

Deep inside, she wonders whether being more open, daring, and true to herself might quiet her apprehension.

She's snooped. Not in the traditional way, but mentally, digging into the intimate corners of what he might want. Chasing clues between pages, she pieces together the lack of transparency she can no longer ignore.

Confirming the facts: *Well, it looks like I already have a fancy wardrobe. Leather. Lots of leather!*

Feeling much braver. *What are you up to, Mr. Marks? What haven't you told me?*

CHAPTER 10

A NOT-SO-FANTASY STORY
BACHELORETTE PARTY DEBACLE

This chapter presents a fantasy session story involving consenting adults only. All scenarios are fictionalized composites inspired by themes from my professional practice, and identifying details have been altered to protect privacy. The story explores adult BDSM dynamics, trust, and power exchange within a safe, consensual, and controlled environment.

A debacle. "Until it Wasn't!"

When your good friend owns an erotic stripper service and asks you to fill in as a dancer, you say yes! I figured I had danced around my house as a fantasy stripper enough times that I should be able to pull off an afternoon bachelorette party. It was a group of women, after all. How hard could it be?

Until the morning of the event arrived. *I am mortified! Who am I kidding?*

Quickly, I adopt the "fake it until you make it" mentality and get my ass in the car. I decide that if all else fails, I can fall back on my security blanket to entertain these people… *my black suitcase full of tricks.*

It is Saturday afternoon, and we roll up to the suburban house around 1:00 PM. My stomach takes on its own choreography, and I am desperate to bail out of the situation. There is absolutely nothing I can do to relieve my nerves. Staring out the window, I contemplate my plan.

The panic sets in. *Plan? I have no plan. I can't do this. I am going to suck!*

I zone out on my driver. He makes it very clear to me that it is not an option for me to be late to this party, and suggests that I immediately get out of the vehicle. As he walks to the trunk of the car to grab my magic case, he gestures with his thumb for me to get out of the car. With my suitcase and speaker in his hands, he firmly states, "Let's go!"

I think to myself. *Shit! Here goes nothing. Or something.*

I could hear my heart cracking a whip against my chest as I made my way through the front door of the house. Silence greets me, and I confirm that the evil eye is not singular. All eyes are on me, and what feels like pure judgment hits me like a Florida lightning storm.

At least 20 women sit in chairs, forming a horseshoe. Expressionlessly, a diverse age range of beautiful *Goddesses* stare me down, and I ask myself if I am in the wrong house. I expected a few men at the party, but that's what I get for assuming. A younger woman approaches me, bewildered by her decision to bring me to the party, and I can tell she is uncomfortable. After making her acquaintance, she brings me into a side room to prepare for my show.

Flipping out. *My show. What show? Am I out of my right mind? I know I am in big trouble with these women, and the thought of stripping down to my tiny G-string is a terrible idea.*

What the fuck am I going to do?

I make the decision to fall back on what I know best. After all, I am a Dominatrix who meets strangers for a living and molds to any given situation. Why should these women be any different?

I search for something more conservative to wear and slip into a black, long lingerie dress, lacy panties, and black stilettos. With the speaker in hand, I grab my chunky suitcase and roll it back out to the center of the room. I see a barstool nearby and decide this is going to make the perfect perch for me to sit on.

It is time to cue the music!

Scared out of my mind, I mumble. "I don't think I have ever felt more uncomfortable in my entire life!" I rise to my feet and begin to sway my body in some awkward form of nonsense. Approaching each woman around the horseshoe like I am kneading some kind of air dough. Erotically, I lift the hem of my gown up and down, as though I am really going to attempt to take this thing off.

Dying inside. *WTF! Pathetic. This is a failure.* After one lap and back through the horseshoe, I have had enough. *I knew this wasn't going to work! Oh well, at least I can be honest with Jax, when she asks me about this party. I tried!*

Plan B: *Tricks!*

Lowering the volume on the speaker and changing the music to a mild tempo, I climb back onto the barstool. In awkward agony, each woman shifts in her seat. I introduce myself to the group of ladies and make it very clear to them that I am not a professional stripper. Instead, I tell them that I am a *Professional Dominatrix*. I watch as their faces begin to display confusion, shock, and interest.

I am not exaggerating when I say that all but one woman sat straight up in her chair when I gave them my truth. And that one woman, Grandma was about 88 years old and confused by the whole situation.

I start a dialogue with the group of women. Asking them if they have any idea what a Professional Dominatrix is and what BDSM means? I get a few low whispers out of the crowd, but most of the women sit there perplexed. I use simple terms to define my profession as a Dominatrix and begin to explain all the kinky details. After a brief explanation, I hop off the barstool and unzip my suitcase. I take out my riding crop and whack the stool loudly. Now I have their attention!

Half of the women begin to giggle and talk amongst themselves. Quickly, I pull out a beautiful flogger. I visit each woman and modestly dangle the leather tassels, as if asking permission to lightly touch them across their arms and legs.

Hearing sounds of joy, I know I am onto something, and I must keep going. Next, I make contact with their skin with the riding crop and feather tickler. As my tickler and crop tantalize each woman, they get a small taste of what it feels like to have the leather slapper connect to a piece of their flesh.

Questions from the women begin to pour in, and together we start an open dialogue. They want to see more!

Down on the carpet, I begin to pull my implements from the suitcase. One by one, I lay them out side-by-side, explaining to the women how each piece of equipment is used during BDSM play. I bring out floggers, leather and wooden paddles, feather ticklers, restraints, rope, blindfolds, handcuffs, a cane, clamps, and an additional riding crop.

I explain to the group of women how important it is to engage in consensual and negotiated playtime and how they need to protect certain areas of the body when playing with the equipment to avoid bodily or organ damage. Using my own body, I show them examples of how to use the playful tools. Curious, they want to touch each piece of equipment, and suddenly, they are all up and out of their seats. *These women are out of control!*

Laughing hysterically, the women begin to grab my BDSM equipment and Dominate one another. Playing with all the BDSM toys, women are being tied up, spanked, blindfolded, and handcuffed. They are having a blast playing with all the kinky toys. I can hear the *Goddesses* talk about how much fun they are having. Some women comment that they would love to do this with their husbands. They discuss whether they think they are submissive or Dominant.

I continue to be showered with questions and several of the women express how they want to hire me to come to their homes. They love the idea of doing this again and sharing the experience with their friends. The party is alive and thriving!

I take a moment and sit back up on the barstool. I watch as these women set their insecurities, inhibitions, judgments, and timidness to the side. It brings me great pleasure to witness their *freedom*. Curiosity, knowledge, a safe space, and effective communication worked together to afford these women an opportunity to let loose and enjoy the moment. An unfamiliar subject has brought itself to life and will impact these women for the rest of their lives. I know our time together will be unforgettable.

It is time for me to zip up my suitcase full of tricks. I thank the women for being gracious and patient with me. I roll my suitcase back into my private room and get ready to leave.

While packing up my bag, I hear a light knock on the door. Opening the door, I am happy to see Grandma welcoming me with a huge smile. She grabs my wrist and places a short stack of folded-up cash into the palm of my hand. Quietly, Grandma reassures me. "You did well, and it looks like everyone had a great time with those swatting things!"

I give her a chuckle and a big hug. "I think you are right!"

My driver is back at the front door and ready to collect me and my magical *bag of tricks*. My time is up, and my days of being a stripper are over! He prompts me to get into the blacked-out sedan that is waiting for me outside the house. I must leave my new friends.

After stepping over the threshold, I can hear the women gather at the front door of the house. I stop and turn around to wave goodbye. The end feels like a new beginning, when I am greeted with cheers, happiness, and laughter from a once overwhelmed and annoyed group of women, now excited and bidding me farewell.

The judgment has been forgotten and washed away. I am no longer the "stripper for hire" whom everyone was appalled to see. I leave today with a deeper sense of purpose. I took off their blindfolds and helped them to embrace a new perspective of understanding and acceptance in an unfamiliar world. Together, we cultivated an environment where conversations could flow freely and without reservations.

Pulling away from the house, my driver is curious. "How did it go?"

Enthusiastically. "It didn't start off so well, but I am happy to say the group of women ended up having a great time. A really nice time!" I briefly explain everything that happened at the party and assure him that Jax is going to be happy with the outcome of her event.

From the moment my eyes landed on the group, I misjudged these women. We had equally misguided notions of each other, and our judgments flew like arrows, aiming straight for the heart. Fortunately, this did not prevent us from sharing in a positive experience and ultimately bonding like longtime friends.

And there I was, full of doubts, insecurities, and fears. I was my own worst critic. I judged myself before having an opportunity to settle into the situation. Mentally, I set myself up for failure, and I assumed I was inadequate for the job. I needed to get out of my own way, to quiet the negative voices inside my head. I recognized that being myself is enough. I witnessed women gravitate towards my knowledge, even though they were unfamiliar with the topics. My enthusiasm, confidence, and excitement with the *Goddesses* welcomed them on a new journey, and I will never forget this group of women. An unforgettable experience, indeed! And valuable lessons to learn!

Did I quit the stripper acts? *Nah!* I had two bachelor parties booked, so I took on the challenge. And then I quit!

By participating in the two extra parties, I stuck to my commitments and faced my fears. Only I didn't have to face these fears alone. I pulled strength from the memories I had with *The Goddesses.* The bachelor parties were a breeze compared to the Goddesses; once you've conquered a room of skeptical women, a room of rowdy men is easy work.

I still think about those memories to this day. I will forever hear their laughter and excitement. A mental gift I will repeatedly reopen!

REFLECTION: RAINA MARKS

Okay! A full-circle moment between a group of women with a happy ending. That doesn't happen too often after awkward beginnings.

I know I'm guilty of being judgmental. I've always been quick to judge others and jump to conclusions. At thirty-seven, you'd think I'd be better at this by now. Being less judgmental is something I've been working on, and reading about The Goddesses is a good reminder to avoid assumptions.

She exhales through a quiet laugh. *Looks like the Dominatrix is human after all! I was wondering if she ever felt insecure or fearful. I know a lot of women experience moments of self-doubt and struggle with keeping up their confidence, even a Professional Dominatrix. But maybe that's a part of a lie many of us live in: pretending we're fine, while we're low-key cracking under the pressure to hold it all together.*

And just like that. *Ring. Ring.*

The phone breaks through her moment of reflection like a warning bell. Raina answers with practiced ease, a smile in her voice. "Hi! Did you have a nice flight?"

She listens, nodding, twirling the edge of the towel around her knee. "Oh, nothing much, just relaxing by the pool, reading a book."

Her eyes flick toward the title. *Whyyyyyyyyy?*

She quickly turns it face down. "Did you already check into the hotel?"

Hotel Suspicion, that is: with your sudden call to elsewhere.

A pause. "Yes, that's good! Do you like your room?"

Just make sure that the room sees you and only you!

More silence. "Great, I'm happy to hear you're settled in comfortably."

Her fingertip taps a steady rhythm on the book's cover, like a metronome keeping time with her rising doubt. "Are you ready for your meeting?"

Eager to hear. "Oh, it's a dinner meeting with a new business associate? I see. That's nice, I hope it goes well."

Wonder what happened with Gerald? The guy you said you were meeting!!!

Her mouth says what it's supposed to, while her body stays rigid. "Do you want to call me after you're done?"

Another pause. A slight hesitation in his tone. "Oh, it might be really late?"

Late my ass!

She forces a soft chuckle. "That's fine. I'm sure I'll be awake. Go ahead and give me a call. Love you too!"

The phone goes silent, but her thoughts do not. *Late?* Her brow creases. *How late is late? Bleep! Bleep! Bleep!*

The tight coil of her gut snaps like a rubber band. *I'm definitely in my head now. Should I have asked more questions? Would it have made a difference? Am I growing suspicious? Or just finally… paying attention?*

CHAPTER 11

EFFECTIVE COMMUNICATION: HOW I SPEAK TO HIS SECRETS

Author's Note: *This chapter offers an overview of personality and character traits and does not capture their full complexity. This section lays a foundation, not a final answer, because personality and communication are layered and evolving, just like the people who carry them. If you are navigating deep emotional challenges or unresolved trauma, please consider seeking support from a licensed therapist.*

Part I

The Power of Safe Space

Imagine a world where you could communicate with your partner in a way that enhances emotional, mental, and social well-being. I've seen proof that transparency and honest dialogue benefit relationships. Men cheat on their partners… with me!

Effective communication requires more than just talking and we must share our thoughts and feelings honestly, clearly, and respectfully. My clients seek a safe space to explore parts of themselves they've buried in secrecy. They gravitate toward me because I offer an environment where desires can be voiced without the fear of the "real world" collapsing.

The Honest Mirror

Before you can truly connect with someone else, you need to understand yourself first. Who are you right now, not who you wish you were, or who you used to be? Real communication doesn't start with a strategy; it starts with self-awareness.

Humans are multi-layered. It's time to stop making excuses and walk down the staircase of your soul with ruthless clarity. But remember, as you descend into the depths, bring compassion and empathy for yourself at every step.

Ask yourself the hard questions:

- What conversations do I avoid having out loud?
- Am I using communication to connect or to control distance?
- Where do I rely on screens to protect me from discomfort?
- What version of myself am I protecting instead of confronting?

Transparency isn't just about other people; it's about catching yourself when you lie to the one person you should know best: **You.**

Active Listening

When I am with a client, I tell them: *"I'm fully present. I'm paying attention not only to what you say, but also to what you don't."* The more they feel heard, the deeper they submit.

I pair this with **Effective Enthusiasm.** Technique alone is cold. Positive, genuine enthusiasm opens people in ways a whip cannot. When I greet a man with authentic excitement, I'm telling him: *"I'm here for you, and I'm eager to hear what you have to say."* This warmth lowers the defenses he's been building all day at the office or at home. It's the antidote to the fear of being misunderstood.

Honesty and Transparency

Do you want to deepen trust, encourage communication, and boost your integrity? Then you must align your actions with your words and stop covering up secrets.

People often use these words interchangeably, but in my world, there is a clear distinction between the two. Understanding that difference is the first step to preventing a relationship from fractures.

- Honesty is reactive. It's telling the truth and answering the question asked of you. It keeps you from lying, but it doesn't always tell the entire story. You might not be lying, but you aren't exactly revealing everything that matters.
  - The Honest Client: When I ask, he says, "Yes, I'm married." He's telling the truth, but he's leaving out the most important part.

- Transparency is proactive. It is about clarity and the willingness to be open about your actions and decisions before you are forced to be. It eliminates guesswork and holds you accountable. When someone is transparent, they share the truth before it's requested.
  - The Transparent Client: He says, "I'm married, and my partner doesn't know I'm here. I need discretion, but I also understand the risks."

As I've said for decades: "Don't leave honesty out of your truth."

John in the Dungeon: The Power of Presence

Let me tell you about John and Sarah. From the start, there were things they didn't talk about. It wasn't because they lacked care, but because honesty felt risky. Sarah kept her real feelings to herself to avoid conflict; John held back parts of himself he feared would be judged. Over time, those unspoken truths piled up like debris. The trust thinned, and a faint distance settled in.

When John finally found his way to me, it wasn't an act of defiance, it was an unburdening. He sought a controlled environment where he could finally reconcile with the parts of himself he had suppressed for years.

Inside my space, spectacle doesn't matter. Presence does. I focus on creating a calm, steady environment where judgment is left at the door. I ask him why he's here and what he's been carrying. Mostly, I listen. I pay attention to his words, but also his pauses, his body language, and the moments where he almost stops himself. I don't want a performance; I want him.

Sometimes, when he hesitates, I'll say something simple: *"You're not strange for feeling this way. A lot of people do. They just don't talk about it."* That is usually when I see the reframing in his body. His shoulders drop, his breathing changes, and he realizes he doesn't have to defend himself here. Through transparency and honesty, John begins to detail his desires. This makes it exciting, like we are finally getting somewhere.

Trust builds slowly through tone, eye contact, and consistency. These moments exist for safety, not control. In that space, John finds something better than an escape, he finds the permission to finally be honest with himself. He stops pretending parts of him don't exist and looks at his unmet needs without shame. For many people like John, being seen and accepted exactly as they are is where real change begins.

Takeaway: Transparency isn't just telling the truth. It's creating a space where the truth can actually be spoken.

Something to reflect on: Ask your partner, *"What's something you've never felt safe sharing?"*

The Survival Gear: Building the Foundation

A strong relationship isn't built on talk; it's built on the grit of honesty. For Sarah and John, survival would mean moving past the surface and getting intentional. They would have to stop just "talking" and start showing up with emotional presence.

The Essentials:

- Own Your Truth: Know your beliefs, core values, and boundaries before you open your mouth. You can't be transparent with someone else if you're still foggy with yourself.
- Lead with Transparency: Don't wait to be asked. Share the fuller picture proactively. This eliminates the guesswork that creates anxiety and distance.

- Create a Sanctuary: Build a safe space where silence is allowed to have its place. Speak clearly, but listen like you mean it and tune into the emotions vibrating underneath the words.
- Ditch the Script: Throw out the old programming and the "way we've always done it." Stay curious. Lean in. Ask the real questions that actually matter.
- Flex and Adapt: Meet people where they are, not where you want them to be. Use language that invites them in rather than putting them on the defensive.
- Honor the Rawness: Celebrate vulnerability when it shows up. If someone is brave enough to be open, honor that moment. Touch thoughtfully, with consent, to steady the connection.
- Keep the Engine Running: Communication isn't a "one-and-done" event; it's a constant practice. Tackle problems as a team, because it's the two of you versus the problem, not you versus your partner.
- Name the Goal: Be explicit. Say what you want, what you need, and the role you are playing in the moment. Clarity is what keeps a relationship on track when things get intense.

Part II: Patterns in Practice – Lessons from the Dungeon

Every man who walks through my door is a unique puzzle, but over twenty years, certain patterns have become clear. These aren't just "kinks"; they are communication styles, attachment wounds, and personality traits playing out in real-time.

Rick: The Power of the Written Word

A few days before our session, Rick sent me an email. It was careful and thoughtful, the kind of message you can tell someone rewrote a dozen times before hitting send. The subject line read: "A thought I've never shared."

In that email, he described a fantasy he had carried quietly for years. His words weren't written to shock; they were honest and deeply personal. He ended with: "If this feels like too much, or too strange, I understand." That sentence mattered more than the fantasy itself. Rick wasn't looking for permission to act; he was looking for reassurance that he wouldn't be judged for who he was.

Takeaway: The truth is often easier to confess to a screen than a face. Digital communication gives people time to edit what they are saying, and also ways to delete and delay. This creates a "buffer" between who they are and who they're afraid to be seen as.

Something to try: Invite your partner to write about a desire they've never shared. Respond with curiosity, not judgment.

Victor: Words as a Love Language

Victor is a calm, controlled man. You might assume he connects most through physical intensity, but I noticed something else: what moved Victor most wasn't touch. It was my words.

A simple sentence spoken at the right moment, "You did exactly what I needed tonight," could soften him in a way nothing else did. For Victor, words of affirmation were essential. Once I understood that, language became just as intentional as the physical work. The connection deepened because he finally felt seen and valued.

Takeaway: Love languages aren't just for "vanilla" relationships. They shape trust and connection in every dynamic.

Thomas: Emotional Triggers and Attachment Styles

Thomas came in asking for intensity, specifically to be pushed to his limits. But the first time I withheld praise after a scene, his body handled the impact fine, but his emotions didn't. He shut down. He felt invisible without verbal recognition.

Beneath his aggressive exterior lay an Anxious-Preoccupied attachment style, a deep fear of rejection shaped by his past. For him, submission wasn't just physical surrender; it was trusting someone to hold his emotional truth.

Takeaway: Notice your reactive patterns. Ask: "When do I shut down or get defensive?"

Ethan: The Trap of Passive Communication

Ethan was charming and used all the right words: consent, clarity, connection. But during the session, he stopped speaking entirely. He didn't seem to be surrendering, but I did notice him showing me avoidance. He went quiet under pressure because his default style was passive. He wasn't hiding from me, but I could tell he was protecting himself from judgment.

Takeaway: Passive communication can look like submission, but it is often just avoidance. Finding your voice transforms both confidence and connection.

Mark: The Quiet Ones

Mark is quiet. He comes across as introverted and hesitant; he fidgets, avoids eye contact, and speaks softly. Sharing himself feels risky. I know that what he feels goes beyond revealing secrets and is wondering how he will be received.

When I work with a man like Mark, I slow my pace and soften my tone. My body language says, *"It's okay, you can breathe here."* I ask simple questions and give him the space to take his time. Under that structure, he relaxes. The man who barely met my gaze becomes present, alert, and engaged. People like Mark don't need to be pulled out of their shells; they need a safe space where they feel they can step out on their own.

Takeaway: Reserved individuals thrive with patience and calm. Their comfort often shows in their body language, not their words.

Something to try: Keep questions simple. Give space for slow answers. Create a structured, calm environment to help someone feel safe opening up.

Lance: The Storm and the Spark

Lance arrives with a swirl of energy: curiosity, charisma, and a layer of anxiety underneath. He is open, imaginative, and hungry for stimulation. For him, intellectual challenge is part of the arousal. I don't just ask what turns him on; I ask, *"What's the most unsettling thing you've ever imagined but never told anyone?"*

He is extroverted and thrives under attention, but beneath that confidence lies self-doubt. I don't want to push him and look for ways to ground him. For Lance, aftercare is a chance to process and reflect. He doesn't want to escape himself, but rather he wants to sharpen who he is. He needs trust to take risks, and he needs reassurance to stay steady. I remind him: *"You don't have to be brave. You just have to be willing."*

Takeaway: Knowing someone's personality—their openness or their extroversion—helps you guide them. Structure and creativity must go hand-in-hand.

Something to try: Match your approach to your partner's specific traits. Debrief after intense moments by asking, *"What did that experience bring up for you?"*

The Starting Ground

Here are some ways designed to help you navigate the layers of personality and desire. Use these tools not as rigid rules, but as a foundation for deeper connection.

The 7 Cs of Effective Communication

- **Clear:** Stop talking in riddles. Say exactly what you mean so your partner doesn't have to play detective with your emotions.
- **Concise:** Respect the moment. Get to the point before the emotional weight of the conversation becomes too heavy to carry.
- **Concrete:** Use facts, not vague accusations. "I feel ignored when you're on your phone" is a bridge; "You never care" is a wall.
- **Correct:** Check your "facts" before you throw them. Ensure your information is accurate so the conversation stays on track.

- **Coherent:** Let your ideas flow. If you jump from one grievance to another, you'll both get lost in the weeds.
- **Complete:** Don't leave out the hard parts. Provide the details needed for a real understanding, even if they're uncomfortable.
- **Courteous:** Your tone is your energy. You can speak a hard truth without being cruel.

Personality in Practice: The OCEAN Model

Understanding a partner's core traits allows you to meet them where they are. Using a visual reference can help you see where you and your partner sit on the spectrum of personality. This is a birds-eye view of the five main traits that shape how we move through the world.

Example: Once Sarah uses this lens to see that John is high in Neuroticism, his behavior finally makes sense. Don't mistake his withdrawal for indifference. It isn't a weapon used to punish you, it's a sign he's lost and looking for a solid place to land. He doesn't need to be fixed; he needs the grounding he felt when he was with me.

- **Openness:** High openness thrives on novelty and exploration. Low openness isn't "boring," it's a need for routine and predictability to feel safe.
- **Conscientiousness:** High conscientiousness needs order and clear expectations. Low conscientiousness isn't "lazy," it benefits from supportive guidance and flexibility.
- **Extraversion:** High extraversion flourishes with social engagement. Low extraversion requires quiet, reflective spaces and the autonomy to recharge.
- **Agreeableness:** High agreeableness thrives in harmony. Low agreeableness isn't "mean," it needs time, consistency, and clarity to build trust.

- **Neuroticism:** High neuroticism needs emotional centering and stability. Low neuroticism does well with independence.

Non-Violent Communication: The Language of Life (NVC)

Beyond the technical, there is a way of speaking that strips away the weapons we usually carry into a conversation. It's about listening and requesting without the hidden edge of demand.

- **Listening:** Truly hear what the other person is saying without interrupting or judging.
- **Observing:** Pay attention to their body language, tone of voice, and the words they choose.
- **Feeling:** Tune into their emotions and acknowledge them. This helps the other person feel seen and understood.
- **Requesting:** Make clear and respectful requests to further the conversation or action.

Non-Verbal & Visual Language

Body language is its own dialect. Facial expressions, gestures, and eye contact share what words cannot. For those who struggle with speech, Written or Visual aids (images/videos) can bridge the gap and spark honest sharing.

The Action Plan: Moving Toward Transparency

- Lead with Proactive Honesty: Don't wait to be caught or questioned. Offer the fuller picture before it is requested.
- Listen for the Unspoken: Pay attention to the tight jaw, the averted eyes, and the written cues. Sometimes the most honest expressions happen in a letter or a silence.

- Recognize Triggers: Learn the attachment styles and love languages that drive your partner. Speak their language intentionally, not just when it's convenient for you.

- Create Rituals for Openness: Build "safe zones" for dialogue. Use pre-conversation check-ins and post-conversation debriefs to process the intense emotions that come with the truth.

- Adapt the Delivery: Adjust your timing, tone, and eye contact. You are speaking to a human being, not a brick wall; match the person standing in front of you.

- Stay Curious and Flexible: Observe their routines and conflict styles. Ditch the old programming and rewrite the script based on the person your partner is today, not who they were ten years ago.

Recognizing Your Communication Style

Before you can change the dynamic, you have to name the habit. Most of us fall into one of these four patterns when the pressure is on. Be honest about which one is yours:

- Assertive: Confident and respectful. You are direct about your needs without being a bulldozer. This is the goal: balance.

- Aggressive: Forceful and Dominating. You use words to control or intimidate. It's a shield made of fire, but it burns the bridge you're trying to cross.

- Passive: Submissive and avoidant. You stay quiet and over-accommodate to keep the peace, but you lose yourself in the process.

- Passive-Aggressive: Indirect and sarcastic. You withhold the truth and use resentment as a weapon. It's a slow poison for trust.

Emotional Triggers: The "Why" Behind the Walls

Communication fails when we react instead of respond. You have to know what pulls your trigger before you can stay grounded.
Ask yourself:

- What specific words or tones make me angry or defensive?
- When do I feel the urge to avoid or shut down entirely?
- How do I manage my internal "noise" so I can actually hear what is being said?

Character & Psychological Style

- Locus of Control: Does he believe he's the captain of his ship (Internal), or does he feel tossed around by the waves (External)? If he feels he has no agency, he needs structure and encouragement to find his own voice.
- Risk Tolerance: High-risk men thrive in the unknown; low-risk men need the safety of a slow, steady pace. Don't push a man who needs stability into a storm he isn't ready for.
- Integrity and Courage: Real transparency requires the courage to sit in discomfort. If his "courage muscle" is weak, he needs a safe space and gradual exposure to the truth, not a trial by fire.

The Social Dance: Meeting the Style

- Reserved vs. Expressive: Some men wear their hearts on their sleeves; others lock them in a vault. Respect the pace. A safe space isn't about forcing the door open; it's about making the room so safe the door opens on its own.

- Leaders vs. Followers: Some need to guide; others need to be led. Both are valid. In my space, a leader might need the responsibility of a task, while a follower needs the direction to finally shine.
- Empathetic vs. Detached: Some feel everything; others analyze it. If he is detached, meet him with logic and space. If he is empathetic, meet him with presence and connection.

The Search for Intensity and Validation

There is a pull toward experiences that feel deep, intense, and all-encompassing. The rush is just the distraction; the real story is what those experiences reveal about who you are when you're finally forced to be honest.

The need to feel truly seen, wanted, and meaningful often fuels this search for intensity. In the Dungeon, men find this through physical and mental surrender. In your relationship, you find it through radical transparency. It's less about the thrill itself and more about using those powerful connections as proof that you are valued. Intensity is often just a shortcut to feeling significant.

The Hidden Drivers: Attachment & Love Languages

We all carry a imprint for how we love and how we fear.

- **Attachment Styles:** Whether someone is Secure, Anxious (fearing abandonment), or Avoidant (fearing closeness), their style could be a survival mechanism. When Thomas shut down in the Dungeon, it wasn't because he was "bad,' it was his Anxious attachment screaming for validation.
- **The Five Love Languages:** Love isn't one-size-fits-all. Victor didn't need a hug; he needed words of affirmation.

Understanding if your partner speaks through acts of service, quality time, gifts, or touch is the difference between a connection that thrives and one that starves.

The Traffic Light: Communicating in Real-Time

In the Dungeon, we don't guess about safety; we use words or a color-coded system to communicate intensity. In your everyday life, you can do the same. Most people don't know how to say, "I'm overwhelmed," until they're already shouting or shutting down. Establishing a "Traffic Light" for your dialogue gives you a way to signal your internal state before the communication collapses.

- Green: I'm safe. I'm present. Keep talking.
- Yellow: I'm getting uncomfortable. My defenses are rising. Slow down, change your tone, or give me a moment to breathe.
- Red: I'm flooded. I've reached my limit and I can no longer hear you. We need to stop this conversation now and come back to it when I am regulated.

Emotional Aftercare

A difficult conversation can leave both people feeling raw, exposed, or exhausted. In my work, aftercare isn't something I feel is an option and I like to make a priority. This is how I help us center the truth and transition from the intensity of the session back into the world. Your relationships need this same stabilization.

Don't just walk away once the truth has been spoken. Practice emotional aftercare. Offer a simple hug, share a meal, or say, *"Thank you for being brave enough to tell me that."* It reminds both of you that the connection is more important than the conflict. You aren't just "done" with the conversation; you are safe with each other.

Digital Transparency: More Than Words

I see it in my inbox before I ever see it in their eyes: the desperate urge to connect filtered through the safety of a glass screen. My clients are often men of immense power, yet they are paralyzed by the very technology that was supposed to set them free.

Modern communication gives us more access than ever, but it also gives us more places to hide. We don't gain clarity through constant contact. Clarity can come from intention, timing, and the willingness to be fully present, even when it is uncomfortable. Being transparent in a digital world isn't just about what you say. You must be honest about why, how, and where you are saying it.

Difficult conversations do not belong in text messages. That is where tone gets lost, intent is guessed, and silence is misread. When there is a pause or the three little dots fade in and out, it can feel like rejection. Short replies often feel like a form of punishment. Most people are left trying to figure out a way to not fill those empty spaces with fear and imagination.

When emotions run high, we need presence, regulation, and centering. We don't need speed. Some conversations require eye contact, a steady voice, and the courage to sit in discomfort instead of hiding behind a screen.

Hybrid Intimacy: When Emotional Closeness Outpaces Reality

Many modern connections live in a hybrid space that feels part real and part imagined. Emotional intimacy can grow quickly through constant messaging, shared thoughts late at night, and private conversations that feel deeply personal. In truth, emotional closeness without stability can distort reality. Technology isn't creating the problem. The issue is a lack of clarity about what the connection actually is.

People begin to feel understood without being fully known. They feel connected without being accountable. This is where boundaries blur and assumptions form. Emotional cheating often begins here, long before anything physical happens.

Technology doesn't make people cheat; it just makes it easier for cowards to sample a life they aren't brave enough to actually build.

Conclusion: The Courage to Connect

At its core, effective communication transcends words. It is built on energy, intention, and the courage to speak from a place of truth. Whether they realize it or not, when these men are in my presence, I am guiding them through the behavioral layers they are too afraid to unpack at home.

I care. It's not pretense. These men know, see, and feel that I genuinely do!

DSC: DON'T STOP COMMUNICATING!

REFLECTION: RAINA MARKS

If you had asked me what I thought about the communication between me and my husband, I would have confidently stated that we're excellent communicators. Now, I'm not quite so sure!

Raina leaves the pool and finds herself back in the kitchen. She makes a beeline for the nearest drawer and yanks it open. *Chaos.*

She stares at it blankly. The infamous junk drawer: batteries, expired gum, and pens that probably don't work. *Ugh! Kind of feels like my brain right now.*

She digs through, searching. Singing out: "Where is my highlighter?"

Raina, book in hand, begins to flip the pages. Her eyes scan the words faster than her heart can process them. *I need to read this chapter again.*

Out comes a bitter, breathy laugh. "Effective Communication," she says aloud, almost mocking the words. "I've seen proof that transparency and honest dialogue do benefit relationships. Men cheat on their partners… with me!" She shouts it toward the open kitchen, her voice bouncing off tile and cabinetry.

"Aaahhh! Say that out loud three times!" She groans, head in hands. "Seriously!"

She finally locates the highlighter, uncaps it like a sword, and begins slashing neon light across the pages. Highlighting with urgency, she mutters: "This. And this. Oh, and I want to remember this."

Closing the book slowly. *A little homework never hurt anyone!*

But then, the dissonance creeps in. *I have so many mixed emotions about this Dominatrix. A part of me despises this woman. Another side of me… gets it. The parts where she supports and provides them with compassion, and a safe space to express themselves. And maybe even helps them learn how to be honest, transparent, and emotionally present.*

I wonder what these men would be doing without someone like her in their lives? My first thought? They wouldn't be cheating. If only that were true. But… realistically? The desire would still be there, and I think they'd just be cheating in other ways.

Placing her hand flat on the book: *What's even harder to swallow is the idea that they share so many things with her. Their secrets, their truth, and a lot of information their partners have most likely never been given the chance to hear. On top of that, these guys are talking about us. That's intimate!*

We're not exactly transparent with each other either. Not really! You think you know your person until you read something like this and realize that, maybe you don't.

This book is about men cheating on women… but the words? She looks up at the ceiling. *At times, they reflect right back at me. I've had thoughts before. The momentary "what if?"*

I believe my husband would be devastated if I were carrying on any kind of relationship outside our marriage. It wouldn't matter if it were emotional, physical, or otherwise. I know it!

I haven't been completely transparent with him either. Unfortunately, our marriage is not perfect. I have needs and desires that aren't being met. But have I told him all of them?

A small, sharp exhale. *No. Not all of them. And whose fault is that?*

Her reflection stares back from the dark window. *Mine.*

Pacing back and forth: *We should've been effectively communicating from day one. Not just "How was your day?" or "Did you pick up the milk?" but real shit. All those needs, secrets, and fantasies. The parts we think are safe to keep to ourselves.*

She closes the book with intention. *I'd like to think we could be more honest and transparent. Because we can't fix what we won't name.*

CHAPTER 12

SIGNS YOUR MAN IS CHEATING

'**ve lost count of how many times I've heard some version of:**

"She doesn't understand this side of me."

"If I could share this with her, I would!"

"We haven't had sex in months… years…"

"My wife would never be kinky with me!"

"What I do, would gross her out!"

"I've given up on the chance of the two of us satisfying my needs."

"I hint at the idea of the two of us playing dress up, but she says no way!"

"It's best I just keep things to myself."

"We did something kinky once, but never again."

"It's just this one thing!"

That one thing being: ME. I want to help you understand more about the kinky, cheating man.

I don't moralize. I'm not here to police anyone's fidelity. But I am a witness, and from where I'm standing, the view is… interesting.

My perspective comes from my profession, where discretion is part of the service and transactional. If your man is cheating with a Dominatrix, you probably won't catch him with lipstick on his collar or secret love notes in his glove box. It's not that kind of affair.

It's quieter, more controlled. **I perform and I charge.**

You're up against a professional-grade secret. My client isn't cheating with a girl from the office who might get messy; he's cheating with a business. Businesses are built to be discreet and he's paying for a managed experience.

I'm going to tell you exactly why your "gut feeling" is actually your highest intelligence. Your brain can work on a level he can't outsmart.

These are some of the patterns you might begin to notice.

The Three Pillars of Deception

Your man knows how to carve out the perfect window of opportunity for himself. I am confident when I say, "He is able to keep the normalcy of his patterns, making it very difficult for you to see any signs." He's methodical, premeditated, even. Whether he visits me before or after work, on his lunch break, between meetings, or while you're otherwise occupied, he's a master at creating space for his secret adventures.

Clients don't have to worry about their identities being uncovered, because 99.9% of Dominatrices won't blow their covers. That's one of the reasons why men pay prostitutes, strippers, and Professional Dominatrices—to keep us quiet and to avoid any messy hassles.

In my 20+ years as a Dominatrix, I have never, not once, heard a man say that he has been caught by his partner for cheating on her with me. And that's not due to these men being exceptionally sneaky or their partners being oblivious. The nature of this kind of cheating is different, because it's contained and controlled.

Pillar I: Tactical Logistics & Physical Trace Management

The cheater clears his path ahead, making sure all necessary texts and calls are made before stepping through my door. He's calculated and precise!

In the Dungeon, he has a lot to say to ensure no physical evidence follows him home.

I hear:

"I don't want you to wear any perfume on the day of our session. I don't want any lingering smell on my body."

"I'm going to keep my shoes and socks on. This way, I don't have any hair stuck to my socks that I bring home with me."

"Don't get your face too close to mine, I don't want any makeup residue on my face when I leave here."

"Please don't wear glitter stuff when I schedule an appointment."

"Don't leave any whip marks on my bottom, I don't want my wife to see any bruises."

"I gotta run a little bit early, something has come up! I booked an hour with you today, but I have to leave fifteen minutes early to pick something up for my wife."

Potential Signs:

- He's extra careful with his appearance, but not for you. He suddenly doesn't want you hugging him right when he gets home. Won't let you get close to his face. Brushes you off with "I'm sweaty" or "I just need a shower."
- He smells fresh from unusual soaps, lotions, and/or perfumes.
- He suddenly has hard boundaries around his body. Won't take off his shirt. Doesn't want you near his thighs or back. He says he's sore from the gym, but the marks don't match a workout. He may be hiding bruises or rope impressions—small, brief signs that fade fast.
- Money starts going missing, but there's no obvious affair trail. He's pulling out more cash. You notice less on the credit card but more ATM withdrawals. There's no lingerie receipt, no hotel charges, because he's paying for his kink in a clean, quiet way. Usually in cash. And if it's on a card, the business name won't raise a red flag.
- You find strange objects, but nothing romantic. A cock ring in the glove box. Nipple clamps. A lockable box. These aren't things you picked out together, and he's not bringing them into your sex life.

Pillar II: Digital Shadows & Operational Discretion

If he finds himself in an unusual jam, he doesn't hesitate to answer or silence your calls or texts. With today's technology, he can text or talk to you freely at the beginning, in the middle, or at the end of a session. Since I am aware of his secretive situation, it's an easy transition.

I hear:

"No, I'm not going to give you my real name. I have to protect myself!"

"It's great that your establishment has an unassuming business name that appears on my credit card."

"Do I have to sign a waiver?"

"I might have to take a call in ten minutes."

Potential Signs:

- He's suddenly very private... but calm about it. He guards his phone, starts deleting texts or call logs, and avoids letting it out of his sight. But here's the twist: he's not anxious like someone covering up a messy affair. He's focused. Relaxed. He already knows how to cover his tracks.
- You see unfamiliar names calling his phone. The Dominatrix may be calling him back to confirm or book his appointment.
- He instantly closes the computer when you enter the room.
- He uses unusual email accounts and deletes his browser history every time he uses the device.
- He has unexplained time gaps. He says he's running errands, staying late at work, hitting the gym... but something doesn't line up. He's always just out of reach during specific windows of time—same days, same hours.

Pillar III: Psychological Shifts & The "Odd Contentment"

The nature of this kind of cheating feels systemic. In most cases this isn't a one-time slip. The cheating client believes he's entitled to both worlds: the loving partner at home and the "special exception." He cheats because he wants to remain emotionally unexposed, keeping his deepest cravings in a box where they can't complicate his life.

I hear:

"This isn't about love."

"I want to separate myself from everything else."

"I can show parts of myself to you that I don't have to show others to get that release."

Potential Signs:

- He's become… oddly content. He's not picking fights. He's not acting out. He's showing up, but emotionally, he's not as available. He's getting his needs met elsewhere.
- He stops initiating sex or no longer cares if you don't want sex.
- He avoids deep conversations about intimacy. He changes the subject. Deflects. Says everything's "fine." He's not open about what turns him on anymore, because someone else already knows.
- There might not be any emotional red flags, just a subtle disconnection. With a Dominatrix, there's no emotional affair. No long texts, no sneaky romantic plans. But you might feel like he's hiding something deeper. Not his heart, but his needs and fantasies.

The Revelation

Even in the most carefully hidden arrangements, the truth has a way of leaving traces. If something does feel off, trust your body before your mind starts making excuses for him. Your intuition is a powerful tool, and it's often right. Not every sign means betrayal, but ignoring your gut? That might be a betrayal to yourself.

To the woman standing in the center of that uncertainty: you are not foolish. I know how deeply women bend themselves to understand, to rationalize, and to forgive. You are not lacking, and you are not to blame. You are whole and deserving of a partnership built on truth.

Communication is key in any relationship. If he's seeking something outside of what you have, it's time to find out why. It's a personal journey, a complex dimension of emotions and agreements that only you and your partner can truly navigate.

REFLECTION: RAINA MARKS

And the hits keep on coming! Raina tosses the book aside. *Breathe, Raina, breathe!*

They sure do try to master the art of secrecy and finesse in the seams of their daily lives. Don't they?

Makes you want to question everything: the late meetings, the quiet phone calls, the way he might look away when you ask what's wrong.

Are there signs that my husband is cheating? What have I missed? Have I missed anything? Nothing seems unusual. Nothing stands out. Maybe I've stopped looking. Or maybe I've convinced myself that if I don't ask, I won't have to know.

Feels like a slow erosion. Like a persistent decline that wears away at the foundation of a relationship over time. What a way to clip away at the trust, intimacy, and emotional connection. Do they truly understand how this can undermine a woman's security, love, and confidence in the relationship? This compartmentalized life they insist on living... without us!

A sudden thought catches in her throat. "Am I oblivious?" she whispers. Then louder, steadier: "Well… at least now I have a better idea of what to look out for!"

Splash! Raina hits the water, creating waves that match her emotions. Drifting down at the deep end of the pool, the weight of her clothes pulls her further beneath the surface: a submersion of everything she's been thinking and carrying.

Heavy like her thoughts, she tosses each piece of wet clothing up on the ledge of the pool.

Whatever! I can either float to the bottom of the pool and try to hide or I can... freedom! I have nothing restricting me in this moment, and no one is here to judge me for swimming naked in my own pool!

Her bare body cuts through the water. She feels fluid, unapologetic, and free. Each stroke from end to end brings her deeper into herself.

She points her finger at the shallow end. *There is nothing to do but look forward. What matters now is how I take responsibility for my role in this relationship. And I want to make sure he is taking responsibility for his!*

We need to… communicate!

CHAPTER 13

TO GUILT OR NOT TO GUILT

In my play room, less than 10% of men admit they feel guilty for cheating.

Does your man feel guilty? Sometimes. Some days. Not always.

Guilt is the elephant in the room that he tries to ignore until it sits on his chest. It's a mix of regret, responsibility, and self-judgment that either forces a man to grow or, in my world, forces him to pay for a release. Guilt goes beyond what happened; it lives in how you carry it inside your being.

Whether your man carries a hive of buzzing guilt or none at all, there's a pretty good chance he won't refrain from fulfilling his desires, needs, and fantasies at some point. In one way or another, life reveals its unyielding presence through the friction of unmet needs. He may find himself unable to break free from the chains of his kinky thoughts or growing dependency.

Ensnared in a perpetual cycle of being stimulated and desperate, he grapples with his relentless cravings. Despite his intentions, the allure of his vice proves too potent to resist. He is no longer in control and fights against the insidious pull of his compulsions.

For many men, when they reach their peak level of horniness, the guilt typically evaporates somewhere between their mind and their cock. They may lose their self-conscious emotions and no longer care about how they perceive themselves. They have misplaced the digits to their moral code.

If these men feel guilty, they typically will experience less sexual gratification. I guarantee you, most men do not want to tamper with their sexual arousal. They will leave their guilt at my Dungeon door, tune out the contrition, and tune in to the satisfaction.

Guilt isn't a constant state. For cheaters, it rises and falls based on shifting circumstances. His remorse, or lack thereof, is often dictated by the situations in his daily life:

- **Relational Friction:** Are the two of you constantly fighting? Has sex become empty or repetitive? Does he resent you for not partaking in his fantasies, or is he simply tired of hearing "no"? Has he begun to rewrite the history of your relationship to make himself the victim?

- **Internal Rot:** Has he lost the capacity for remorse? Has cheating become a lifestyle norm rather than a mistake? Does he feel his professional success or financial provision entitles him to a secret life of private pleasure?

- **The Shame:** Does the weight of his guilt actually become the fuel for his next surrender? Is he seeking a professional to punish him for the very things he feels guilty about? Does he use the "dirty" feeling of his secrets to heighten the intensity of his next session?

- **Compartmentalization:** Is he using secrecy to keep his "saint" and "sinner" personas from ever having to meet? Does he believe that by paying a professional, he is actually "saving" his marriage from his darker desires?
- **Chasing The High:** Is he stressed at work or bored by a mundane life? Has the pursuit of a dopamine high rendered him cognitively blind to the consequences?
- **The Need for Autonomy:** Does he simply want privacy? Does he want the freedom to explore what he cannot share with you, or is he using secrecy to keep his "public" and "private" selves from ever colliding?

This list is exhaustive, and every factor contributes to the unfortunate reality of the choices he makes.

Types of Guilty Men

Mr. I'm Guilty

For the guilty man, his conscious mind has sounded the naughty alarm, and he's standing naked with the weight of his choices pressing down on him.

I hear:

"I really tried not to come here today!"

"I have been thinking a lot about our time together, and I think this is the last time I will be seeing you."

"I feel extremely ashamed for cheating on my wife. I just don't know how to control myself!"

"I feel so guilty!"

"I wish I could talk to my girlfriend about my fantasies, but I know she won't be interested."

"I'm only here because I am having problems at home."

"What's wrong with me? Why do I like you Dominating me so much and why can't I stop?"

"Do you think I will be able to stop obsessing over this fetish I love? I can't stop myself!"

"I haven't been here in six months. I have been trying to figure out a way to stop seeing you."

"I haven't seen you because I have tried to just focus on my wife instead of on my own desires."

"I'm nervous, I'm afraid I will get caught!"

"I really don't understand why I am the way I am!"

"It's not like I feel great about being here!"

"I feel guilty, but I don't know if I would feel remorseful if I were to get caught."

The Layers of His Guilt

Cheating isn't just about the act. It is the mental toll and the compounding weight of the double life he's leading. If your partner is cheating and feeling guilty, trust that there is a list.

He feels guilty for the *Betrayal:*

- For lying to you and not being upfront about his double life.
- For breaking your relationship agreements and violating the family's trust.
- For spending the family's money on his secrets.
- For being a sneaky, kinky little fuck.
- For going against his cultural morals, his upbringing, and his own internal value system.

He feels guilty for the *Emotional Shift:*

- Because he does love you and wants to be a loyal man, but simply isn't.

- For no longer desiring you the way he used to or not finding you attractive.
- For falling out of love with you and the guilt that comes with that drifting.
- For the dark thought that you're "not enough" to keep him faithful—though he'll never say that out loud.
- Because he likes what he is doing without you, and he enjoys the world he has built in the dark.

He feels guilty for his *Lack of Control:*

- For being a cheater—plain and simple.
- For his "bad boy" behavior and the shame of being "perverted" or "broken."
- Because he is ashamed of his own cravings and his inability to "be normal."
- For not being able to stop paying me for my time.
- Because he just cannot STOP.

And it doesn't stop there. For the guilty man, the reasons just keep piling on, burying him under a mountain of his own making until he finally realizes he is no longer in the driver's seat of his own life.

The Internal War

These men are at war with a lifetime of programming. Many were conditioned from an early age to suppress curiosity, to toughen up, and to silence anything that didn't fit the traditional male mold. When they finally step into a space like mine, a space that reflects their most vulnerable, erotic truths, their internal alarm system goes off. They ask themselves: *What does this mean about me? Am I broken? Am I weak? Am I perverted?*

For some, the act itself doesn't matter as much as the symbolism of being Dominated and the choice to submit. They might be exploring forbidden practices like anal play, feminization, sissification, or even just being emotionally transparent with a woman. These are lines many men were taught never to cross. When they do, the shame can be paralyzing.

Desire does not wait for permission. These hidden cravings do not make a man a monster, but they do make him undeniably human. The tragedy is never the hunger itself. The tragedy is the method he chooses to feed it. When a man resorts to cheating, he is no longer just seeking a release because he is actively stealing it. In that process, he systematically breaks the trust he once swore to protect.

The Broken Promise

Then there is the man who carries a different kind of weight. Beyond the battle with cultural stigma lies the heavy truth of a broken sacred promise. This guilt hits differently. It isn't necessarily a fear of being caught that haunts him, but the reflection staring back in the mirror. Sitting in my sanctuary, his heart is split in two: the craving for something he feels he can't express elsewhere, and the aching awareness that he has betrayed someone who trusted him.

He may try to justify it, *"She wouldn't understand"* or *"It's not like I'm in love with you,"* but eventually, the wall breaks down. The truth that surfaces is the real conflict: he knew better and he did it anyway.

This cheater isn't always looking to escape accountability. Sometimes he wants to sit in the discomfort and say the truth out loud to someone who won't judge him. I become the witness for that truth. I don't tell him it's okay, and I don't justify his actions. Instead, I create an environment where he can be transparent and take a deeper look at what drove him to cross that line.

I see past the shame and into the part of him that just wants to feel accepted. Slowly, session by session, we unpack the *why* behind the fantasy. Sometimes the biggest release isn't physical; it's the moment they realize they can be both kinky and kind, submissive and strong, and still worthy of respect. It is often this very realization that leads them to the decision to never return to my Dungeon again.

Here's a few examples of these guilty cheaters.

Mr. Sulking Sinner

I hear:

"I thought I could change!"

"I'm back. Again!"

"I really didn't want to do this, but I can't stop myself!"

"Being here with you, goes against everything I believe in!"

"I feel awful that I can't stop!"

"I feel weird about myself all the time."

"Mr. Moody" is caught in a deep internal tug-of-war. He tries to bury his kinks, pretending his urges will disappear, but repression rarely works. Eventually, the temptations win and he's back.

These are the men who show up monthly, quarterly, or maybe once a year for what I call "moody sessions."

The man walks in like a storm cloud, heavy, slow-moving, and blinking guilt like a neon sign. Usually, he is in no rush to play; he wants to talk first. Out pours a list of justifications and internal battles: why it took him so long to return, how hard he's tried to "be normal," and how exhausting it is to wrestle with something he cannot delete from his mind. I find it interesting that his guilt isn't just directed toward his partner, but toward me, for his failed attempt to eliminate me from his life.

He is ashamed that he cannot turn it off, and that his cravings have a pulse of their own. He explains how he almost canceled the appointment and thought about walking away from kink altogether. But once again, here he is.

These sessions require a different rhythm. I guide him out of his head and back into his body, holding space for the guilt before helping him release it mentally, emotionally, and physically. Once he drops the shame and lets himself surrender, his entire energy settles. He rises, literally and figuratively.

Success: the guilty man is momentarily satisfied. However, in many cases, the guilt soon surfaces again, and he struggles to stay in a playful headspace. This puts us right back where we started, revisiting his guilty conscience.

Mr. Regular *Guilty* Cheater is: Consistent

I hear:

"I love my wife, but she's just not into kinky things."

"In the beginning of our relationship, I could get my wife to do certain things, but that didn't last very long."

"I love my girl. She's hot! I've tried buying her expensive boots, but no matter what, she just won't wear them. But I keep trying!"

"My girlfriend is amazing, but if I told her what I was into, I know she would break up with me."

"I wish my wife would do what you do!"

"How can I get my girlfriend into these kinds of things?"

"I don't want to deal with home crap; it's just easier for me to come to you."

"I don't really feel like I'm cheating; it's not like I'm having an affair!"

"You are my only escape when I can't deal with the outside pressures."

"GOD, I love you!"

"I wish I could marry you, Mistress!"

"Why rock the boat? It's easier to come to you for my kinky needs."

"I am just so fucking bored! I can't help it; these fantasies are never going to leave my mind."

"You are my addiction!"

"Cheating has become a normal part of my life."

"I'm not cheating if there isn't any sex involved."

"I am so stressed out. If I don't come here, I'm going to lose it!"

"I just need a break!"

"This is my thing, my time; no one needs to know!"

"Take me away from reality, Mistress!"

"I'm such a bad boy for being here, Mistress! Punish me!"

This repeat client schedules a session with me on a weekly, bi-weekly, or monthly basis.

"Mr. Regular Cup of Joe" rarely shows any real signs of guilt. This is the cheating man who walks through my door most often: the not-so-guilty guy. Early on, he might have squawked out a line or two about feeling badly, but that fades fast. As time goes on, the seriousness in his voice disappears. Confessions start to sound more like jokes or complaints than actual remorse.

These clients aren't just addicted to the kinky fun; the experience has become a necessity for their state of mind. They rely on the mental and physical relief they get from our time together. After a session, they feel like new men, ready to go back to their daily lives. For them, cheating has become a normalcy. I have become as common and as necessary as their habitual morning cup of coffee.

Mr. Privacy

I hear:

"Can I just get some fucking privacy?"

"I need time, my alone time!"

"There is always something or somebody getting into my business."

"I have zero privacy, and I want something that is just mine. My secret. My time. And I don't want to have to explain myself to anyone!"

"Mr. Privacy" is desperate to reclaim a piece of his life that belongs only to him. Amidst the clamor of obligations and responsibilities, he finds a way to escape the prying eyes of the world, slipping into the seclusion of the Dungeon to protect these stolen moments.

With calculated intention, he carves out time to step away from the demands that suffocate him. Interestingly, this man does not believe he is acting out of selfishness; instead, he views it as a desperate need to nurture his own private time. He is tired of accommodating everyone else and craves the power of being a man who does not have to answer to anyone.

The act of escaping those who constantly intrude on his life makes him feel like he has regained control. If only for a moment, he defines our time as his own secret, where he alone sets the boundaries and the rules.

Mr. Not Giving Two Fucks

I hear: Nothing most of the time. But when I do!

"I'm just an asshole and I know it!"

"I don't feel guilty!"

"I know I shouldn't be cheating, but I will do whatever it takes to get what I want!"

"Guilt should stop me, but it doesn't!"

"I don't really think about it anything except for what I want to do!"

These guiltless men cheat with ease, as if the act is casual and the consequences are optional. You won't hear a single word suggesting that guilt or the women in their lives would ever stop them from walking through my door. They never hold themselves accountable because, in their minds, there is nothing to be accountable for. To them, the betrayal isn't a burden; it is simply a choice they make without a second thought.

Recognizing the Guilty Cheater

Can you recognize the guilty cheater? Based on what these men have told me and what I have witnessed behind closed doors, here are the hints that the mask is slipping.

The Deflector (Hiding the Truth):

- He brilliantly creates a façade of false information.
- He avoids specific topics or refuses to answer your questions.
- He becomes defensive or unusually submissive when approached.
- He is becoming unrecognizable—no longer the man you know.
- He flat-out lies, even when you see right through him.
- He leaves you guessing, confused, and unable to detect his true motives.

The Over-Compensator (Managing the Guilt):

- Your bedroom activities take on a whole new level of kinky interests.
- He is suddenly interested in pornographic material or introducing it to you.
- You suddenly become an object of intense affection, adorned with unexpected gifts.
- He becomes unusually passive-aggressive, sad, or even depressed.
- He develops an unusual "pep in his step" or becomes communicative on topics he'd normally avoid.

- He asks for constant reassurance or displays sudden insecurities.

Guilty or not, you are dealing with a man mostly unfazed by moral implications. This man remains impervious to the potential devastation his choices may cause. He is steadfast in his pursuit of personal gratification, brazenly indulging his impulses with a callous disregard for the sanctity of his commitments.

If you were prioritized over his fleeting pleasures, you would not be left in the wreckage of his wake.

My Role in Their Story

Do I feel guilty about being the professional Dominatrix in your man's life?

No. I do not.

There is a common confusion that needs clearing: a "Mistress" is traditionally a woman in an affair with a married man. But in my world, Mistress is a title of authority, discipline, and trust. I am not your man's secret lover. I am his Dominatrix. I give the orders, make the decisions, enforce obedience, and take the tribute.

When men walk through my door, I don't ask about their marital status because their domestic contracts are not my concern. The truth of their outside lives reveals itself on different timelines. Some men collapse into their reality the moment the door closes, while others require a slow burn before I see the lives they live outside my space. Many of my clients are cheating, but that decision is theirs, not mine. I am not the keeper of their morality. Every man who enters is the sole owner of his own integrity.

This is not a traditional affair. There are no intimacy statements, no emotional dependencies, and no stolen kisses in the dark. I don't fall in love with your man, and I have no desire to replace you or take him from your relationship. What I offer is something your partner often doesn't know how to ask for within your shared dynamic.

I embrace this work with pride. I'm committed to safely guiding people through their shadows, not around them. Without a safe, carefully maintained space, suppressed desires often leak out in riskier, more damaging ways. With me, we don't need to worry about that!

As many clients tell me: *"I get what I need here, and I go home a better man."* They mean it. What they find with me is an overall release, not emotional entanglement, but safety and fulfillment. Shame is not my tool, and it is not my place to smother them or myself with judgment. I've seen the relief and the emotional grounding that comes from this work.

My presence in your partner's life doesn't mean you've failed or that you aren't enough. It means there is something he hasn't voiced, perhaps because he is paralyzed by his own vulnerabilities, afraid of the judgment that follows truth, or simply lost in the confusion of his needs. Or, he's just a jerk!

Regardless, I hold that space. *Safely. Professionally. And with integrity.*

REFLECTION: RAINA MARKS

Feeling guilty. Raina glances at the crumpled heap of damp clothes: cashmere clinging to linen like regret to memory.

So much for that cashmere sweater! I guess I shouldn't have taken it for a swim. Should've left it on the chair like a sane person.

She rolls her eyes dramatically and sarcastically whines out: "Oops. Just ruined the sweater Mr. Whatever-He-Is-Up-To surprised me with last week." *The hubby is going to be pissed about this one!*

Maybe I'm going to be pissed off about a few things myself! Honestly, he should be less worried about my sweater and more worried about where his dick has been or wants to be. Did I just think that?

Almost no remorse? These men have a lot of nerve living these lies so casually. Like their emotional double lives are just another Monday meeting.

Rethinking the words she just read in the last chapter. ***"Grapples with his relentless cravings!"*** *I will give my man something to grapple with and make him think clearly down the path between his mind and his cock if he cheats! He'll learn what a real punishment feels like. And not the sexy kind.*

Unleashing the rebel. She drops the book beside her and stands tall, bare and bold. "I'm not getting dressed," she announces to no one but herself and the birds in the trees. "This is my house. And from now on, it's a *Nudie Duty Sunday* for the rest of the day. From here on out, it is my duty to myself to feel free and in control!"

Her reflection in the sliding glass door catches her off guard. *I sound like a child. Who am I right now? Look at yourself, Raina. You're stark naked in front of a giant window, talking to your damn self.*

She shrugs. *I know. I see myself. Can't blame it on the wine—I only had one glass. It's the book! I'm blaming the Doom'inatrix. No… I'm blaming the cheaters!*

Peeved, her tone hardens. *Come on. Excuses, excuses, excuses! Just stop already! Communicate. Stick to your commitments. Be honest. It's not that hard. If you know you can't stay faithful, then don't pretend to. Don't lie! Just… don't cheat. No one deserves to be manipulated and lied to like this.*

If these men are truly so desperate to fulfill their needs, and they know they can't do it within their relationship, then end it! Be single! Find someone open to a different kind of agreement. Don't destroy someone who thinks they're building a life with you.

She takes a long breath in. And out. "I need to calm down!"

Easing into stillness, she lies back on her lounge chair.

Let me settle into the thought that… this woman wouldn't feel guilty for indulging in my man's secrets and fantasies. His lies and deceit. I'm not quite sure how I feel about that. Honestly? There's a part of me that's relieved they aren't having traditional affairs. But another part of me? Outraged. Cheating is cheating: emotional, physical, or otherwise.

This whole situation is a double-edged sword. The Dominatrix gives him "Fantasy Therapy." Some safe space where he can be his full, honest, kinky self. I want him to have that freedom… but not at my emotional expense. Not at the cost of my trust. I want to be the one who helps him feel right inside of his world. Or at least come to our own negotiations about how he is going to handle what he needs. I want to be the one he confides in. If he needs help exploring this side of himself, I want him to come to me first.

Would I feel differently if "kinky time" weren't involved? If he went to a sex therapist and shared all his fantasies and secrets without telling me? If I didn't know, probably not! Either way, it's the secrets. The lack of transparency. And respect!

The fact that he can open up to another woman while keeping me in the dark would really hurt. Not just the kinky gratification, but the absence of me in his truth. Even if he says it's for the greater good of our marriage, I'm not sure I could ever forget the secrecy. It would burrow under my skin and live there.

Well, this is turning into quite the adventure!

CHAPTER 14

FANTASY SESSION STORY
A SERPENT'S TORTURE

This chapter presents a fantasy session story involving consenting adults only. All scenarios are fictionalized composites inspired by themes from my professional practice, and identifying details have been altered to protect privacy. The story explores adult BDSM dynamics, trust, and power exchange within a safe, consensual, and controlled environment.

Character Development: *This client is a man in his twenties. Other than the fact that he loves pain, I do not know anything else about him.*

I find the colors mesmerizing as each hue highlights a different part of his body. The pigments rich in color define the snake that wraps his creamy skin from head to toe.

"I am happy you are here again. I really love our sessions." It is always a special hour when he makes his annual appearance to see me here at the Dungeon.

Commanding him: "I want you to remove all your clothing. Place your clothing on the spanking horse!"

He nods and smiles but remains quiet. Standing at 5'7, his eagerness for pain is vivid by the markings of his full-body tattoo: a graceful guardian in a symphony of colors.

I lay out a rainbow of waxed candles onto the counter. I pull a nearby candelabra to the center of the counter. This will be the perfect igniter for all my candles. These are not your usual candles; rather, they are specially crafted for use on the body. I take a cotton sheet and drape the bondage table for protection from the wax. Slowly, I graze my hand across the sheet to smooth out any wrinkles and summon him to lie on the table.

I see he is now comfortable, and it is time for me to begin. Like weapons, my long nails trace the serpentine's beauty. I watch his flesh become flushed as I scratch my pointy blades over the inked details.

I pick up the first candle and spark the wick. I know that he enjoys a lot of pain, so I will be sure to hold the candle just a little more closely to his skin than usual. The closer the candle, the hotter the wax droplets. *Perfect!*

Starting at his neck, I move in closely and brush his cheek with my fingertips. Slowly, I tilt the black candle to the left as he watches a single drop of wax fall: a quick sting to the serpent's crown. The moans from his mouth give me a sign that he is pleased.

"Do you want more?" I ask him.

Hearing him hiss out the word "*yessssssss,*" I continue.

With the burgundy and black candles in hand, I trace and fill in the head of the snake. Drip by drip, I make the vibrant kaleidoscope my own. I watch as the head of the snake disappears underneath the wax. With my liquid flames so close to his skin, I risk burning him if I do not concentrate. I put these two colors back on the counter and pick up another color.

Towards the heart's rhythm I go. The purple essence heats up his skin, and I penetrate his nerves a little bit longer with the hot wax. Placing my hand over my client's heart, I light the red candle. I find the heart of the snake and pack in the crimson tint. He sees the intensity in my eyes when I pierce his soul with a gentle sigh of wickedness. The candles weep a symbol of both pain and pleasure.

Green and blue droplets of wax begin to cover the slithering silhouette. Inch by inch, the colors leave light trails as he reminisces about the needles that once intricately stabbed his skin. To satisfy him, I will trace every speck of the reptile's scaled form with my burning wax. I will not miss a spot! Melting whispers flicker upon the Dungeon walls, and it is time to carefully examine my work.

Pleased: "Beautiful!" I place a sheet onto the floor and slowly guide my serpent back onto his feet.

X marks the spot. "Stand right here in the middle of this sheet and do not move!"

Before me stands a coil of splendor. Hovering behind him, I hold up three lit candles in each hand. I hit his shoulder blades with the hot wax like firing torches, lighting up a night sky. The flames become one, and I can smell the burning embrace. He is no longer the cold-blooded vessel that crept his way into my zone looking for his painful fix. I have succeeded at giving him what he came here for: **pain.**

It is now time for the finale.

Standing in front of him, I raise my hands above his head. Coming down hard and fast, I claw at his flesh and begin to rake off the attached wax. Colors begin to cascade and hit the floor like a rainbow falling from the sky. Left behind is a remarkable sight of beauty and a piece of living artwork.

REFLECTION: RAINA MARKS

Raina twirls under the open sky, bare as truth, grinning like a woman who's just remembered she's allowed to be wild. *I'm kind of feeling like that majestic serpentine now! Au naturel!*

At least this story has made me curious. Her hips sway a little. *Should I go grab a candle?* she muses, already halfway to the door.

Racing with laughter, she dashes barefoot through the hallways, tracking remnants of pool water onto the hardwood floors. *Music! I need music! And a candle! Where are my matches?*

She tears through a bathroom drawer. "Aha!" she grins, holding up a lone matchbox like a golden ticket.

"Ms. All-of-a-Sudden Risky Briskly" is back at the pool, with her candle lit.

Moments later, the flickering scent of amber and vanilla fills the air as indie pop pulses through outdoor speakers: giving the moment an edge of cinematic mischief.

With no one around to judge or interrupt her personal revolution, she lets loose—dancing, dipping her toes in the water, playing with the flame.

This isn't performance. This is a plot twist: a shedding of all the hesitation, the silence, the years of tucking herself away to be something other than her full self.

Unaware and free-spirited, Raina is beginning to awaken a part of herself that has been asleep: inhibited by fear, dulled by apprehension, and bound by silent compromise. Now, finally, she's embracing a moment to let go. To just be!

A drip of warm wax hits her thigh. *Sting.* "Yikes! That hurts!"

Breathing through the sensation, curiosity remains. *That's quite the red spot left on my thigh. Let me try it on my stomach…*

Another drop. "Yow!" *That's even worse. She's not kidding: A Serpent's Torture is really torturous!*

She winces and laughs at the same time. *And he did his whole body? His endorphins must've been flying off the charts.*

Challenging the unknown, she flips to the next page. "What's next?"

She scoffs.

CHAPTER 15

LOST AUTHENTICITY: THE DOMINATRIX AND THE DECEIVER

I have spent time with hundreds of men. Throughout my journey, I have found that authenticity is not a simple 2 + 2 = 4 equation. In reality, the sum of who a man is usually doesn't add up at all.

I call bullshit on the 90% of men who act like they can't be upfront about what they want. Most can trace the roots of their fantasies or name the reasons why they fixate on certain desires. These needs don't just pass through; they pulse through their veins until one specific thought ignites the spongy erectile tissue, frenzied for release.

The Performance of Honesty

Authenticity is showing up as yourself, even when it would be easier to perform or stay silent. It means choosing honesty instead of approval. These cheating men often like to think of themselves as authentic; they speak in confessions and share "deep, secret truths." But what they're really offering is curated vulnerability, selective honesty that serves their needs without risking their comfort.

True authenticity requires accountability. I am screaming this word: **Accountability!** It demands the courage to be seen in your full complexity, even when it is inconvenient.

Many men choose to outsource their kinky intimacy to me. Their self-awareness is a closed loop, just enough to find me, but not enough to face themselves. They aren't lacking awareness; they are prioritizing appetite. They feel "real" in my sanctum only because it costs them nothing beyond the fee. It is far cheaper to pay me with currency than to pay their partners with the truth; the transaction is simply a calculated investment in the maintenance of their own lie.

Their inauthenticity is fueled by fear. The fear of being judged, excluded, or rejected. They believe their partners would never accept their "dirty little secrets," so they lie. Authenticity is not a matter of kink or conformity. It's truth. These men either never stop to question what authenticity means, or worse, they've convinced themselves they're already living authentically. Their authenticity is lost somewhere between my chamber walls, reality, and again, their cocks.

The Narcissist's Decision Matrix

Narcissism isn't a rare trait; we all carry some level of it. But for some, that spark of self-preservation grows into a fire that burns everything in its path.

The narcissist typically believes he is being authentic, and perhaps he is. His words may be genuine reflections of who he is, but they are not always kind. Authenticity without empathy is just cruelty wearing a name tag. He shares his identity on a need-to-know basis, and usually, you don't need to know. Hurting you doesn't register on his decision matrix. There's no pause, no guilt, and no afterthought. In the absence of compassion, insensitive behaviors flourish into ugly bouquets. For these men, the truth is optional.

Mr. "Inauthentic"

"Mr. Inauthentic" has made peace with his deceit. He lies with ease, saying exactly what others want to hear, and plays the role of the unbothered, confident man. But underneath that facade, he's a shapeshifter, constantly toggling between versions of himself depending on who's watching. Whether it's a loud ego or shy hesitation, the energy feels staged, a frantic performance he hopes I won't see through. But we aren't sitting at the craps table; I'm not betting on his act, I'm dismantling it.

With me, it's easy to justify. I am the Dominatrix, paid to perform, not to judge. I fit into a tidy little box designed for his gratification, but what that box doesn't hold is the weight of his actual reality. That reality, he carefully keeps out of sight, even from himself.

The New Girl

I hear it constantly:

"I met someone new and I don't need my kink anymore!"

"I fell in love and I want to be faithful!"

"I know she's the one and our sex is enough."

They convince themselves that restless fantasies disappear the moment a new woman enters their lives. At first, the relationship is fresh and validating. Until it's not.

Here We Go Again! Eventually, the relationship dulls and the cravings return. They fall back into the familiar rhythm of secrecy. The new girl becomes a silent background character in the same old story. Diving into a new relationship to fix his inner chaos is just a well-dressed lie. Sooner or later, he's back with me getting his kinky fix and the new girl is just another victim of those lies.

Unfortunately for her, he once again thrives on performing inside his two lives or vanishes without an honest explanation. *Nothing says emotional maturity like ghosting when things get too real. Ugh!*

REFLECTION: RAINA MARKS

I used to think being "the one" meant I was special. But a couple of those relationships taught me I was just next. It's easy to feel chosen when someone isn't honest about what they're really choosing you for.

Truth is Just a Question Away

To get past the surface, charm, and ego, you must ask questions that invite vulnerability and consistency. Use these layered questions to see if his actions align with his performance:

The Inner Self:

- Define authenticity?
- What makes you believe you are an authentic person?
- Who really knows the real you?
- What do you do when no one's watching?
- Is there a part of you that you fear people might not accept?
- What's something about you that most people misunderstand?
- What's one thing you're afraid to lose?
- How do you define success, and has that changed over time?

Growth & Accountability:

- When's the last time you changed your mind about something important?
- What's something you're still working on within yourself?
- Have you ever hurt someone and taken full accountability for it?
- When was the last time you admitted you were wrong, and how did you handle it?
- What's something you've had to unlearn about yourself or relationships?
- When was the last time you felt deeply disappointed, and how did you handle it?

Relationships & Patterns:

- How do you feel about emotional vulnerability?
- What would your ex say was the hardest part of being with you?
- Have you ever ghosted someone, and if so, why?
- What kind of partner do you not want to be?
- What do you think it means to earn someone's trust?
- Do you notice any patterns of narcissistic traits in yourself?
- How do you usually respond when you feel disrespected?
- What does "showing up" look like to you in a relationship?
- Are you still working on getting over a past relationship?

Integrity:

- What's something you've never told anyone, but you want to?
- Do your actions always align with your words? Can you give an example?
- What's more important to you: being right or being honest?
- Have you ever promised more than you could deliver? What happened?
- What are your values when it comes to how you treat women?

Financial/Time Transparency:

- How do you feel about total financial transparency, or do you believe some "privacy" is necessary to maintain your independence?

His inability to be authentic is not your fault. You did not cause his secrecy by being "too much" or "not enough." A man hiding his truth is a reflection of his own fear and avoidance, not your value.

As people are not looking for a performance; we want presence. If a man's outer self is out of sync with his inner world, it will show. If he is still hiding behind ego and survival habits, make it clear: I'm not judging you, but I won't bond with a façade.

REFLECTION: RAINA MARKS

I think a lot of people never stop to consider what being authentic actually means.

These men! They appear so genuine, so honest, so emotionally available when they're in that controlled space with the Professional Dominatrix. Outside that carefully staged room, their integrity mostly vanishes. It makes you wonder: how transparent are they with others?

Her throat tightens. *Looks like her clients reveal a side of themselves that they couldn't, or wouldn't, show to the women who love them. They choose a woman in a Dungeon over their partners at home. They cherry-pick which version of themselves to offer the ones who love them, and they only offer the parts that are convenient.*

Their authenticity? It feels lost. They actually look... just bad!

I don't know! It's not necessarily a lost cause. But both people have to be willing. Maybe people can come back from this if they're brave enough to go all the way in. If questions are asked. If truthful answers are given: the ones that strip away the act and pierce through what's being withheld.

She flips. *Time to tan the backside.*

CHAPTER 16

SUBSPACE VS. HEADSPACE

To understand why your man seeks me out, you must understand where he is trying to go. There are two primary destinations: Headspace and Subspace.

Headspace is a state of mind. Every client who walks through my door arrives in a specific headspace. He steps before me ready to surrender, asking to be taken out of his own will to control and into a compliant state. He remains focused and present, but he is looking for elation and release.

Subspace, by contrast, is a pleasurably altered state of consciousness. As adrenaline and endorphins flood the body, the submissive becomes immersed in a physical and mental haze. He achieves his ultimate goal: an experience that feels entirely outside of himself.

Think of it this way: Headspace is the mind fully engaged in the role. Subspace is the mind and body surrendering together.

Entering the Haze

Subspace looks different for everyone. Your man may already be experiencing it with you without you realizing it. Certain words, gestures, clothing, or tones can act as signals. He slips into that altered state and suddenly becomes deeply receptive.

Think of an intense kiss, the kind you melt into completely. It pulls you out of your thoughts and drops you fully into sensation. You lose yourself and the world fades away. You feel your body begin to hum. That euphoria is a mild glimpse of what subspace feels like. Imagine lifting stress out of your body, stepping out of the busy mind, and letting yourself settle. Everything around you goes still, sounding like a faint echo. Tension is replaced by calmness as your muscles loosen. Your body becomes heavy in a comforting way, as though you are floating inside a warm, gentle haze.

Who wouldn't want that feeling?

The Fragility of the Fix

Nothing feels better than being able to quiet the mind and fully surrender. For some men, these euphoric states become deeply compelling. The intensity driven by endorphins and adrenaline can feel intoxicating, which is why intention, boundaries, and aftercare matter. Without them, it is easy to chase the high rather than understand what it is revealing.

Without grounding or integration, some men struggle to regulate what follows. Frustration, defensiveness, or withdrawal can take hold. This does not stem from failing to get a fix. It stems from the experience opening something they do not yet know how to hold. Or, want to let go!

I have seen what happens when someone becomes attached to the state itself. If too much time passes without reaching that depth, some men grow irritable, distant, or closed off. This frustration isn't always about sex; it comes from losing access to a place where the mind finally felt quiet. Without awareness, that longing leaks out as anger or pressure rather than being named for what it is: an underlying emotional need.

My boundary here is clear. Subspace is not something I provide on demand, nor do I engage with emotional volatility as a pathway back to it. My work is founded on consent, regulation, and responsibility, never entitlement. What matters isn't the intensity of the high, but whether someone has the tools to make sense of what it stirred.

REFLECTION: RAINA MARKS

Hmmm… been there, done that!

The Look of Surrender

Subspace can take a man into a dreamlike state. His eyes may glaze over, and often he stares off into space, grows giggly, or becomes very quiet. Speech can become fragmented or fade altogether. His body may soften or become limp. Movements become slower and his reactions are often delayed. In this trance, his body takes the lead. Emotions feel magnified and time loses its usual shape. He may lose track of minutes, struggle to articulate thoughts, and experience an increased tolerance for pain. Judgments fade. As his capacity for reason dissolves, the burden of responsibility shifts entirely to me.

The Sub-Drop and The Landing

Sub-drop is the post-scene hangover that follows the high. This feeling is real and should never be ignored. It is a full-body, full-brain experience. After a session, emotions rise and fall as the body comes down from a hormonal peak. Dopamine, endorphins, and adrenaline recalibrate. This shift can leave someone feeling raw or unsettled if they are not properly supported.

Because of this, aftercare is not optional. In 99% of my cases, it is a must. It is how you help someone transition from the intensity of play back to reality.

After each session, I make sure my client is grounded, safe, and emotionally regulated. Generally, I offer a cool-down period that includes quiet time, reassurance, or simple presence. Sometimes we speak; sometimes we sit in silence. This allows him to regain composure before returning to the world outside.

These clients are my responsibility. I make sure they leave my space in a stable and safe headspace.

REFLECTION: RAINA MARKS

Aha moment. *I've felt this before! Only I didn't know it was called Subspace.*

I'm hot! I need my pink flamingo floaty!

Dragging her bubblegum bird into the pool, Raina takes a leap onto the inflatable blow-up buddy.

Slipping into a daydream: *A few weeks ago, my husband got home from a night out with the guys. He was dressed in my favorite leather jacket, dark jeans, and these really nice boots. I'm always sexually aroused by the smell of his cologne that has embedded in his leather jackets.*

I remember him walking through the door and coming straight at me. He was so sexy! He picked me up off the couch and carried me into our bedroom. He commanded me not to speak and pulled up my long dress. I started to grab at the button on his pants, but he told me: no!

I couldn't take my eyes off his hands as they were gently caressing my body. He must have spent at least 30 minutes passionately kissing and caressing me. He was taking his time with me! I could see his rock-hard cock pressing against the tightness of his jeans. I wanted it! I wanted it badly! But he wouldn't give it to me.

I was desperate! Desperate for him to remove his clothing and come into me. Only he kept maneuvering his clothed body around mine. His leather redolent with aromatic temptation had me heavy and weak! I was lost!

My whole system was out of control, and I must have had a dopamine hit as big as a volcanic eruption. I became inundated with the desire to be taken by him. I would have done anything for him to make ravenous love to me.

Eventually, he spread my legs apart and pulled my panties to the side. His hot breath penetrated my succulent entry. But still nothing! Inch by inch, he crawled up towards my face. Touching. Gripping. Peering deeply into his eyes, he leaned into my lips. No kiss, just a breathy whisper: "I love you, Raina!"

Garbled noise. #%$&* and !?@*! *Damn, it was so exciting! Oh crap, this pool water has cooled down a lot! I can see why someone can be drawn to this type of euphoria. I sure am! I want to do that again!*

Raina takes an intermission and heads back inside for a bathroom break. At least I think that's what she's doing. *Wink! Wink!*

CHAPTER 17

FANTASY SESSION STORY
UNDONE BY YOU

This chapter presents a fantasy session story involving consenting adults only. All scenarios are fictionalized composites inspired by themes from my professional practice, and identifying details have been altered to protect privacy. The story explores adult BDSM dynamics, trust, and power exchange within a safe, consensual, and controlled environment.

Character Development: This client is a married man. He has no children and is unhappy in his marriage.

"I cannot believe I am finally here with you. I have been in a brain fog all day. I could not stop thinking about being in your presence. Your beauty captivates me Mistress!"

I see that he is already in a dreamy state of bliss. Unable to take his eyes off my black spandex catsuit, he awaits my commands. So, I get right to it!

Grabbing his arm: "Come with me! I want you to stand in the middle of this red rug, with your hands behind your back, and your head bowed down to the floor. Now, wait here!"

I start the music and begin playing my pulsing sounds of electronic, ambient, and world music elements: a perfect one-hour combination of atmospheric soundscapes to pierce his soul.

I walk by the bondage table and grab the blindfold. "Do not move!" I place the blindfold over his eyes.

Moving my body into his, I tenderly touch his arms. Pausing to ruminate my essence around him, I gently place the side of my neck against his jawline. I know the smell of me is ripping away at his desperation, making him want to get his hands on what he cannot have: me.

Patience allows for my touch to speak a language of its own. No words could suffice; he is now under my erotic spell. Slowly, I begin to unbutton his shirt. One by one, the buttons become an unlocked gateway to his flesh. His shirt hits the floor.

Delicately, my fingernails penetrate his skin. His heartbeat, rapid and hungry, beats to his growing anticipation. Leaning into his chest, I stare him down. Only the shields that cover his eyes block his view from knowing that my mouth is a quarter of an inch away from his. I drag my right pointer finger against the inner lining of his belted pants. I give a slight tug on the belt that seals away his dirty companion. Letting out a quiet giggle, I tug once more at his belted khakis. My face makes contact with his and I whisper, "If only!"

He is ready for it! He is ready for me to take off his pants to expose his hard cock. With a quick jerk on his belt loops, I drag him over to the front of the bondage table. Pushing him up against the side of the table, I gently grab his throat. It takes me a few seconds to have his pants down to his ankles. I am ready to let the games begin.

Teasing him: "One more piece of fabric out of my way and I will have that hard cock right where I want it."

"Yes, yes, do it!" he cries out. The problem is, he has talked himself straight into a trap.

My hand grips his throat a little more tightly. "First of all, you will not tell me what to do. Secondly, I did not give you permission to speak. Furthermore, when you address me, you will address me properly by saying, Yes, Mistress! Where are your manners?"

I push and guide him up onto the bondage table. I leave his pants wrapped around his ankles and his shoes on. I love a little trick that saves me time. With his ankles bound by his pants, he feels the restraint and continues to surrender to me. Carefully, I rise up and over him. Straddling him, I have him pinned down to the bondage table. I raise both of his hands up over his head and cuff him to both sides of the bondage table.

Down at his ear, I faintly whisper: "Looks like you are not going anywhere, slave."

I swing myself around and sit on his thighs. I have a plan for his belt and slide it out through the loops and set it to the side. I take the rope and separately bind his ankles. He is securely bound to the bondage table and can no longer escape. I squeeze him with my inner thighs before reaching around to smack his cock. Like a spider, I hop off the leather table. It is time to turn up the heat!

Grabbing the rider's crop, I hit the bondage table with force. *Whack!* "You will take my pain and you will like it!" I circle the entirety of the bondage table, continuously slapping its leather foundation with my riding crop around his body.

Fearful, he squeals. The crop contacts his inner thigh. A few more taps on the head of his cock, and it is time to have him pull down his boxers.

Debating: "What have we here? Should I be disappointed, slut, or should I be relieved that my desire to ever fuck this useless cock is nonexistent?"

Before putting it around his neck, I take his belt and smack his pathetic cock. Slipping one end of the belt through the buckle, I slowly slide the belt down to tighten it around his neck. This makes for a fabulous collar and gives me something to pull on.

I grab his testicles and tie them up with my thin white rope. Taking a mini flogger, I begin to hit his insufficient nub with the rubbery tassels. Continuing, I whip his testicles again and again. I feel an instant desire to pain his nipples. I grab the tweezer clamps and constrict both of his fleshy peaks.

The mumbling tells me that he might have something to say. "Speak, slave. What would you like to say?"

Barely able to speak: "It hurts so badly, but I do not want you to stop!"

Reminding him: "I don't need your permission; you are now in this whether you like it or not!" My laughter sweeps through the room.

I let him stew in the moment before intensifying my actions. I guide his body slightly onto his side to expose his right butt cheek. Spanking him with a leather paddle, I explain to him that I will not stop until his butt cheek is rosy red. Reaching in front of him, I grab the ends of the testicle rope and give a good pull.

Begging me, he cries out: "No, Mistress, no!"

Placing a ball gag into his mouth: "Another fuck up! I gave you one warning. You have failed!"

I walk myself around the other side of the bondage table and position him to expose his left butt cheek. I begin to paddle his ass, only this time twice as hard.

With every smack: "If I wanted to hear you, I would ask you to speak. If I sensed that you had anything important to say, I might care to listen. However, I do not want to hear your voice. You have one job, pain slut, and that is to take what I give you."

Whack! "Without complaint!"

Like a shot of dopamine, he descends deeper into a subspace. He feels reality begin to blur into the quietude of his mind. Weightless and transcending the mundane confines of life, he discovers a profound sense of peace.

Laughing: "Is it what you thought it would be? Being here, in my presence?" And what do I hear? Silence. Just the way I like it!

Until this: grabbing the chain that links the nipple clamps, I give a swift pull. The ball gag muffles his sounds of shrieking agony.

I untie his ankles and uncuff his wrists. Pulling off the blindfold, I command him to lower his arms to his sides. Slowly, I make my way around his body, gently touching different parts of his flesh. After a few minutes pass, I command him to sit up on the bondage table. I swing his legs around, allowing them to dangle off the side of the table. With both hands, I grab each knee and spread his legs apart. I remove the testicle rope and move myself in between his legs.

Staring at me, I see that his eyes are glazed and he is lost.

Staring back at him, I pull him closely to me by the lead of his belt. "You are lucky we are almost out of time. Otherwise, I don't think you would be able to walk out of here!"

The haze of my laughter wraps the room in a seductive embrace. Gently, I bring him down to his feet. Taking a moment to stabilize his position, I turn him around and press him up against the wall.

Taking two towels off the counter, I place one at his feet and the other in his hand. "Well!" I say and point to his cock.

I turn to clean up my gear as moaning sounds penetrate around the ball gag still in his mouth. *Hmmm.* "That was fast! Bring your limp body back over here and lie back down on the bondage table."

As he rests, I begin to show him aftercare. I offer him a warm wet towel and a bottle of water. Gently, I touch over his nipples, massaging out any leftover pain. I ask him questions to make sure he is not feeling any unusual discomfort. I watch over him until I feel he is emotionally, mentally, and physically stable to stand up.

When I feel enough time has passed, I bring him to his feet and have him sit on a nearby leather bench. We continue to speak about our session, and he expresses how amazing he feels. He speaks of the subspace he fell into and how he feels like he is in a euphoric state.

I recommend that he take it easy for the rest of the day and enjoy drifting through the cosmos.

I command him to get dressed and leave the premises.

REFLECTION: RAINA MARKS

Raina, wearing nothing but her towel, lounges against the cool granite of the kitchen island.

I understand why these men want more. More of these intense and euphoric subspace feelings.

She could imagine it now: a place where the mind quieted and where the outside world didn't matter.

I haven't stopped thinking about how it felt to slip away and forget everything. It really did feel like it was just the two us and the rest of world vanished for a moment. My man was definitely taking me there!

Standing at their bedroom door, she is reminded of their presence. The presence that now feels like their absence.

Opening the dresser drawer, she holds up two options: sheer cover-up or this beautifully crocheted kimono?

Holding them to her body in the mirror, she considers each carefully. One is all illusion. The other, artful transparency. *Kimono it is!* she decides, tossing the other back in the drawer. *But no undies! Why can't I stop thinking about food?*

Tapping her finger on the refrigerator door. *I'm not sure if "Duty Free day" means I can eat anything and everything I want, but…*

She swings it open. *Nothing here that I want. Pizza! With everything on it! Including a ranch on the side.*

A grin spreads across her face as she picks up her phone. *Pizza is ordered! And to all you ranch-pizza-dipper-haters—don't judge me! We're reading a book about non-judgment, remember?*

Letting the designer in her take control, she curates the perfect poolside sanctuary. She uses fresh-cut flowers from the garden, woven mats, antique plates, and neutral linens to give everything a laid-back, summertime feel.

Looking around, the words expel from her lips: "Where is my book? Ah, here you are, my little cognitive stimulator."

CHAPTER 18

SONIC SEDUCTION: FRISSON AND SOUND FREQUENCY

The Skingasm!

Ethereal music is a vital part of my seductive force. He surrenders to the intoxicating rhythm as I caress his senses, a symphony designed to embrace both mind and flesh. I erotically ignite a frisson of pleasurable melodies to awaken his deepest desires.

I hear it in their voices:

"You just sent shivers up my spine!"

"I love the music you play!"

"It's like I am lost in a trance here with you."

"You take me out of my stress."

"I'm lost!"

The Electric Rush of Frisson

Frisson is that sudden electric rush that tingles through your body, the unexpected thrill that catches you off guard. It is a moment where emotion, sensation, and meaning collide, sending a shiver down your spine. It is brief, intense, and unforgettable, reminding you that you're alive in a way words sometimes cannot fully capture.

There is a method to my madness when it comes to your man's mind, body, and soul. I have a reason for everything I do. I intentionally provoke his physiological arousal through a delicate mix of music, rituals, stories, room temperature, and my simple presence.

Frisson refers to a psychophysiological response: that involuntary shiver or thrill ignited by an intense surge of positive stimuli. This emotional response is associated with the release of feel-good chemicals like dopamine and endorphins, creating a euphoric sensation that reaches into his innermost self.

Those who feel frisson are often more open to new experiences and notice beauty in music or art more deeply. A song or a moment might stir something inside them, not just emotionally but mentally. When that connection happens, the body responds with goosebumps, tingling skin, or subtle changes in the eyes. This physical experience of pleasure touches both mind and body.

The way this happens is unique to each person. The reward system shapes pleasure and motivation by releasing neurochemicals, while the sympathetic nervous system prepares the body for a heightened experience. Chemicals like norepinephrine and adrenaline guide how the brain and body respond to these intense moments. Frisson is not limited to music; other sensory rewards can spark it just as strongly.

The Power of Sound Waves

Why not play on a few more of his endorphins? The sound of the singing bowl begins to pulse through the room. The higher frequencies whisper ecstasy, and the lower tones tug at his primal longings. As he surrenders to his fantasy, he feels himself vanish into a state of fulfillment.

Sound Frequency refers to the rate at which sound waves vibrate, measured in hertz (Hz). It determines pitch: the higher the frequency, the sharper the sound; the lower the frequency, the deeper and more resonant.

Sound Waves are the oscillations per unit of time. Together, they don't just shape how we hear; they shape how we feel. The right frequencies can nudge hormones, calm the nervous system, and bring the body back into balance. They melt away stress and quiet negative emotions. These vibrations reach deeper than the ears, touching mental, physical, and energetic levels to guide a man into deep relaxation or meditation.

Creating an atmosphere that helps my play partner relax is essential for building a deeper connection. Music and sound therapy set the tone, but I often incorporate instruments such as chimes, bells, gongs, and singing bowls. These elements create a soothing, immersive environment that allows my play partner to fully engage and let go.

The Frequency of Healing and Release

Various frequencies have unique effects on the body and mind:

- 174 Hz: Known as the healing frequency, this can relieve pain and stress, promoting deep relaxation and a sense of security. It has powerful grounding and calming effects.

- 396 Hz: Often associated with releasing guilt, fear, and shame, this frequency helps clear negative beliefs and emotional blockages, creating space for transformation.
- 432 Hz: Known for promoting relaxation and concentration, this frequency helps reduce stress and release emotional tension.
- 528 Hz: Often referred to as the "miracle" frequency, it is believed to reduce anxiety and support transformation.
- 639 Hz: Known for enhancing connection and relationship healing, this frequency supports compassion and harmony, encouraging emotional bonding.

There is a vast array of sound frequencies out there for you to explore. Both my client and I are deeply influenced by these sensory impressions. True care transcends superficial interactions because it focuses on safeguarding inner peace and emotional balance.

It is just one more reason why my clients come back to me, even when some know they shouldn't.

REFLECTION: RAINA MARKS

The method to her madness! Part of her seductive force! Erotically igniting! I read these words again and feel like the Dominatrix is straight-up entrancing these men.

She pauses, licking a stray drop of ranch from her fingertip. *Goosebumps! I get them! It looks like I'm part of the population that experiences frisson.*

This is all just another level: getting all this deep relaxation and stress reduction. But do the cheaters really deserve all this? Nope!

Pizza Slice #2. She glances over at her phone, picturing her husband's sometimes weary face as he walks through the door after work: tense shoulders, short replies, the hollow way he says "I'm fine." *Maybe he just needs some music therapy?*

Pizza Slice #3. *Makes you think. What would it be like to have a play session?* She sits up straighter, contemplating the idea. *I can appreciate the idea of being clear—crystal clear—about needs. No filtering, no trying to sound palatable or polite. Just… honest.*

Dragging the last slice through a generous pool of ranch dressing, she savors it slowly. *Ha! Cheers to the ranch lovers. We're not so different from the thrill seekers, really. We know what we like, and we're tired of apologizing for it.*

I get the draw, but cheating makes my skin crawl. I struggle between disgust and understanding. These men are given permission: permission to feel, to explore, to drop the armor. Great… but!

Food coma incoming. Okay, I'm done. Three slices in, and it's time to stop pigging out.

Her eyes drop back down to the book in her lap. She turns the page and cracks up laughing. *Post-nut-waaaat? That deserves another sparkling water and maybe a side of judgmental curiosity.*

CHAPTER 19

WHAT THE FUCK IS POST-NUT CLARITY?

I feel like many of us have heard some version of the following:

"That was great. I needed that. I gotta go!"

"Oh man, I'm late! Bye!"

"So, you're doing well? You look great. Just been busy on my end!"

"I think I just want to be alone."

"I just need to sleep!"

"That was exactly what I needed. Take care!"

"I'll text you later!"

"It's getting late, I have to be up early!"

Uncomfortable laugh. "Bye!"

There's a moment that can come on suddenly right after an orgasm: a pause, a shift, a dip in emotional connection. I've felt it in my personal BDSM play and my intimate relationships. It is a moment where once a man's orgasm is over, he becomes unrecognizable. "Mr. I Will Do Anything" suddenly becomes "Mr. No Way in Hell," and he is checked out.

Post-nut clarity, or post-orgasm clarity, is that raw, unfiltered stillness after release. The urgency fades, the noise flatlines, and what's left is the truth. That "truth" sometimes surfaces insight, discomfort, regret, or relief.

For many, the pattern is real. Post-nut clarity stings, revealing an emotional rift you can't ignore. One minute, there's heat and closeness; the next, there is silence, distance, and that sudden drop. You might be left wondering: was any of that real, or just chemistry and need?

Lust can blur, love can steady, and climax can make things clearer.

The Psychological and Biological Reckoning

Now that the "evil" is out, what is going on with these men?

There's a transition in their mental and emotional states that clears away the desirous smoke. This change is driven by neuro-chemical shifts: dopamine withdrawal pulls the rug out from under his excitement, while a surge of Prolactin acts as the ultimate buzz-kill, shutting down desire instantly. In these men, the "cuddle hor-mone," Oxytocin, never stands a chance. Prolactin signals the end of the road; without oxytocin to anchor him, he has no reason to stay.

A man's brain picks up on every bit of sensory input from his genitals, mixing it with erotic thoughts. These catalysts activate key brain areas: the hypothalamus, amygdala, and nucleus accumbens. Together, they turn sensations into full-body responses, shaping everything from attraction to the clarity that follows orgasm.

As arousal builds, the brain releases dopamine, the chemical tied to motivation and reward. When the dopamine hits, it narrows his focus, pulling attention toward whatever feels good in that moment.

Testosterone intensifies the effect, making the pull toward gratification harder to ignore. Meanwhile, his genital sensory cortex becomes hyper-aware, a physical storm takes over: adrenaline spikes, his heart rate climbs, and his breathing quickens. This biological surge of desire creates a tunnel vision where logic fails, making him increasingly willing to take risks—even cheating—in a relentless pursuit of the high.

The prefrontal cortex, the brain's decision-maker, often takes a back seat during arousal. When it does, impulse takes over. This part of the brain teams up with pleasure centers, amplifying intensity while quieting the signals that say "stop yourself." The result is a laser focus on immediate gratification and fewer brakes on impulse.

The Post-Nut Collapse: Connection vs. Conquest

When sex is nurtured by love and real intimacy, the aftermath can look different. The man may seem calmer and present, experiencing an afterglow full of affectionate behaviors. He isn't scrambling for the next conquest; he's deepening a connection.

For many men, especially those chasing conquest, post-nut clarity isn't some grand revelation. It's emptiness. The chase was the high and that desperate wanting was the fuel. Once they've gotten what they came for, the edge dulls, the thrill vanishes, and intimacy suddenly feels unnecessary. The high of the hunt disappears the second they "win," and what's left isn't insight. *It's disinterest.* It was never about the connection. They weren't seeking a person; they were seeking an ending.

Some men may feel embarrassed, guilty, or regretful after they achieve their "pleasure payload." The physical tension is released, but so is the illusion. Choices that seemed thrilling moments before become irrelevant or foolish. That's not intimacy, but it sure the heck is selfishness rolled up into biology and ego. Their ego is fed, and they're already hungry for the next chase.

Stepping Off the Ferris Wheel

When I was younger, I found it challenging to re-center myself at the end of intimacy. It wasn't until I understood the biology that I found clarity in their behavior. Most people have felt it: being left staring at the aftermath of a once-horny person. It's confusing, awkward, and fucking frustrating!

When men chase the "great cream escape" and then withdraw, it can leave us feeling used and invisible. Like our bodies were just checkpoints on the way to the next high. Understanding the game lets us step to the side of his horny Ferris wheel before we get spun dizzyingly around. Great intimacy is a beautifully shared exchange, not a conquest. It's when both people leave fuller than they entered.

When the dopamine breaks and he drifts into his biological fog, do not chase him into the mist. This is your moment of *Aftercare*. Reclaim your space, re-center your energy, and remember that his withdrawal is a chemical reflex, not a reflection of your worth. You are the catalyst of the entire experience, and your value remains long after the act is over.

The Strategist: A Game of Tease and Denial

Now that we've decoded the biology, let's explore a way you can work with it. Would I even be me if I didn't give you something delicious to try?

Try this for fun: tease and deny your partner.

Seductively woo your man into a state of sexual tension. Keep him horny and biting at the bit by denying him the pleasure of ejaculation. That aching edge he hovers on? That is your playground. It's the slow burn, the way you stretch out desire until it's trembling. Take control of his body's rhythms and make him wait.

You can start the build-up with flirty texts. When he is physically under your control, use a combination of verbal and physical play.

A brush of skin, a whisper, eye contact, your hand grazing exactly where he wants it: then nothing but air. Let him taste just enough of what he craves to keep him hungry, then pull it away before he can grasp it. Repeatedly tease and deny him, but refrain from any type of release.

Don't just tease him for the sake of the game, do it to recalibrate his internal wiring. By denying the climax, you keep the dopamine "high" from breaking. You are essentially keeping his brain's logical brakes disconnected, leaving him in a primal state of total focus. In this gap of denial, he doesn't own his mind because he can't satisfy his brain's demand for an ending.

Remember: do not let him cum!

Show him he does not own his pleasure. Make him beg for it, then tell him "no." Hold onto that hungry tiger for as long as you can. You decide if, when, and how he reaches that breaking point. He's no longer in charge of his release or his escape. You are.

In those gaps of denial, everything he feels will heighten. Watch him become desperate. Every nerve should feel electric and every thought consumed.

The Truth in the Dust

Post-nut clarity doesn't end with the orgasm; the truth it reveals demands action. Understanding the game means you're no longer just a player. You are a strategist. The next time you see that familiar flicker of disconnection, remember that you don't have to wait for clarity to take control. You can see through it or play with it on your own terms.

Real intimacy isn't the chase or the release. True presence shows itself when the dust settles. It is a power within your grasp, if you dare to hold it.

For readers curious about the brain science behind arousal, see the References section at the back of the book.

REFLECTION: RAINA MARKS

LOL. "Now that the evil is out!" That's one way to look at it!

Raina nudges the pizza box to the back of the table with her elbow, glancing at the mess for a split second before deciding: *Nah, not today.*

Not cleaning up. Back to lounging. *He is zonked out. The clarity is out. Or maybe… he's just out the damn door?*

Mr. Disinterested. Her jaw clenches. *I've been in this situation. Let me dangle my pleasure carrot.*

I mean, sure. The tease and denial thing? I like that part. It's playful. Keeps the tension alive. But post-nut clarity or disinterest? That? That can feel like emotional abandonment laced with hormones and some twisted conscience crap.

I don't think I've really ever thought about this too much. This whole post-orgasm mental pivot. Men suddenly getting quiet, pulling away, turning on the TV like they didn't just devour our bodies a minute ago. It can be subtle or thrown in our faces, but it's there.

I can't count how many times I've felt sad after sex. That ache in your chest when you're still connected, in the intensity, and reaching, but he's already slipping away into his own world.

There was that hollow feeling left behind when he's had what he wanted. It didn't feel like intimacy: it felt like a vacuum. I gave my attention, my body, my trust, and what did I get in return? Sometimes, a cold disinterest. Like I was a checkpoint or a prize to be claimed. I definitely wasn't seen. When that happens, it twists something inside me and makes me question myself. I hate that!

She shakes her head. *Makes me think about this one guy I briefly dated. He insisted on making me climax first. Every time. Said:* "I'm useless after I cum, Raina. You deserve more than my leftovers." *I thought he was exaggerating… until I realized he wasn't wrong.*

Her mind drifts back to her husband. *I've felt that ache too many times in my own marriage. And I told myself it was fine. That was just how men are. Just how my man is. That it wasn't personal. We are fine!*

I have often wondered why my husband was inclined to have make-out sessions without intercourse. His words: "Trust me, you want to keep me on edge. The passion will last longer, and so will I! I'm like a hungry animal, and my hunger builds over time."

He is right. Once he ejaculates, the passionate kissing and intense affections disappear. Don't get me wrong, he's still loving, but it's just not the same.

I think having my own secret set of tools might be a good idea. And a lot of fun!

Hang on a second! This whole tease and denial thing she is talking about sounds very familiar. That's what my husband did to me! His "carry me from the couch to the bedroom" shenanigan. He teased and denied me.

Looks like Mr. Marks is going to get a taste of his own medicine!

CHAPTER 20

MY AROUSAL: TURNED ON BY TRUTH

Is my pussy wet? Maybe. But I'm not exactly reaching down there for a weather report.

I am often asked if I get sexually aroused in a session with my clients. Of course, some of my clients are sexy and appealing. My senses might heat up a bit, but that isn't enough to tip the scale on my horny meter or cross forbidden lines with a taken man. That said: "Yes, I have dated single clients outside the Dungeon. It happens."

Overall, most men are interesting, well-groomed, and visit me smelling fresh. Other men stink of rotten ass, have bad breath, and would lead me to believe my kitty is a dried-out desert. No matter the state of their presence or my vagina, I am not looking for sexual arousal or pleasure. Nor am I looking for a relationship. I seek

Dominant/submissive or professional/client relations under our consensual playtime experiences.

I operate from a place of control, performance, and intentional boundaries. I need that separation to maintain clear emotional limits. The dynamic is built on psychological power exchange and ritual, not on romantic or erotic intimacy from my end. My satisfaction comes from the truth, the control, the craft, and the way the experience responds.

My role is to guide, lead, and deliver. I cannot be in a headspace that clouds my ability to provide a safe, structured session. I must stay in an overall state of caution and readiness. Mental, emotional, and physical safety is my number one priority.

During and after our time together, I have to protect my energy. Adding another layer of sexual tension on my behalf would only complicate my time. What I do can be extremely exhausting. I spend a lot of time in a deep breathing state. Thank goodness for blindfolds. When I reach my sensory limit or need to re-center my own energy, I put them on him. It slows the scene down and gives me the shadows I need to breathe, while he remains suspended in the dark, thinking it's all for his benefit.

The Professional Boundary

I am a Professional Dominatrix, not a prostitute. A prostitute sells her body; a Dominatrix sells her mind. My value isn't found in my availability, but in my ability to orchestrate a reality that he cannot create for himself. I did not get into this business to satisfy my intimate needs, fuck for pay, or freely mess around with a bunch of men where I conduct my business. I provide fantasy experiences that are about their fantasies, not mine.

Some assume that a Dominatrix must be sexually aroused to enjoy the work. In reality, much like other professions, the fulfillment I gain is psychological. I take pleasure in the artistry of the scene and the satisfaction of delivering a deeply immersive psychological experience. That does not mean I am erotically engaged. My responsibility is to ensure the client's fantasies are fulfilled. After all, he is spending his hard-earned money to pay tribute for our time together.

Does My Work Affect My Sex Life?

No, not in a negative way. If anything, it has taught me the importance of effective communication and open-mindedness. Through my BDSM studies, I have gained knowledge about the body and the psychological gravitas surrounding sexual gratification. I understand how the brain must properly engage for a person to be emotionally, mentally, and sexually satisfied.

Time spent with my clients has offered insight into my own thought process. These reciprocal relationships have been instrumental to my development as a woman. I have acquired first-hand knowledge from these men that I might not have obtained otherwise. Their honesty has inspired me to be honest with myself. I look deeply into my own erotic zones and am open to exploration. I am comfortable sharing my truth about the secrets of my arousal with my partner. I definitely know what I like and what I don't.

My work doesn't take from me; it teaches me. It has stripped away the shame of asking for what I want. Because I spend my days witnessing the deepest, most hidden desires of others, I have no interest in hiding my own. I don't just know what I like, I know how to demand it.

After a long day of work, the desire to sexually engage with a man is still there. I have never experienced anything in a session that disgusts or impacts me to the point of diminishing my sexual cravings. Every encounter reminds me that desire, in all its forms, is still my own.

When Desire Has My Name

I hear:

"I love watching your movies while I masturbate!"

"I can't help myself Mistress, I think about you all the time when I jerk off."

"Your pictures are so hot! I use them to masturbate!"

"Can you send me a picture of yourself wearing latex? I want to use it later!"

"I wish I could get you off!"

"Let me please you! I think about it all the time!"

"I imagine licking your pussy all the time!"

They go there! I often think, *There's punishment in store for you!*

Men from all over the world let me know that I've been the object of their private indulgences. They share these moments with a strange mix of pride and vulnerability, as though confessing a secret they can't quite keep. They want me to know, and they also use these statements as a tool, hoping for free content, extended playtime, or my attention outside the Dungeon. *I suppose that comes with the territory!*

Is it the chase, the hope to bed me, or something more?

"Date me! Outside of here!" they say, thinking the woman who commands them will somehow step into their world unchanged. Throughout the years, I've had my fair share of sexual advances. Clients' fascination sometimes hardens into obsession, and some refuse to respect boundaries. They seek an experience, but they blur the lines between arousal and reality. Their flattery tests my limits, believing I might eventually give in.

I am obtainable, but by appointment only. I think some of these men love the chase as much as the experience itself. More than a dozen clients have professed their love for me, and a handful have even proposed marriage. I understand why they feel the urge to express these devotions. They are ecstatic to be anyone they want to be without the fear of judgment or life-changing consequences.

I am giving him the fantasy brought to life with a woman he holds nothing back from.

Only a select few ever get to see past the illusion, to glimpse the many layers that make me who I am. Most are content with the version of me that lives in their imagination, and that's exactly how it should be. Not everyone earns access to the woman beneath the role.

REFLECTION: RAINA MARKS

Snickering. *What's the forecast, Mistress?*

Ruminating as she pours a glass of water. *What sexually arouses me?*

Zipping around. *Better watch out, "Big Fly"–SWAT! I really know how to handle this flyswatter. I have a lot of practice here in Arizona with our massive fly population.*

I keep thinking about this. I don't know if I have ever sat down and really thought about my sexual needs. I mean… sure, I know the general idea of what turns me on. I know the strokes, the angles, the rhythms that make me moan. But if I compare my go-to pleasures to the depth of my un-touched fantasies, there's a lot more to this puzzle than I've allowed myself to even consider.

Admitting: *I limit my sexual fulfillment. I know I do. I don't usually ask for a lot of what I want. The idea of asking… ugh, it makes me feel so exposed. It's like standing in front of someone naked and saying, "Here's a part of me I might not even understand."*

It just makes me feel vulnerable. And honestly, it's a little embarrass-ing. So instead of going there, I ask for what feels safe: sex in the shower, a quickie in the car, some naughty texts, or a few fun positions. No risky conversations required!

The last thing I want is to ruin the chemistry between us. To kill the vibe. What if I ask for something and he pulls away? Or worse, looks at me like he doesn't recognize me? What if he doesn't want to do what I want? I'm scared that if I open the door to that level of honesty, I'll face rejection I can't un-hear. And then I'll hold resentment. Quiet, ugly resentment.

It's always been easier to focus on his needs. Keep him satisfied. And to be fair, I do know what he likes; he's said it. Especially early on. He loves oral, has his favorite go-to positions, and I've pieced together the rest. I really try to listen to his body. I take pride in pleasing him. I now know how important it is to check in periodically to see if these needs have changed.

Category is: *Vanilla. Yes, we've dabbled in some light spanking and some dirty talk. Maybe a blindfold. But reading this? It's making me think we are pretty vanilla. What if there's more to him? What if he does have a kink buried under all that routine? What if I'm the one he's afraid to open up to?*

I think I need to write out a list of what I want. Just for me. And then I'll figure out how to share all this with him. I believe he would want to know. It's possible he's been waiting for me to start the conversation.

CHAPTER 21

FANTASY SESSION STORY
GREASY AF

This chapter presents a fantasy session story involving consenting adults only. All scenarios are fictionalized composites inspired by themes from my professional practice, and identifying details have been altered to protect privacy. The story explores adult BDSM dynamics, trust, and power exchange within a safe, consensual, and controlled environment.

Character Development: *This client is a middle-aged man who appears to be financially secure. He has never spoken of a relationship or children. From what he has told me, he is single. However, certain signs point to married.*

The question is: Why am I saying yes? I roll my eyes internally. *You've got to be kidding me. You want me to do what?* After a moment of deep contemplation—the razor-thin edge between a refusal and an invitation—I finally say, "Yes!"

Today is the day! I slip into my lime green latex bodysuit and white patent leather boots. I slick my hair back and clip on a red ponytail hair extension: a ponytail long enough to whip the shit out of this crazy kinkster.

This is probably some of the heaviest makeup I have ever worn in my life. Hues of purple shadows pancake my eyelids, and my blacked-out eyeliner looks like a printer exploded on my eyes. Atop a mask of thick foundation that is plastered all over my face, I am wearing thick red lipstick and red gloss. *Wow, help me! I look like something out of a comic book. Wild and over 6′6 tall in these platform boots.*

Tapping my temple: *Oh, but wait. We have not gotten to the good part yet.*

Before my client arrives, I get prepared for the appointment, which will be two hours of possible hell. So, it's off with the boots for now.

For fear they will slide, I securely weigh down two white sheets with heavy anchors. I grab the empty tennis ball container, a large wine bottle, a small plastic bat, a large hand mirror, and a bunch of bananas and place them on the side of the sheets. I take out twelve tubs of his surprise ingredient, four rolls of paper towels, a pack of cleaning towels, and rubbing alcohol, and I organize them with the other items.

And he is here!

Showing his excitement: "Amazing, thank you for getting everything ready for us today. I am glad that you got the bag of items I left for you. I cannot wait to do this!"

He makes his way into the bathroom, and just when I thought it could not get any more interesting, he comes streaking out wearing only a pair of skimpy leather briefs.

Clapping his hands together: "Ready?"

This fetishist is ready to go, and he wants to get his freak on. He lies down on his stomach in the middle of the play area. I join him on my knees in front of him and grab the first tub. Smearing the petroleum jelly onto my ass, I continue to wonder why I am doing this.

Thick as thick-ass tar, the greasy goop is attaching to me like another layer of skin. I continue to spread the petroleum onto my stomach and chest areas. As he lies there, he begins to thrust his groin against the floor.

Suggesting to him: "I see this excites you! Maybe it is your turn to get a little more greased up!"

Taking the rest of the petroleum out of the first tub, I begin to smear it down the sides of his arms. With eagerness, he asks me for more. So, I make a thick line down his back with the goopy jelly. Taking my fingernails, I scratch the ointment away from his spine, making sure he feels my intensity.

Back in front of him, I continue to lather up my skin, and it does not take me long to cover the entirety of my body. Feeling concerned that no oxygen is getting through to my skin, I gasp at what is happening.

Momentarily appalled. *Best believe there is no way I am leaving this man free of the lubricating grease bath. This level four situation is about to hit a level 10!*

I open another tub of the slippery substance and dip my fingers inside. I pull out every ounce and go towards his face with my hand. "Open wide, slut!"

Shoving the entirety of petroleum into his mouth: "Let the mayhem begin!"

I shriek with mirthful malice and grab the large wine bottle. I hand him the bottle and ask him to show me what he can do with it. I watch his eyes widen as he shoves the glass vessel into his mouth. The ointment oozes out around the sides of the bottle with every oral thrust.

Ugh. "You disgusting pig!"

Only I do not stop there. I begin to smear more of the petroleum onto his body. I command him to stand up, and I grease down his front side. I place him cross-legged in front of me and take another dip into the petroleum with my fingers.

I whisper: "Close your eyes!"

A cap of glistening sheen begins to veil his head. Pressing downward, I pull the ointment over his hair, eyes, and face. As he begins to struggle, I make the decision to give him another bite. I command him to open his mouth as widely as possible. I place the plastic bat into his hand and once again shove a large scoop of petroleum into his mouth.

Laughing: "I know a slut like you can fit this bat into your mouth!"

He begins to penetrate his face with the bat. Fucking his mouth with the bat, he slowly moves it in and out.

Commanding: "Do it faster. Faster!"

The jelly continuously oozes and drips from his mouth. With every jab of the bat, squishing and squirting sounds begin to gross me out.

Gagging: "I love it, Mistress! I want more!"

I smack his thigh with my hand. "Do not talk with your mouth full, whore!"

I grab the bat and replace it with the tennis ball container. It is time to prepare three more tubs of jelly. Before scooping into the three tubs, I assess the situation. *This man can barely see and breathe as it is, and he is asking me for more? How much more can he take into his filthy mouth?*

To make sure, I ask him: "Are you sure you can handle having three more tubs of petroleum shoved into your mouth?" Expelling out words with confidence, he desperately begs me for more.

"Let's go for it!"

Without further hesitation, I drive the ointment straight into his mouth. In amazement, I watch as he practically swallows down the tennis ball container.

Intrigued: "If you can take all that girth into your mouth, let us see how many bananas I can stuff in that dirty trap!"

One by one, I break apart the bananas. I dip each banana into the petroleum jelly before handing it over to him. He takes the encased fruit and pushes each yellow delight into his mouth.

Showing him the fourth banana: "Do you think you can take number four?"

In it goes! "You are a filthy animal! I cannot imagine who kisses that disgusting mouth. Just look at yourself!"

I pick up the mirror so he can see himself. Once again, he begins to fuck his face. He watches in pure delight as he penetrates his mouth with the bananas. With every push of the bananas, he begins to dry hump the air. Repeatedly, he moves his hips forward and backward as his face makes the oddest expressions.

Stopping him: "I have had enough. Stop!"

Our time is up, and I tell him to end the session how he wishes. He spits the bananas onto the sheet. Asking me to put another load of petroleum into his mouth, he picks up the bat. Ramming the jelly deeply into his mouth, he begins to ravish the bat. Looking down, I see that his leather briefs are now at his knees. I hold up the mirror and look away.

Moaning like a desperate animal, the monster inside him strangles his cock.

I can hear the petroleum sloshing everywhere. *How I am going to clean up this mess. Do I dare look back to see his face?*

Slowly, I turn my face, just enough to gaze around the mirror. The spit drools from his mouth like a rabid dog. His eyes are open and bloodshot. The greasy monstrosity stares into the mirror, and within ten seconds, he explodes and collapses into himself.

Sighing with relief that the adventure is over, I chirp out: "Now, clean up this disaster!"

I attend to myself and watch as he attempts to clean up the mess. After wiping off and putting himself back together, I instruct him to take all the leftovers and get out.

I spent the next four days getting rid of the petroleum layers that suffocated my flesh. Even though he tried, I never scheduled with "Mr. Petroleum" ever again.

I have had one simple reply to all his requests: "No fucking way!"

REFLECTION: RAINA MARKS

This woman is insane, and this is absolutely disgusting. I mean, I'm really trying not to judge, but come on! Why? Just... why? And how the hell did he even come up with this idea? What was the thought process? "Hey babe, I want you to lube up my mouth and body with Vaseline while I..." *No. Just no!*

She rubs her forehead. *I'm trying to be open-minded. I swear I am. I'm trying to remember that everyone has their own kinks, their own fantasies, and their own very private needs, but petroleum jelly? In the mouth? While getting penetrated by... what, a lamp leg?*

I am honestly trying to figure out what I would do if my husband ever leaned over and whispered in my ear: "Hey honey, tonight I want to rub this slippery sludge all over our bodies and jam some random object into me while you gag me with it like it's foreplay."

You know what I'd do? I'd laugh. Hard. And then I'd probably grab the jar and toss it out the window. At least this woman has boundaries and is able to say, "No thanks, I'm out!" *Funny enough, even she didn't want to play with that greasy disaster again. So yeah, apparently, everyone has their limits.*

Raina hesitates for a moment. Not of total acceptance, but a soft wave of it. *I'm starting to see the value of people having a place to go to fulfill their fantasies. Although, I will never accept these cheating behaviors.*

As far as the client: some things aren't for everyone. He likes it, so whatever. See how I'm improving? Less judgment. So, I am telling myself!

CHAPTER 22

FROM FANTASY TO REALITY: WHY MEN CHOOSE ME AS THEIR DOMINATRIX

Like a feline, I gracefully toy with the poor little creatures. I am the vixen they can't resist and the one they can't have.

Whether on screen, in print, online, or in person, I don't just catch their eye; I hijack their imagination. I strike their thoughts like a bite just shy of pain. Men are often drawn to the surface before they discover the depth. They choose me because they think I am mysterious and beautiful. That is when beauty bows, and skill steps forward.

At home, they may be a boyfriend, fiancé, husband, or "single." With me, their roles have changed, and they are free to redefine them.

I am a *Goddess of Desires*, manipulating energy and illuminating unlit realities. Like a force of nature, I move through my work with passion, perception, and compassion. My confidence doesn't just fill the room; it reshapes it. I don't merely command. I command respect.

I am satisfaction and serenity in a chaotic world. I reflect their unspoken yearnings, unlocking the need to be both powerful and powerless. I capture their gentleness only to challenge it. With me, they are understood. That, more than anything, is why they return.

The Keeper of Secrets

I've been told I have the face of an angel—one that disguises my capacity for being wickedly untamed. From the first glance, I ensnare them. My intense gaze, the velvet edge of my voice, and my sultry attire titillate the mind and body.

I am the one who understands what they cannot admit to themselves. Unknown to them, yet somehow safe, I become the keeper of their secrets. When they realize this fantasy is real, that is when the game truly begins.

I feed their hunger with deliberate attention. They assume my professionalism absolves them of judgment. Within my walls, they surrender willingly. I honor their vulnerabilities without shame and quickly gain their trust. Here, they feel both comfortable and unleashed. At least, until they are leashed. I understand exactly what they want, and I know precisely how to give it. They are mine to command. It's playtime!

The Refiner's Fire

In my line of work, consistency is paramount. My sessions are reliable, structured, and intentional. I take my craft seriously, providing an environment free of substance abuse and nonsense. Behind my door, there is only us: a space free of expectation or pretense. I make sure the outside world stays outside. They walk in knowing there will be no headaches, no blame, and no bad vibes.

In my presence, they are accepted as they are. I show no disgust, hesitation, or lack of enthusiasm. I honor their honesty and create a space where they can lay down their armor. My clients feel my care in every gesture. Through mind play, I rip control from their core, leaving them begging for more. I balance temptation and pain in ways they cannot foresee.

I am sadistically expressive, taunting and intriguing. I am a woman who instills pain and pleasure according to his wishes, fueled by what he needs. Yet, I am also lighthearted, imaginative, and unpredictable. I can bring joy alongside intensity, reminding them that we are here to have fun.

The Meticulous Ritual

I have a massive dedication to the process. Every detail matters: costumes, lighting, music, and props pull them into the world I create. For me, "enough" is never enough. Impeccable hygiene is non-negotiable; it is a matter of professionalism and respect. I am meticulous about cleanliness, choosing subtle perfumes and even specific chewing gum to ensure fresh breath. Nothing must distract from presence, focus, or consent-driven connection.

I notice everything: words, body language, pheromones. Every cell of their being is under my scrutiny. My focus is sharp and my full presence is non-negotiable. Distraction breaks trust. I do not merely play; I see them and hear them. I allow them to let go in ways they cannot elsewhere. They feel the act of being truly known.

My passion for erotic games pulses through his nervous system. I draw the edge of my knife down a crisp dollar bill, a silent promise of what happens to those who forget who is in command. He won't understand what my wicked laugh conveys until the very end of our ritual.

In the Shadows

"What might I do next?"

Gently murmuring in his ear, I become the enigma. My words stoke his curiosity while I scratch my fingers over his flesh. His breathing intensifies. I don't care if his screams are heard outside.

I move through the space deliberately, extinguishing candles one by one. The room darkens and I draw him into the shadows. I approach his bound body, dragging my knife gently between his thighs. Staring into his eyes, I press the blade into the tip of his cock and remind him he doesn't know me at all. Gripping his throat, I softly scrape his cheek, my sinister laugh penetrating his mind. I warn him not to move.

He's afraid. *Perfect!* It's moments like these where play takes on a serious tone. My sadistic ways love a good moment.

Excited at the end, he proclaims, "I wasn't sure if I was going to get out alive!"

Can we really blame others for seeking a safe, sane, consensual zone to be themselves?

While that need is valid, it doesn't excuse dishonesty or betrayal. The issue isn't the craving; it's how people choose to act on it. When he steps across my threshold, it is never merely about flesh—it is alchemy. My purpose is to awaken what lies dormant and to touch his being with unwavering support. If he leaves more whole and more in tune with his truth, the ritual is complete. My client walks away satisfied, renewed, and most dangerously, drawn back for more.

My promise is absolute: "You are in the best hands, and I will always take great care of you!"

REFLECTION: RAINA MARKS

Meow. Here, kitty, kitty!

"I am a Goddess of Desires, manipulating energy and illuminating their unlit realities."

Raina's eyes widen. *Interesting! Sensual, wickedly untamed, Dominant, and a force of nature. Seems like she's a living archetype of feminine power: an enchantress with some sort of psychological warfare plan and maybe even healing at the same time.*

Her fingers trace the edge of the book. *She's… something. Whatever that "something" defines for me.*

It's hard for me to separate the allure from the discomfort. She's guiding men who cheat, men who lie, and I keep asking myself: does helping them this way really change anything? Or is it just another layer of permission?

She pauses with conflicting emotions. *I can't deny that she understands desire, power, and control in a way some of us might not. Can you imagine that kind of energy exchange? She must feel like a human keypad. They punch in their fantasy codes, and bam—she manifests it.*

These clients are being offered something most people don't ever get: a safe space to be raw, to be real, to say the things they might not even whisper to themselves. They are granted an emotional and kinky bucket to unload their cravings into, and then this woman is expected to mop it up with style. Part of me winces at the thought of her influence over men, but it is the man who should be accountable for himself.

And still… I catch myself thinking about what that kind of clarity, that lack of compromise, would feel like in my own life. Not that I want to be her, or even play with her, but it makes me ask: how much of myself am I holding back?

The afternoon sunlight is starting to fade into a nightcap, and Raina decides to conclude her aquatic escapade. Gathering up her poolside belongings, she heads back into the house.

Tucking herself into her peaceful dwelling, she curls up in her favorite chair. She watches the trees wave hello outside her office window and thinks. *I wonder how the dinner meeting is going? It's almost 9 PM on the East Coast, and Mr. Marks should be deep in conversation with that guy.*

As an interior decorator, Raina feels the pressure of the upcoming week. Pulling her day planner off the side table, she reviews her workload and is pleased to see there is nothing on the calendar for tomorrow.

Monday is clear. Great! I have the entire day to process everything and sit with my thoughts before he flies home.

CHAPTER 23

WHAT'S IN THE SUITCASE, LADY?

Tricks, treats, and everything I need to satisfy my clients!

I hear it all the time: "There she goes again. Religiously pulling that black suitcase in and out of the back of her car." Comically true!

You'd think it's just a black suitcase, but it's far more than that. Every day, I drag it into the Dungeon, its corners scuffed from years of service. It joins a closet already housing seven other colorful suitcases belonging to other women, but mine is special. It's my arsenal, my toolbox, my portable world of imagination. It is more than just gear; it is power and control in one rolling box.

The tools I carry aren't just props. They are extensions of my authority and my creativity. Each piece has a purpose and each item a role in crafting experiences that are safe, consensual, and unforgettable. Being prepared means, I can meet desire with precision, anticipate needs, and guide a scene without hesitation. A Dominatrix without her tools is like a painter without a brush. The magic isn't in the object itself, but in how it is wielded. Wielded well, these tools become the instruments of connection, surrender, and transformation.

Being prepared isn't just necessary for me, it is an absolute must. Each encounter has its own demands. I often need various props, shoes, clothing, makeup, and the hardware of impact to craft a reality that satisfies a fantasy. For my regulars, the suitcase becomes even more tailored, holding specific items for recurring requests so every visit feels seamless.

Inside, the contents are organized chaos. There are separate pouches for lingerie and stockings, wigs and hair accessories, boots, stilettos, and sandals. I carry business suits, latex, fetish wear, masks, planners, pens, and playful erotic games. There are sunglasses, tutus, bikinis, hats, badges, belts, perfumes, deodorant, razors, lotion, soap, and flip flops. It is a wardrobe for a thousand different women, all of whom happen to be me.

Clients often request special items in advance, and I ensure every scenario comes fully equipped. For example, a regular client once scheduled playtime where I would interrogate him as a law enforcement officer. Weeks in advance, I began assembling evidence: fake DNA tests, paperwork, and small props. Every piece is designed to make the scene tangible, immersive, and unforgettable. Nothing is left to chance.

In the interrogation room, truth doesn't always come easy. Sometimes encouragement is necessary. A well-placed, consensual whipping can escalate the energy perfectly. By the end, the suspect is always behind bars: safe, satisfied, and completely swept up in the fantasy.

Even now, my suitcase sits packed, ever-ready for the next adventure. Props and power!

REFLECTION: RAINA MARKS

Charge it on my card. Can I get one of those suitcases? And while we're at it, can someone send me a subby boy to lift it in and out of my car?

On a more serious note. *The sheer precision and thought that goes into every session. It's like running a traveling theater, therapy office, and fantasy playground all in one. I'm exhausted just reading about it.*

Examining her marriage. *How often do I show up unprepared? Not in a physical sense, but emotionally, mentally, sensually? I haven't exactly been hauling around a suitcase full of silk rope and psychological strategies. It's not unusual for me to apologize or tone myself down to make things easier for my man. Maybe I need to better claim my territory, my curiosity, and my power.*

Too often, I settle for routine over spark. I choose the safety of habit over the risk of exploration. I hide behind exhaustion, distraction, or fear instead of leaning into what I want. The idea of a suitcase full of tools suddenly feels like a metaphor for how much more intentional we could be with each other.

And then there's my body. The way I feel when I imagine the thrill of anticipation and surrender. It doesn't come from a place of weakness, but from a place of choice. My curiosity becomes more vivid… more mine. Not just his, not just a fantasy. Mine!

Maybe I don't need a suitcase of props to claim that power. But the thought of it, the idea of intention packed neatly into every corner, leaves me curious in the best way. It makes me want to explore more.

CHAPTER 24

FANTASY SESSION STORY
BOOT BOY

This chapter presents a fantasy session story involving consenting adults only. All scenarios are fictionalized composites inspired by themes from my professional practice, and identifying details have been altered to protect privacy. The story explores adult BDSM dynamics, trust, and power exchange within a safe, consensual, and controlled environment.

Character Development: This repeat client is in a long-term relationship and does not have children. He is deeply in love with his girlfriend, constantly referring to her as the hottest woman in town. He is a wealthy businessman, mostly Dominant in nature, and lives an extravagant, indulgent lifestyle. I have heard countless stories from *him about how much he wishes his gal would wear the sexy boots he keeps buying for her. He has repeatedly made his fetish clear to her, but she never obliges. Frustrated by her refusal, he cheats.*

The thirty-minute session is booked for 10:00 am, and I know exactly what to expect. He has been a client of mine for several years, and his requests have not changed. He is a true fetishist at heart, and thigh-high leather boots are his obsession.

Since he is my first appointment of the day, I can simply put on an outfit that I know he will love and change later for other clients. I slip on my leather trench coat over my cobalt blue lingerie set and pair it with black patent leather thigh-high boots.

To satisfy my mood, I put on low-key techno. I take a sterile wipe and disinfect the countertops and seating areas. I place two specific towels on the bench in front of a floor-length mirror. For my final step, I sterilize and double-wash my hands. With everything specifically in place for this client—including no perfume, lotions, or smelly candles burning—it is now time to step into Mistress mode.

Let the show begin!

I leave the door to the room open. My client is never late. His routine consists of entering the room and walking straight over to the counter, where he will place his car keys. Standing like a propped flamingo, I lean myself up against a wall. He has the same exact smirk on his face that he always does: that kind of side-mouth grin that demonstrates just how eager he is to be here.

Even though he is in his late 50s, his curly blonde hair gives him a younger, more innocent look. He is attractive and quite the charmer.

I watch as he removes his pants and shirt from his six-foot frame, then folds them with perfect precision. No, the socks and shoes do not come off. No, the briefs do not come off. He is 100% committed to not risking anything, sticking to his socks. He places his shirt and pants onto the sterilized countertop.

Strutting my way, he is quite the tease. There is something about the way he is swaying his hips as he walks towards me, wearing briefs, black calf socks, and shiny black business shoes, that makes me giggle.

"*Mmmm*, you look so hot!" he seductively states. "Oh, and you wore my favorite boots, too!"

Favorite boots! I think to myself. *These are the only boots he allows in the session!*

He begins to circle me like a scavenger ready to eat his only meal for the day. His hips are grinding and his hands are motioning in ways that convey the desperate need to touch me. Only that is one of the hard rules: zero touching.

I see that familiar look in his eye. An orchestra of moaning is about to commence. Slowly pacing towards the bench, he finds immediate comfort sitting on his very clean towel.

I am not sure if I am in a seductive BDSM experience or a pottery shop. All this shaping, molding, pressing, and rubbing to his genital area makes me wonder what his cock is feeling like with all that dry, rubbing friction.

Begging: "Show me, baby! Yes! Come here! Please show me!"

Without touching him, I move as closely as possible to his legs. "You like what you see?" With the pulse of each second, I turn my body, giving him every angle I have got.

Showing him more: "You want to rub your cock on my boot? Aw, that's too bad that you can't!"

His moans vibrate out of his chest, and he exhales. "I love the boots, baby! You know I love the boots! You are so hot! So hot!"

The pressing redirects to his hand, placing the other clean towel over his lap. It looks like he is shaking a dirty martini, and pop goes the tent with his raging schlong.

In 10, 9, 8, 7, 6, 5…

He is done!

Within minutes, it's as though he were never here; he is cleaned up, dressed, and out the door.

REFLECTION: RAINA MARKS

Wow. Mr. Boot Boy is done and out the door. No trace left behind. Not even a single hair clinging to the bottom of his socks. Pfft!

I am now that "Fly on the Wall," fluttering about and shaking my ass straight out of this fantasy session story. I feel disappointed and once again, judgmental. Kind of pissed off, really!

It seems pretty straightforward. This guy told his woman what he wanted. He made it clear that he has some kinky obsession with sexy boots. He tried to open the door, and she said no. And that's her right.

But then he made a choice. Not to be honest. But to lie. He crawls into a Dungeon and plays with a stranger wearing the exact style of boots he begged to see on the woman he lives with.

There are so many layers to this subject. Suddenly, it's not about his kinky obsession, needs, or sexual gratification anymore. I look at what he did when he didn't get what he wanted from his woman.

What is it with these men and their emotional immaturity? You don't get your way, so you go pay someone else to fill the fantasy? You say you love your woman, "the hottest babe in town," yet you're betraying her just so you can stare at a pair of boots while you satisfy yourself? This feels like a big fuck you!

After reading, I have reached a point where "the boots" have become a tipping point for me. A man is willing to lose everything over a pair of boots. He couldn't just be more transparent and revisit his desperate need with his girlfriend. Maybe suggest some sexy time online, or end it before he deceives? He couldn't have just self-regulated. Instead? He cheats again and again.

Well, fuck you too!

CHAPTER 25

DEBUNKING THE MYTHS

The following reflects my experiences, knowledge, and professional perspective as a Dominatrix.

The Media

For decades, media has loved to portray BDSM and Dominatrices as dangerous, violent, abusive, mentally unstable, or connected to crime. The focus is almost always on the extremes, which only reinforces harmful myths. Over and over, we see kinky scenes played out in the same way, on TV, in the news, in magazines, leaving behind a digital footprint that can feel uncomfortable, confusing, or just plain weird.

In recent years, some media (especially independent films, documentaries, podcasts, and TV series) have started to show more realistic and respectful depictions, acknowledging consent, negotiation, boundaries, and emotional intelligence in kink exchanges.

There is a misconception created by the disconnect between what is real and what is make-believe. Film and television have an agenda to portray the Dominatrix as the wickedly intense Femme Fatale. The Dominant figure is typically dressed in leather or rubber and frequently wears boots or heels. Commonly, the Dominatrix causes distress to her subject before torturing or killing him. She is the villain, releasing her whip before potentially sexually Dominating her captive play toy.

The mainstream media has a profound influence on how we have perceived this character. Many portrayals leaned on sensationalism to attract attention. Their storytelling space, where stereotypes are created, and their puritanical values fuel the opinions of many people.

So don't be fooled by the simplistic storyline streaming across your screen. For their purposes, many facts surrounding the Dominatrix have been eliminated from the script!

The Dominatrix is a "Hooker with a Whip!"

I hear:

"I find it so naughty and fun!"

"I get to dabble in submissive exploration, without any social ridicule. And I get to fuck while she beats my ass!"

"It's the perfect combination of sexual pleasure and pain."

"And… I get my dick sucked!"

There is a roster of Dominatrices who do not label themselves as prostitutes, yet they will fuck, suck, and stroke your man to climax. The perception that Dominatrices are "Hookers with Whips" has a place in reality. Some prostitutes have leveled up their services by calling themselves a Dominatrix, offering BDSM games with their bag of sexual tricks. For them, it means more money and niche appeal.

Through my personal experiences, I have encountered problems with this. It has hurt my craft. Over time, I began to see a change in requests; potential clients were primarily interested in a BDSM/sex combination. Because I don't offer sexual acts, it is challenging to get new clients who will accept an appointment without hands-on gratification. These men must be convinced they will be satisfied without sexual involvement, or they will go elsewhere.

Then there is the alternate world of the "Willing Mistress." These women provide a full menu: anal play, hand jobs, foot jobs, and nudity. Some even demand to be orally or otherwise pleased by the client. They argue that this isn't prostitution, but rather a "normal" part of kinky play. This creates a messy overlap where the lines between a professional power exchange and a sexual transaction disappear entirely.

So, is the Professional Dominatrix who conducts these behaviors a "Hooker with a Whip," or is it acceptable to keep her titled as a Professional Dominatrix? There is no one straight answer. "Sex work" and "prostitution" are fluid concepts. For some, "Hooker with a Whip" is a dismissive label that fails to capture the skill and artistry of BDSM. For others, any exchange of money for sexual acts is prostitution, and that is that.

The world of sex work and BDSM is not black and white; it is a spectrum. What matters is that we continue to have these conversations, respect boundaries, and recognize that for me, the distinction is clear. One is a transaction of the body; the other is a transformation of the mind. I am in the business of the latter.

The Dominatrix Must Be Mentally Unstable!

Some assume that Dominatrices—or anyone in the BDSM community—must be mentally unstable. In reality, it is often the opposite: most of us are grounded, self-aware, and emotionally stable. I stand by the belief that we cultivate stronger communication skills and a deeper commitment to safe, consensual spaces than the average person.

Many people avoid the subjects of desire, power, and taboo because those spaces unsettle them. A willingness to engage these topics consciously suggests psychological curiosity and emotional literacy, not instability.

Research backs this up. Having unusual sexual interests does not automatically mean something is mentally "wrong" (Moser & Kleinplatz, 2006; Wismeijer & van Assen, 2013). Multiple peer-reviewed studies have found that BDSM practitioners are, on average, as psychologically healthy as or sometimes healthier than the general population. We often show lower neuroticism, lower rejection sensitivity, and higher overall well-being.

The American Psychiatric Association agrees. The DSM-5 no longer classifies BDSM as a mental disorder. Atypical sexual interests, known as paraphilias, are only considered disorders if they cause distress to the individual or involve non-consenting partners.

So why does the stereotype persist? Perhaps it isn't about us at all. Maybe it is about a society that is uncomfortable with sexual power and nontraditional desire. Exploring taboo subjects like power dynamics and paid intimacy doesn't signal instability. I think it reflects courage and a commitment to understanding human complexity. Kink is about exploration, not pathology. And if that makes some people uncomfortable, it is worth asking *why?*

The Bitch

"Are you a man-hater?"

"Are you just careless and mean?"

Am I a *bitch*? No, but men can be a complete pain in my ass, especially when they start mansplaining!

I won't speak for every Professional Dominatrix, but I am not. The myth that a Dominatrix must be aggressive, manipulative, or abusive is simply not true. I do not represent myself that way, I don't claim the title, and I don't carry the attitude.

Consensual playtime requires a mentally stable setting. I have very strict rules for myself: I do not play if I am in a bad mood or emotionally upset. My client's mental, emotional, and physical well-being is my primary focus. To maintain that, I must be centered.

Dominance and bitchiness are two entirely separate traits. A "bitch" often lacks control; she is driven by anger and unchecked aggression. Being out of control is potentially dangerous in a play setting, especially if the Dominant is narcissistically tempered. If a Dominatrix feels she cannot Dominate without applying a "bitch" mentality, she is in the wrong business.

True Dominance is the opposite; it is a state of being in absolute control. As a Dominant, I employ leadership, assertiveness, authority, and awareness.

Of course, context is everything. Playtime affords a safe space for me to role-play as a bitchy woman. I can pretend to be cruel and control the scene with a stable mind, responsibly bringing a man's fantasy to life in a safe, sane, and consensual environment. But when the scene ends, the mask comes off. Leadership remains; the "bitch" was just part of the show.

The Abuser

I hear:

"You must have been abused as a child."

"Do you have a lot of aggression to get out?"

"Did being abused make you abusive?"

Here is my truth.

As a Dominatrix, my clients' mental, emotional, and physical well-being is my top priority. I take full responsibility for myself, my clients, and every aspect of our play. Together, we establish clear rules and boundaries to ensure every experience is consensual and safe.

Yes, I was abused as a child. But no, I do not harbor hidden aggression, nor am I abusive. In fact, it is the opposite: I am deeply protective of those who trust me with their vulnerabilities. My experiences drive my commitment to compassion, empathy, and meticulous care.

Before becoming a mother or a Dominatrix, I spent years in therapy. I wanted to understand my past and ensure I wasn't unknowingly carrying forward trauma. That work confirmed what I already knew: my past does not define me, nor does it make me harmful.

For over thirty years, I have studied mental health, trauma, addiction, and the neurological roots of behavior. This knowledge has deepened my understanding of the line between consensual BDSM and abuse, strengthening my ability to care responsibly for others. That care shows in my consistency. My behavior is grounded, my emotions are balanced, and I respond to stress with clarity. I don't react in extremes; I adapt, grow, and communicate. My history didn't make me an abuser; it made me a guardian of boundaries.

Being A Professional Dominatrix Makes You an Unfit Mother

Judgments like these are a perfect example of why we shouldn't judge a book by its cover. No one can truly know a person based on a label, a title, or a fleeting impression. Stigmas and stereotypes cloud judgment, reducing complex human beings to oversimplified caricatures. Over time, I've learned how vital it is to set aside assumptions about what is "right" or "wrong" for others.

My career is built on consensual adult practices, emotional intelligence, and self-empowerment. This does not diminish my ability to be a loving, responsible, and present mother—I believe it enhances it.

Good parenting is about presence, consistency, and emotional accountability. It means providing stability, modeling integrity, and fostering a strong sense of self-worth through healthy boundaries. Above all, the goal is to create a home where truth is honored, not punished, and where shame and judgment simply do not belong.

My work has refined my understanding of abuse, manipulation, and consent. I am a more conscious mother because my profession has taught me the true cost of human respect.

All Dominatrices Must Be Dominant in and out of the Bedroom

Not true!

It is a common myth that we are Dominant in every area of our lives. In reality, just as a person in the role of a Dominant may be sadistic, they may also be submissive. It's not unusual for those who practice Dominance to explore the worlds of masochism and submission in their personal time.

I know many Dominatrices who take on different roles inside the Dungeon. They may be "Switches," refusing to limit themselves and finding fulfillment in every aspect of BDSM play. Women who embrace both their Dominant and submissive sides often make fantastic Dominatrices. Their love for playing at all levels gives them an intimate understanding of the interplay between roles and the deeper layers of eroticism.

Having submissive tendencies does not hinder the ability to Dominate; I believe the best Dominatrix has a deep, personal connection with both sides. This creates a true understanding of what the client is feeling.

Others perform exclusively as Dominatrices at work while remaining mostly submissive at home. Some live fully as submissives in their private lives, embodying what it means to dedicate themselves to a Dominant partner. If you peeked in late at night, you might see the woman who commanded a room by day curled up at the foot of her partner's bed throughout the night.

Relinquishing control can be incredibly relaxing and freeing. Creating the trust necessary to share one's vulnerabilities is both fulfilling and pleasurable. For many, surrendering submissively is how they feel safe, connected, and desired.

Power is not a permanent state of being; it is a costume we wear and a gift we give. Pick your passion, but always stay true to yourself while doing so.

Lady of Mystery

The mystery remains of the leathery-clad ghost that creeps around the dark night once the sun hides behind the night's calling. We watch in wonderment to see if she will idle long enough inside the darkness for us to find the answers that scratch at our curiosities. Unfortunately, she vanishes into the hue of the evening, and we are left guessing.

If only it were that cinematic!

In reality, the Dominatrix usually goes undetected. Don't be surprised if you are sitting next to her at a restaurant, pushing your shopping cart alongside her, or standing behind doing a school pick-up. We are everywhere!

Our lives are just as "common" as everyone else's. Typically, we live within societal norms and blend right into the crowd. Other times, we look edgy and sport our kinky gear for a night out on the town, just like you might do on occasion.

Just like you, we maintain traditional relationships, pursue educational ventures, and enjoy leisurely activities. We manage the mundane ebbs and flows of life and bask in an array of annoying responsibilities. And yes, we do chores. Unless, of course, a submissive has earned the privilege of scrubbing the floors for us.

The Dominatrix Is a Goth or a Witch

The answer is yes, no, or sometimes.

The Dominatrix can often be seen in the color black. However, this does not automatically signify that she is a Witch or a Gothic

Raven. Wardrobe and makeup choices can pigeonhole us into specific categories, leaving the world with misconceptions of who the Dominatrix is. Yes, we may choose to look Goth or like a witch, but this does not mean we classify ourselves as such. Or maybe we do!

The Gothic Goddess or Witchy Seductress may be dripping in her wardrobe of choice simply to please her own self-image. Her desire to visually express this illusion could go only as far as her own aesthetics, with no mental, spiritual, or other meaning. Others may consider themselves to be a witch, be darkly inclined, or be part of a Gothic subculture.

I won't tell you their secrets, but these mystical beauties can be magically irresistible. They sculpt the world of BDSM into interesting statuaries, leaving their attendees mesmerized by the beauty and the intrigue of the unknown. Manipulating their atmospheres, they curate potions to cast spells of pleasing effects.

Approach if you dare!

The Dominatrix Must Be: The "Super Kinky" Expectation

In my experience, men I enter personal relationships with often expect me to always be the Dominant partner and "kinky as fuck." They automatically assume that my title as a Professional Dominatrix entitles them to have their fantasies fulfilled by "The Mistress" on a daily basis.

The truth is, a Dominatrix is no different from anyone else. Our sexual needs are individual and ever-changing. A woman's cycle, mood, and daily life all cause fluctuations in sexual desire. We are human, not caricatures.

That said, I can say with confidence that many of us are compassionate, aware, and highly communicative in our personal sexual lives. Because we understand the vital importance of boundaries, we are more inclined to set them clearly in the bedroom.

Surprisingly to some, we are not looking for an ongoing BDSM circus act. We ask our lovers to set aside their expectations and stop asking us to balance on a never-ending kinky high wire. Sometimes, we just want to be present without the props.

Vanilla sex is great, too. Sometimes, the most Dominant thing a woman can do is simply exist in her own skin, without the costume, the props, or the performance.

REFLECTION: RAINA MARKS

Myths or not, I'll never look at a Professional Dominatrix or the worlds of BDSM, Kink, and Fetish the same again.

I'm still annoyed! I don't feel like reflecting right now.

Raina leans back, eyes unfocused, replaying the words, the stories, the confessions that now live in her head. What once seemed like a fringe fantasy now unfolded as something so much more layered: an ecosystem of human psychology, emotional vulnerability, structured safety, and radical honesty.

Now, she simply needs a moment to reflect on everything, as we all do from time to time.

CHAPTER 26

WOMEN HAVE ASKED

Before I started writing my book, I asked several women which questions they wanted answered.

Here's what they asked:

Question: How does a man not get emotionally connected or attached when fulfilling his fantasies with you?

Some men do have an emotional connection with me. That's the part no one wants to say out loud, but yes, he can absolutely get emotionally connected.

Some people don't compartmentalize as cleanly as they pretend to. Often, different types of intimacy, whether real or staged, create connection. Even when it's transactional, even when it's "just play," the moment a man brings vulnerability, craving, or emotional release into the space, something gets exchanged. It may not be love, and it may not be commitment, but it is undeniably a connection.

I think he connects simply because he is human. Deep down, in most cases, he wants to be seen in ways he doesn't allow himself to be seen in the rest of his life.

Trust is the foundation built between us, even if it's a paid transaction, and he easily becomes attached to the idea of having someone he can trust with his secrets. Without trust, it is difficult to form a connection; trust is our building block to furthering any level of playtime intimacy. This means trusting the power exchange, respecting boundaries, and understanding that the connection is real, but not romantic. It is built on consent, clarity, and mutual emotional safety, not emotional possession.

Question: Before we met, my man visited a Dominatrix for years. I'm willing to play with him, but how do I gain the confidence to Dominate him?

Confidence is a multi-layered feeling. Self-assurance is key to believing that you have the abilities and qualities to securely produce what is being asked of you. This is an extremely involved question, and I can only scratch the surface of the topic.

Be honest with yourself. If you feel you are unable to be Dominant, then stop there and have that conversation. Alternatively, if you do not want to participate in these play acts, then don't. Do not force the situation just because your man has asked you to participate in a role to fulfill his fantasies. It is your choice. You do not need to involve yourself in activities that make you feel uncomfortable. Set boundaries and effectively communicate your needs and concerns.

If you are willing to proceed, communicate with your man and ask him as many questions as possible. Be inquisitive about his needs, desires, and fantasies. If you do not have the answers, you most likely will not have the confidence to perform. You might need to build and sustain your confidence before jumping into these kinky activities.

Write down what your participation looks like inside the play experience. When we have a clear understanding of what is being asked of us, we can better prepare for the task. Once you have a clear understanding, the knowledge will help you find the confidence to move forward.

The two of you need to consensually agree on what boundaries and rules you will be following. If you don't have the answers yet, that's okay. Research. Explore. Experiment. The internet provides a variety of videos, books, workshop listings, and articles. You can even visit a Professional Dominatrix to take lessons and ask questions. Take small steps, but be transparent about where you are in the process. Don't fake it to make it. Only you will know when it clicks.

Being asked to participate in acts that feel unfamiliar can stir up deep feelings of inadequacy. You might start questioning yourself, wondering if you're enough or if you'll ever truly measure up. You want to please your partner, but instead, it feels like you're falling short. That gap between desire and self-doubt is where emotional exposure lives. That is where vulnerability rises to the surface. Over time, that kind of pressure can quietly build walls in your relationship, making it harder to voice your needs, your limits, and your desires.

If your mind is spiraling and you can't get grounded, say something. Be honest. Press pause. You can always revisit the idea later, when it feels like a choice rather than a performance. If there are parts of the fantasy you are open to exploring, communicate that too. Clearly.

Confidence doesn't just appear overnight. Self-assurance is built through safety, trust, alignment, and doing. Honor your pace. Stay with your process. Move in a way that feels real, not rushed, and definitely not forced.

Getting out of your own way is key to shutting down the noise in your head. The more you feed negative self-talk, the faster you'll convince yourself that you're not enough. That mental spiral kills potential confidence and disrupts the flow of what could have been a playful, empowering experience.

Most of us have an ever-evolving relationship with our bodies. Body image issues come and go, and when they hit, they can drain your confidence fast. A lot of that comes from cultural conditioning. We're spoon-fed narrow, unrealistic ideals of how we should look.

Start here: Release the idea that a Dominatrix or any Dominant has to look a certain way. There is no "correct" aesthetic. What matters most is how you feel in your skin. Choose wardrobe pieces that make you feel powerful, sexy, and comfortable. You don't need to squeeze into something tight, skimpy, or painful just to match someone else's fantasy. If heels or boots wreck your feet, wear them sitting down or don't wear them at all. It's your call.

Confidence doesn't come from forcing yourself into a mold; it comes from owning what already makes you feel good mentally, emotionally, and physically. Never let a man dictate what you wear, in fantasy play or real life. Don't sacrifice your confidence for clothing that makes you shrink inside yourself.

Whether he means it kindly or not, I can't help but roll my eyes when a man says, "I think you look great in that skintight bodycon dress I bought you!" *You mean the dress I've never worn? The one you expect me to wear to titillate your senses?* Sure, the gesture is nice. But all I hear is the "I" in that sentence. It's all about him and what he wants to see. I often confirm for myself: "I would never buy that dress for me."

Men often think that because they say the outfit looks great, we should automatically feel great in it. It doesn't work like that. Most of the time, we don't. Real confidence doesn't come from someone else's opinion, especially not when stepping into a Dominant role.

You don't need a man's validation to decide what's sexy, powerful, or acceptable. You decide what feels good in your body. You decide what feels right for you. Own that. Wear what you love. Do what empowers you. Your comfort, your confidence, and your joy make it sexy, not his reaction.

And while we're here: use your voice. Ask for what you need. Say what you desire. But first, be honest with yourself. Name the insecurities. Acknowledge the doubt. Get clear on your needs, your fears, and your fantasies. Self-honesty is the only way to build real honesty with a partner. Whether you're in the Dominant role or not, this still stands: you set the rules. You set the boundaries. You decide what's right for you.

The keyword here is *willing*. Build the Dominant dance around your willingness to participate. You're the conductor of your own brainwaves, so make them work for you.

How do you know if a man carries prior emotional or physical trauma when he comes to you for a session? What if he doesn't tell you, you don't suspect it, and you unintentionally amplify his trauma?

That is part of the risk that comes with this work. Some men won't tell me what they are carrying, and others don't even know themselves.

Many men come to me because they want to feel safe enough to explore parts of themselves they have kept hidden. Others come because they are running from pain or shame, or they don't even realize they are carrying trauma until something in our session exposes those feelings. If I accidentally trigger something, what matters most is how I handle it.

I have to read body language and trust my instincts. I listen to what my clients say, and I pay close attention to what they are not saying. It is important to carefully observe their actions and watch for contradictions. Often, I will test the waters and plan from there.

If a man comes to me with something unresolved, all I can do is create a safe space where he can let something go, ask for what he needs, and explore. I am not a therapist, nor is it my responsibility to heal him. I always do my best to support his mental, emotional, and physical needs, but I maintain the line between play and pathology.

I ask questions. This helps me screen clients and hopefully opens a transparent line of communication before we begin our playtime. If something surfaces, I pause and check in. "What are you feeling or is something releasing from inside you?"

This is why aftercare is offered at the end of every encounter, unless we have agreed otherwise beforehand. This helps me notice if something feels off or heavy. I can see if he avoids the transition, becomes overly needy, or lingers at the door. It is important to give him tools to ground himself. I make it clear that if he has further questions or needs support, he may return to me for help.

I cannot control what happens after my client leaves. I can only control what I give him while he is with me. That is enough, because I am human, doing human work. I do my job with all the mess, the magic, and the responsibility that entails. At some point, I have to let go. I am not his ultimate savior. I cannot fix him, and that is okay.

Question: My partner and I have a very active sex life. I recently found out he is visiting a Professional Dominatrix. What does he need besides our sexual intimacy? What does the practice of BDSM give him that our sex life does not?

It is completely natural to feel confused, hurt, or even betrayed after discovering your partner is seeing a Professional Dominatrix. However, BDSM often fulfills needs that go far beyond traditional sexual intimacy. What he is seeking may not be about sexual gratification at all. Instead, it is often about power, vulnerability, control, or emotional release. These are experiences that are not always present in conventional relationships.

He may not need "more sex," but a different kind of psychological or emotional experience. BDSM can offer surrender, roleplay, discipline, or ritual, all of which serve deeply intimate, non-sexual needs. This does not mean your intimacy is lacking. Your connection might be strong, but BDSM can exist as a separate layer of personal expression, identity, or emotional regulation.

This discovery opens the door to an important conversation if you are willing to safely discuss his needs without judgment, and if he is transparent about why he is seeking these experiences. He may be looking for psychological exchanges rather than physical acts. Concepts such as surrender, structure, or the experience of being controlled can provide emotional intensity or relief from anxiety, stress, or the heavy pressure of always being in control in his daily life.

With a Dominatrix, the dynamic is strictly professional and ritualized. This offers a safety to explore taboo fantasies or aspects of himself he may feel uncomfortable expressing in a romantic relationship. He may be exploring deeper parts of his identity tied to submission, humiliation, pain, or specific fetishes. These are experiences that do not always fit easily into standard relationship patterns.

BDSM can impact him emotionally, physically, and mentally in ways that "vanilla" sex may not, offering something different or kinky to fulfill his needs. The key is to approach the situation with curiosity rather than blame. Create a safe space and approach him with as little judgment as possible.

Start with effective communication and ask your partner these same questions: What do you need besides our sexual intimacy? What does the practice of BDSM give you that our sex life does not?

It is obvious that he feels something is unmet in the relationship. He is desiring more than just traditional intimacy and has stepped out to satisfy that craving. By creating space for honest dialogue, you can move toward the truth together.

Question: I think my partner is interested in BDSM. He won't talk to me about his desires or fantasies! How can I engage him in a conversation about his interests?

Revisit Chapter 11, "Effective Communication: How I Speak to His Secrets," in this book. When it comes to uncovering his kinks and hidden interests, how you communicate makes all the difference. Try to use these tools: verbal, nonverbal, and intuitive. Getting to the core of what he wants might take time, so meet the process with patience, curiosity, and an aim for limited judgment.

Compassion, kindness, and a softer approach can go a long way, especially with men who struggle to open up. Some of them aren't necessarily closed off, but they may feel intimidated, scared, or even embarrassed. Show him through your energy, your presence, and your words that he can trust you with his truth.

I've found that some men respond best when they are led, not pushed. And it is not always with words. If he's shy or hesitant, try a different angle. Skip the talk and create the experience. Surprise him with a kinky gift and set up a scenario. Let playfulness do the heavy lifting when conversation feels too vulnerable.

Above all, don't give up. Once he feels safe and believes you're genuinely with him in this exploration, he will most likely open up. It may happen slowly, but it can happen. Your steady, nonjudgmental presence is the key.

Question: Why does my man want to fulfill his needs and desires without me?

Maybe you are wrong! Maybe he would prefer to fulfill his needs and desires with you. You might be assuming he doesn't want to simply due to a lack of effective communication. Ask him. Ask him this exact question: "Do you want to fulfill your fantasies and needs with me?" You might be shocked by the answer you receive. If the answer is yes, then ask him: "What are your fantasies, needs, and desires?" If the answer is no, then ask him: "Why not, and how can I turn that "no" into a "yes"?"

This is a powerful question, and it speaks to the heart of emotional and relational complexity. When a man seeks to fulfill his needs with someone other than his partner, it is usually not as simple as a lack of love, attraction, or commitment. Rather, it often reflects unmet needs, unspoken truths, timidness, or unexplored parts of his identity that he doesn't know how or doesn't feel safe enough to express within the relationship.

Men have shared with me that their wives or girlfriends often struggle to have the real, uncomfortable conversations. Sometimes, it is easier to shut down, get defensive, or avoid what feels too hard to face. I have heard it more times than I can count: "She just didn't want to hear it." While there may be many reasons for that, the result is often the same: missed opportunities for deeper connection. When communication breaks down on either side, the emotional distance can grow quietly between you. Both people must stay open to sharing even when it is uncomfortable.

Men have also expressed that they have had in-depth conversations with their partners about their kinky thoughts. They were excited to hear that their partner was willing to participate. However, over time, the woman opts out of the games, and the man is left on his own to find that satisfaction. Eventually, he is no longer on his own, because he finds someone like me.

From day one, ask the uncomfortable questions. People do not always ask the right questions. Get to it and get in it! Put in the work. Relationships take effort, and both parties must do their due diligence to have an honest, respectful, and healthy relationship. Most men do want to fulfill their fantasies, needs, and desires with their partners. Most couples simply do not effectively communicate.

Let me say this again: Most couples do not effectively communicate. This is a big problem!

Question: Does a man's connection to BDSM make him feel "dirty?"

I often remind him, "He's a dirty, dirty boy!" But what does "dirty" really mean? Is it about a man who is desperately horny, ready and willing to participate in unusual sexual acts that intensify his urges and gratification? Does he get a thrill from acting out what he feels is naughty, or does he feel liberated and fulfilled? Or does "dirty" actually result in shame and guilt? The answer varies; it could be any of the above, depending on the man.

A man may feel "dirty" about his connection to BDSM if he hasn't reconciled it with his identity, values, or self-worth. But in a healthy, consensual, and accepting environment, BDSM is not a source of shame. Instead, it becomes a gateway to self-understanding, liberation, and deeper intimacy.

"Dirty" might feel morally wrong if a man is drawn to kink but has grown up believing his sexual exploration is perverse or abnormal, especially when it involves Dominance, submission, pain, or taboo play. BDSM is often misunderstood as abusive or immoral, which can make him feel isolated, ashamed, guarded, rejected, or conflicted. If he was raised with strict religious or moral teachings, his interests might feel sinful or shameful, even if they are completely consensual and healthy. He may fear being seen as aggressive, weak, or deviant, especially if he enjoys being submissive or vulnerable.

Society often links masculinity with control, stoicism, and emotional detachment. A man who enjoys being Dominated, humiliated, or emotionally exposed in BDSM may feel like he is breaking the rules of what it means to be "a real man." When he hides his kinky quests, even from himself or his partner, it can lead to feelings of being dirty, broken, or unworthy, especially if his needs feel incompatible with "normal" relationships. If he is cheating on his partner, all of this becomes even more complicated.

Other men find freedom, healing, and empowerment in their BDSM journeys. They create intense connections and satisfy deep emotional and psychological needs. I've heard from many clients that our visits together have strengthened their confidence and communication skills, offering catharsis and relief from the control and performance-based stress of the outside world.

Question: Can a man's desire for kink surpass the emotional intimacy he shares with a loving partner? Is a man's connection to kink more important or better than having meaningful sex with someone he loves?

The truth is, it depends.

BDSM and emotional intimacy fulfill different needs. Kink taps into identity, not just arousal. It can feed a man's psychological or primal self, offering control, surrender, or catharsis in a way that traditional sex does not. Emotional sex, on the other hand, feeds the relational or soulful side of him.

For some men, kink is more than a preference; it is a core part of who they are sexually and psychologically. Power exchange, submission, or Domination may feel like truth in action: raw, intense, and revealing. They may feel seen or accepted in ways that emotionally connected sex alone cannot provide, especially if their thoughts feel taboo.

I have seen this play out in two very different ways with my clients.

Man number one is in love with his partner, and the sex is amazing. He is willing and able to set aside his kinky activities, at least for a while. He might say, "I can usually only set my kink aside at the beginning of the relationship." For him, the thrill of new love and emotional intimacy is enough to satisfy his needs. But if that emotional spark fades even slightly, kink inevitably resurfaces, sometimes secretly.

The second type of man is different. He is in love and has amazing sex, but BDSM is non-negotiable. He cannot feel fully satisfied without exploring his kinky urges alongside emotional intimacy. Love and affection alone are not enough; kink is part of who he is sexually, and it always matters. It is not unusual for him to figure out ways to involve the simplest act of BDSM inside the bedroom, without his partner knowing the depths of his desires. He will fuck and fantasize or even cheat.

The real challenge and the real magic lie in integration. Many men do not want to choose between love and kink; they want both. When a partner can hold space for emotional intimacy and authentic BDSM exploration at the same time, the connection can be richer, deeper, and far more fulfilling than either could be alone.

Question: Do people still consider BDSM taboo?

Taboos related to sex impact sexual preferences, specifically those that fall outside typical sexual norms. Yes, BDSM still carries taboo weight in many circles, but it is becoming more understood, respected, and explored, especially as conversations around sexual identity and emotional expression continue to evolve.

The BDSM world has moved away from just being about "leather and whips" and has become much more focused on mental health, technology, and "soft" power.

In the United States, I have seen a shift in sexual expression. We may not be living in a fully sexually liberated culture, but things are definitely loosening up. From what I have experienced, BDSM has started to shed some of its stigma, especially within younger, more open-minded, urban communities. I am noticing that more people are curious and actually willing to have honest conversations about kink, power dynamics, and desire. It is not fully mainstream, but the edges are smoothing out.

Sex-positive spaces, online communities, and a growing number of kink-aware therapists are making it easier for people to explore BDSM in safer, more informed ways. The shame is not gone, but it is being challenged, and that matters.

Societal controversy over sexual taboos is either a never-ending discussion or a forbidden topic, depending upon the culture. Social customs are known to restrict or prohibit any association, discussion, or connection to these topics. Religious doctrines, morality, political correctness, and traditional standards of cleanliness commonly motivate these mindsets.

The resistance game still exists within various cultures and most likely will not ever change. I have clients who willfully escape this resistance and turn a blind eye to their cultural morals to satisfy their fantasies. These men step outside their cultural beliefs and secretly submit themselves to me. It seems their fantasies outweigh what they were taught to believe is right and wrong.

Many people still believe that BDSM falls under the categories of "consensual domestic violence" or "consensual violence" of some other kind. Because many are never taught about consensual kink, they equate physical intensity or power play with harm and trauma. They feel that BDSM will never be an acceptable lifestyle choice, and many do not wish to speak on the topic at all. However, please understand that consent, communication, and trust are the foundation of BDSM, not abuse.

Throughout our lives, we develop a psychological map that details our emotional, mental, and physical history. We explore our sexual map by navigating in between what we feel is right and wrong. Our erotic layout expands if we dare to color outside the lines. Some people may express their sexual passions more openly, while others continue to keep their urges silenced in secrecy.

The shadowed figures on the wall play out the fantasy whilst the lover once again slips into the missionary position. Do you dare to grab the hand of your shadow and step outside your "normal" sexual encounters?

To taboo or not to taboo, that is the question. And my answer is: to each his own!

Question: How can I hear my man and not judge him for his fantasies? Do I need to let him go or accept his fantasies into my life?

Revisit Chapter 11, "Effective Communication: How I Speak to His Secrets," in this book. Creating a safe space for honest, effective communication is the first step. It opens the door for both of you to learn more about each other's desires, needs, and fantasies. These conversations should never be one-sided. They are an opportunity for you to speak your truth too and to share your own needs, boundaries, and curiosities.

Keep an open mind. Listen with the intention to understand, not just to respond. That alone can help ease your initial reaction to judge. Hear him out fully before you make assumptions. Once you have heard him, give yourself time to process. You do not need to decide anything on the spot. This goes both ways; make sure he hears you out as well!

It is completely valid if what he is asking does not feel good to you. If something does not bring you pleasure or, worse, makes you uncomfortable, honor that. Be honest with yourself first, and then with him. Set boundaries that feel true to who you are. Only you can decide what you are open to. Only you know if his fantasy fits within your emotional and sexual landscape.

That said, do not underestimate the power of negotiation and compromise. Just do not mislead him. If there is room to meet in the middle without betraying yourself, it might be worth exploring. Flexibility, creativity, and mutual respect can go a long way in making two different worlds work together.

Remember that not every fantasy has to be a dealbreaker. You might find that what he is asking, such as wearing stilettos during sex, is more playful than threatening. But if something is a hard no for you, that is okay too. You get to decide what is worth salvaging and what is not.

What if a small step leads to a deeper connection? What if honoring each other's desires actually brings you closer? You will not know unless you try, but it is worth the effort to find out.

Question: At what point should two people be honest with each other about their needs, desires, and fantasies?

Honesty and transparency start from day one and should be afforded to the other person throughout the entirety of the relationship. Like people, questions evolve over time. What may not feel appropriate to ask or share on day one may feel appropriate to ask or share on day twenty-one. Just do not wait too long! The goal is to ask the intimate, uncomfortable, and deep questions from the onset of the relationship, because early honesty builds a stronger connection, clearer boundaries, and deeper compatibility.

Others may wait to share their needs until trust and mutual comfort deepen, particularly as a relationship becomes emotionally or physically intimate. It is my opinion that waiting too long to get the data can create conflict and excuses of the heart if you find yourself already falling in love. I have witnessed this time and time again with my clients, and the results are negative. A client who has not been honest explains that he feels it is too late to tell his amazing new girlfriend about his dirty secrets. He loves everything about her, but he does not think she is kinky or open to exploration. As a result, he is back in my Dungeon, cheating once again.

In my experience, most cheating men who come in for my services have always been, and will always be, into their kink or fetish. These desires do not just disappear. These men are aware of their truth and can openly share their secrets. I know this because they share all of this with me.

Do not get duped or potentially devastated by what has not been unpacked by the other person. Really press for the information and read between the lines. Do not make excuses or tell yourself something is acceptable if you truly know it is not. Do not mislead, and make sure you are not being misled. Ultimately, intimate needs are not a one-sided experience, and both participants need to be honest and transparent with each other.

Question: If my man were your client, how would you teach him to fulfill my fantasies?

First and foremost, he has to care about fulfilling your fantasies or feel there is a genuine opportunity to fulfill them.

I am in a unique position to help guide not only my client's exploration of BDSM, but also to empower them to show up more confidently, honestly, and attentively within their intimate relationships. Men need to become aware of their needs, limitations, and insecurities so they do not project them onto their partners in negative ways. In many cases, I guide them on how to initiate honest, non-judgmental conversations about their desires without pressuring their partners or turning the moment into a performance test.

During my time with a client, I demonstrate how trust and communication can build erotic connection. He sees that being present, respectful, and attuned creates awareness, safety, and openness. This is something he can carry into his personal relationship.

Often, men need to build their confidence or gain specific knowledge. Through me, he begins to understand how to use language, anticipation, and playful Dominance or submission to bring fantasies to life. Through my actions and, at times, my direct explanations, I invite him to start the conversation with his partner about light roleplay, shared storytelling, or introducing kink elements gradually.

I encourage him to see female pleasure and fantasy not as pressure, but as an invitation. If he is intimidated by strong or sexually expressive women, I work with him to reframe that power as a turn-on rather than a threat.

I am not just giving him control or submission; I am instructing him how to serve with intention, listen without ego, and create safe, erotic spaces. I want him to understand how to be both strong and soft, Dominant and submissive, devoted and creative. It is ultimately up to him whether he applies any of this in his current or future relationships.

Women need to be honest about their desires, needs, and fantasies, first with themselves and then with their partner. It is beneficial to communicate and teach your partner how to mentally, emotionally, and physically touch and satisfy you.

Women experience desire differently, both internally and externally. What works for one woman may never work for another. It is not possible to teach men how to fulfill women's fantasies as a generic class. I can give him general information, verbal whispers, erotic tips, and sensual expressions, but that does not mean he will execute them in a way you find romantic or sexually exhilarating.

Often, women feel intimidated, guarded, or insecure about sharing their needs, even when they desperately want them met. This can leave you feeling unsatisfied. Finding ways to eliminate these feelings will only benefit you. Ask yourself which forms of communication can best help you tell and receive information.

There are men who are constantly taking the temperature of their women, trying to understand what they need and want. He will do just about anything to make her happy, and not just in the bedroom. These men are always trying to figure out their partner's current mood, menstrual cycle, and overall emotional state.

Realistically, what worked for you last week may not work this week. More often than not, these men define the situation as a guessing game. They tread cautiously through the erotic fields to avoid rejection, frustration, or fighting. In other situations, they give up and submit to a systematic sex routine that feels safe, or they stop asking for sex at all. I try to help them recognize that being a giving lover starts with emotional responsibility, communication, and support.

If "Mr. Trial and Error" steps in, give him grace; you might love the result. However, never surrender to sexual activities you do not enjoy or those that cross your boundaries. Formulate an honest approach where you can negotiate and ask for what you need. If an unexpected act makes you uncomfortable, stop it immediately. Your "No" is just as erotic as your "Yes," because both are yours.

Question: Many of us grow up with the man "wearing the pants" in the house. The man might play the Alpha Male, "Cultural Alpha Man," part because of how he was raised or because he is naturally Dominant. I am not sure an Alpha Male would accept his wife being Dominant. Have your Alpha clients said that they would be open to their wives being Dominant? My strong sense is that men tend to compartmentalize easily. They are raised to hold back their emotions and do so accordingly in front of others. Behind closed doors, these same men will exercise their freedom and right to be Dominated by you. I wonder what he holds back or if he can truly be Dominated?

Yes, the *Cultural Alpha Male* can be Dominated. In fact, many of these clients want to be. These men come from vastly different backgrounds and cultural or social groups. Many have given me their tributes over the years in exchange for me taking control over them. The alpha male often arrives in the Dungeon not to surrender in body alone, but to safely leak out what he might not be able to show anywhere else.

"Mr. Alpha Dominant" stays steadfastly consistent with societal norms in his everyday life. No one would ever believe that he would be kneeling at my feet. These men exercise the freedom to choose when and who will Dominate. They seek out pleasure games to satisfy the urges that otherwise suffocate their minds.

Typically, these men have been taught to suppress their feelings since boyhood. They are instructed that strength is stoicism, that vulnerability is weakness, and that expressing emotion makes them less of a man. What lies beneath the bricks may hide their tenderness or something else entirely. They may feel plenty, but they keep it locked behind a vault of masculinity.

This is the beauty of compartmentalization. In the privacy of my space, this same man who commands boardrooms and makes authoritative choices all day can melt into submission. This is not him being inconsistent; it is him finally being allowed to be whole. He does not have to reconcile these two selves for anyone but himself, and that is the freedom he is really paying for.

Other than setting certain limitations—no bodily marks or evidence that could lead to them getting caught by their partners—these men become flexible over time on how they wish to be Dominated. Even then, it is a negotiation wearing his own armor. The performance of power is all he knows, and anything deeper feels like a risk he was never allowed to take.

In my experience, these alpha types will not dump their deepest vulnerabilities in the first session; they give them in measured, earned doses. Before they completely surrender, they want to feel safe. I must earn their trust and respect. They may kneel, but they still keep a watchful eye on my integrity before handing over every inch of themselves. These clients typically do not display manipulative submission. He won't "top from the bottom" or test you with power games; if he gives you the reins, it is genuine. However, a select few will instantly test me. It is common for their impulse reactions to stay composed, even in intense moments, because mastery over himself is part of who he is. Even though I am Dominating these men, it is clear their submission is a gift, one that can be ripped from my hands and taken back at any time.

Being "alpha" does not mean these men do not crave the release that comes with surrender. Power is exhausting and control gets heavy. Even the strongest men want a refuge where they do not have to lead. My clients have strong needs to submit to the power exchange; it feels like a breath of fresh air to them. They are tired of "wearing the pants" in their daily lives and want to relinquish control. Most of them have expressed a wish for life not to be so demanding. They share that they would not mind setting aside a large amount of their Dominance on a regular basis.

For this alpha man, submission does not make him weak. It takes strength to let go. It takes trust to hand over control. When an alpha male chooses to submit, it is not from losing power; it is from giving it intentionally. Just like cheating is intentional!

These clients ask for a variety of play activities. Typically, they immediately set their boundaries and, from that moment on, let me take charge. For example, some of these alphas want a specific form of weight play. They ask me to put all of my weight onto their entire body. With me holding them down, they are quiet and want to be positioned so they cannot move. They fully switch off and tune into their release mode.

Will the alpha male accept his wife or girlfriend as the Dominant participant? From my experiences, yes and no. According to some of my clients, they will accept their partners being Dominant in the bedroom. Many of these men will not accept their partners taking on a Dominant role in other aspects of life. Firstly, they may only love the power exchange as a playful release. Secondly, societal norms do not afford him this pleasure. Thirdly, it is not likely that his wife would agree to playing this full-time role, or any Dominant role for that matter. Power, like any other intimacy, is a composition. It requires two willing partners and a shared resonance. Whether the alpha in your life wants to kneel or lead, the truth remains: he can only go as far as your mutual honesty allows.

REFLECTION: RAINA MARKS

Okay, I've finally calmed down. I've learned this much: silence can be a weapon, but it can also be a tool. And I needed it to find my footing.

Everything I've been reading got under my skin. These stories weren't just stories anymore. They finally sank deeply into my mind. And they were loud. These men, these betrayals, this game of secrets and substitutions… it angers me.

But what pissed me off more was the part of me that understood it. The part of me that knew how easy it was to avoid the hard conversations. To water down the truth so no one gets uncomfortable. To hold it all in instead of being honest. So yeah, I needed a minute!

I appreciated the thoughtful questions in this last chapter. There's a lot that stood out to me. Especially this one specific topic: the "C" Word. Confidence! A never-ending revolving door on an important subject. A multi-layered inner-verse.

Ask me about my confidence on any given day, and I'll give you a different answer each time. Like so many of us, I grew up swimming in self-doubt, constantly comparing myself to every other girl in the room, hoping to find acceptance with who I was inside and out.

I used to stare into the mirror and ask myself: "If I were a man, would I find myself attractive?" Some days the answer was yes, but most days, it was a hard no. That journey was anything but smooth, but even when I was quietly breaking inside, I found ways to stash bits and pieces of confidence somewhere deep within me. Even if I couldn't show it on the surface, I was always holding onto something that reminded me I was still worth fighting for.

I really can be my own worst enemy. No one critiques me more than I do.

The brutal words I've spoken to myself:

- *You're fat and that's unattractive.*
- *Your hair should be thicker.*

- *Your lashes should be longer.*
- *Your skin is dry; you need a tan.*
- *Go to the gym more.*
- *Your butt's not perky enough.*
- *Maybe you should get the fat sucked out of your thighs.*
- *Your face has too many pores. Too many wrinkles. Maybe you need Botox.*
- *Your lips are too thin; get fillers.*
- *Your teeth should be whiter. Your feet are weird.*
- *Your boobs are not big enough.*
- *Your acne is disgusting—do something about it.*
- *You don't dress well.*
- *Your shoes are ugly.*
- *Why aren't your nails done?*
- *And seriously, that underwear? Where's the sexy lingerie?*
- *You don't even carry a designer bag.*
- *You're not sexy enough to pull that off. Don't even try!*

That list? Endless.

It took me years to learn just how loud and cruel that inner voice could be, and how much damage it could cause when left unchecked. Today, even as a grown woman, I still have those moments. But the difference is: I've found ways to love myself through the discomfort. I've learned to catch those thoughts before they spiral and sometimes, to shut them down completely.

Sometimes I wonder: what if someone actually said those awful things to me, out loud, to my face? I would crumble. My body would freeze, my breath would vanish, and I'd retreat into a cocoon of devastation.

If hearing those things from someone else would destroy me, why do I tolerate that voice saying these things inside my own head?

The truth is, I wouldn't allow another person to speak to me that way. And that's exactly why, when my inner critic starts to run wild, I remind myself: I am the one who loves me the most, so that's enough brain bashing.

There is no perfect formula for confidence. It's not like I'm heading towards a specific destination. It's a process, right? A daily, sometimes hourly, negotiation between grace and grit. I am constantly realigning. My mind is always adjusting, my body is changing, and my expectations should evolve right alongside that.

I've learned the importance of being kind to myself. Letting my insecurities have their moment, but not letting them write my story.

CHAPTER 27

THE MECHANIC
THE INTERVIEW PART 1:
LET'S START AT THE BEGINNING!

Disclaimer: *All sexual content and fantasies described involve consenting adults only. Identifying details have been changed or omitted to protect privacy. The purpose of this interview is to explore adult BDSM, fetish, and power-exchange dynamics in a professional, consensual context.*

What year were you born?

"I was born in 1982."

How old were you when you began to sexually fantasize?

"I had certain early experiences that shaped my attraction to lingerie, which later became central to my adult fantasies."

What is your fetish?

"I have a lingerie fetish."

Do you remember where your fantasy came from?

"Yes, I was nineteen and my sister would have her college friends come over. The girls would use the pool a lot. One friend was very beautiful. I loved her voluptuous body, and her curves excited me. I would watch her at the pool as she came in and out of the pool. The woman had very big breasts, and I would watch them float at the surface of the water. Her bikini barely fit her, and this aroused me. One day after swimming, she left behind her bra and panties. The set was made from white lace. I took the set and hid it in my bedroom under the dresser."

How did the panty set develop into your fetish?

"After I found the panty set, I would fantasize about the voluptuous girl when I was in the bathtub. I imagined her wearing the lingerie while submerged under the tub water with me. Eventually, I got brave enough to pull the panty set out from under the dresser and play with it late at night when I was in bed. I would think about the girl squishing me with her body, and I would rub my cock and balls with the soft lace."

Did your fantasy evolve after you first played with the panty set?

"Yes, I would steal panties out of the laundry hamper inside my house. I didn't want to destroy my original panty set, so I would use the other panties to masturbate into. Once the panties became too soiled, I would throw them out on my way to school."

I want to make sure I am understanding this correctly. At nineteen years old, you were aroused by a girl with a voluptuous body, and this turned you on. Since she visually excited you, you began to associate her voluptuous curves with the lingerie she left behind. The undergarments became the erotic object that you used to masturbate while fantasizing about the curvy girl. This, in turn, created a fantasy in your mind that gave you sexual arousal and eventually sexual gratification.

Is that correct?

"Yes. She is the reason I have a lingerie fetish."

What is a lingerie fetish?

"I think about lingerie all the time. I would rather use silky panties than my hand to rub my dick. I like to take all kinds of pieces and rub them on my body, dick, and testicles. I also like to wear the pieces myself and have it shoved in my mouth. I like to shop for lingerie for myself and for women. I love to look at voluptuous women wearing garters and lace. Erotic situations that involve lingerie turn me on, especially if a beautiful woman is involved."

What is another word for lingerie play?

"Underwear fetishism. This is a sexual fetishism where people like stockings, pantyhose, bras, different types of underwear, and other types of undergarments."

Do you watch pornography? Specifically, lingerie fetish videos?

"Yes, I watch regular pornography. And I look for any kind of lingerie videos I can find. I watch your fetish movies, Mistress."

What is your favorite lingerie to use during your playtime?

"That's kind of endless. I really like "used" lingerie the best. I have purchased panties from women who sell their undergarments. It's even better if I can buy panties that a man has cum in. I love it when a woman takes her panties off and stuffs them into my mouth. I have kept panties from ex-girlfriends that are worn. Otherwise, I will go to thrift stores or regular stores to buy my pieces."

Do you ever wear lingerie when you are out in public?

"Yes, all the time. I will even wear panties when I am at work. Sometimes I will wear nylons too!"

Give me an example of how your fantasies have evolved over the years.

"Now, I like to be publicly humiliated. I love it when a woman takes off her panties and makes me go into the bathroom to put them on. I like to be told to wear panties when I'm at work. When I am out running errands, I like to be commanded to ejaculate in my pants and wear the panties all day. I like to take risks with my fetish, but it's usually a Mistress that tells me to do this stuff. I like to be teased for having a small dick. The humiliation excites and embarrasses me. This is something new I have really grown to like. I would also like to watch a man fuck a woman while she teases me."

How often do you think about this fantasy?

"All the time!"

Was there a time when your fantasies and desires began to change?

"It happened after I developed my fetish. I was walking past a newsstand, and I saw a fetish magazine. There were so many women in the magazine. I took the magazine with me, and I began fantasizing and masturbating to the photos of the ladies. After this I started to think there was more out there I could do and I might not have to do it alone."

Did anything else come from finding this magazine?

"Yes, eventually. I came across a commercial Dungeon that was being advertised at the back of the paper."

What did you do after you discovered the commercial Dungeon?

"I would call the Dungeon periodically to ask them questions. I would explain part of my fetish to the desk lady to see if it would be possible to play out my fantasy. She explained to me that they could do my fantasy and I should come in."

How did that make you feel when you called the Dungeon?

"I got sexually aroused and nervous. The thought of going there one day made me very excited."

Did the experience of calling the Dungeon add to your original fantasy?

"Yes, because I felt like I would be too embarrassed to tell these ladies my fantasies in person. I felt humiliated, and I would masturbate to these feelings."

You say you felt embarrassed to talk to the ladies in person. Why?

"I was ashamed of having a small penis. The thought of them teasing me for my dick being so tiny humiliated me."

At what age did you first visit a commercial Dungeon?

"I was 22 years old."

How much money do you think you have given to Dominatrices over the years?

"A lot! Thousands and thousands of dollars. I am sure it's over $90,000.00."

Why do you see a Dominatrix?

"To fulfill my fantasies, I can't get other people to do. To get out of reality. To not face my problems for a while."

Are you addicted to your fetish?

"I think so!"

What is your favorite thing about your fetish?

"The incredible orgasms I have, and the fact that I never get tired of my fantasies."

Do you ever feel ashamed of yourself for being a fetishist?

"Yes, at times. I question myself and why I can't stop. I feel like something is wrong with me when I can't tell a girl because I'm afraid she won't like me. It can feel like a burden."

Have you ever told a woman about your fetish?

"I have. The problem was, she immediately told me I was gross. She judged me and made me feel like a loser. That was the end of seeing each other and I creeped her out."

Have you ever cheated on a partner with a Professional Dominatrix?

"When I was in a relationship but fell out of love, I started seeing a Dominatrix again. If I'm in a relationship that I feel has ended, is about to end, or is not going anywhere, I will go on with my business and see a Dominatrix. I don't feel that it is cheating. But I suppose it is cheating."

How do you feel about cheating on your partner?

"In order for me not to cheat, I have to be in love and in a fully committed relationship. I think she would need to understand my fetish and play with me too. Otherwise, there are no guarantees. I think I would eventually cheat."

Is there an exception to your rule, where cheating is concerned?

"Not really! If I am in a relationship that I know is not going in the right direction or that is basically over, I will step out of the relationship. I don't want to be a cheater, but eventually I crack."

If you're in love with a woman, can you live without playing out your fantasy?

"Maybe, for a little bit. I would have to really be in love with her. Honestly, I don't think I will ever be able to give up my fetish!"

So, are you telling me love isn't enough for you to change your fetishistic ways?

"No! At the end of the day, I will always want to play with lingerie."

If you're in love with a woman, will you still play out your fantasy in your head while you are fucking her? Will you still play with lingerie by yourself?

"Yes. There is no way I will ever stop thinking about my fetish or playing with it. However, I would eventually like to talk to her about my desires and see if she will play with me. Whether she's involved with my fetish or not, I will always play with lingerie by myself."

If you could tell your potential partner one thing, what would you say to her?

"I am kinky. My fetish isn't going away. It would be nice if she would participate in my fantasies, but if she doesn't, that's fine too. However, she needs to accept that I will be playing by myself or going to a Dungeon."

Do you think that most cheating men who step out with a Dominatrix are not in love with their wives or girlfriends?

"I think most of them probably love their wives or girlfriends. I think there are so many things that can get in the way of the relationship to make a man cheat. Like falling out of love, resentment, no excitement, and a stressful life. It's not just about a kink or a fetish. I believe though, if a man is kinky, he won't stop whether he loves her or not."

What's the difference between an orgasm with a play partner and an orgasm by yourself?

"The main difference is that I am not alone. When I am with a partner, it's more intense and satisfying. That person becomes a part of my fantasy. My fantasies are much more fulfilled when I play with someone else."

How often do you think about sessioning with a Professional Dominatrix?

"You always pop into my head. You are much more than a Dominatrix to me, you feel like a friend. You understand what I need, and it's not just about my fetish. You help me with so many aspects of my life."

Is fulfilling your fetishistic fantasy with me better than sex with a woman?

"Not really! It depends. Sex with someone new can be pretty intense, even without panties nearby. But sex is even more enjoyable if I can involve my fetish somehow. I need my fetish!"

Tell me a few ways I have changed your life.

"I used to be really shy, but I'm not anymore. Coming for sessions has helped me overcome my shyness. I can approach women more easily, and I am more open to talking about my fetish to strangers. Well strippers! I can only hint about my fantasies with the people I date. I am a lot more honest about what I want and I think I'm a better communicator.

I can't just talk to anybody about my fantasies. There is no way I'm going to talk to guys about them. You gave me somewhere to go and someone to be honest with. When I first went to you, you didn't know me. But when I told you my fantasies, you knew what I wanted. I felt because you are a professional, you understand what I and other men want. I feel less judged by you.

You support me in my real-life situations, and this helps me to handle things better. You help me in my relationships with other women. You have helped me with work and my overall health. And you always help me with life advice."

Are there any other reasons why you have sessioned with a Professional Dominatrix all these years?

"I do it to reward myself. I feel that I have earned the right to spend my money on what makes me feel good. When things are difficult, seeing a Mistress has helped me through the pain. It's a great distraction!"

What is your favorite thing about having me in your life?

"Everything! I just love having you in my life. Thank God, I have you in my life!"

How do our sessions feel now, after all these years?

"Our time together feels different now. I started out feeling very curious, and just wanting to explore my fantasies. My needs have evolved. Our time together is no longer just about satisfying my urges. I can't imagine going to a Dungeon and having a session with another woman who wants to be on her phone or who doesn't really care about me. That wouldn't work for me at all. You are still my favorite escape, but you are so much more! I can have deep and important conversations with you. I know you understand. You help me a lot. You help me with my pain. You help me through my problems. You know the kinky world I want to be in. This is your life. You get it!"

REFLECTION: RAINA MARKS

I find it fascinating to witness the connection this man has developed with his Dominatrix. What began as an exploration of fantasy has clearly grown into something far more personal. It's equally interesting to read his reasons for seeking out this dynamic. Looks like over time, he's become somewhat emotionally dependent on the relationship.

It seems that somewhere along the way, he stopped viewing her as just a woman in a Dungeon throwing out demands. She has become a trusted confidante and a safe place for the parts of himself he doesn't share elsewhere. What's especially striking is how natural it feels for him to confide in her beyond their scenes.

Hopefully, he can find a way to be completely transparent about his fetish before starting and then ending relationships. Instead of compartmentalizing it into a secret box.

If we were to read a hundred of these interviews, I think we'd see a pattern: most of these men won't give up their kinky obsessions. They rely on their time with her, not only for erotic release, but also for emotional fulfillment.

Looks like some men go to therapy, and some just book a session with Mistress.

CHAPTER 28

FANTASY SESSION STORY
SPLOSH! SPLOSH!

This chapter presents a fantasy session story involving consenting adults only. All scenarios are fictionalized composites inspired by themes from my professional practice, and identifying details have been altered to protect privacy. The story explores adult BDSM dynamics, trust, and power exchange within a safe, consensual, and controlled environment.

Character Development: This client is a fetishist and has been married for over ten years. He loves humiliation and playing with food. He has been obsessed with his fetish since working in a pizza restaurant.

My commands take on a whole new meaning when it comes to placing an order. And this does not mean I will be dining in this afternoon!

Ordering him: "Before our session, you will go to the market and pick up the following ingredients: pizza dough, eggs, refrigerated linguine pasta, vanilla pudding, and one gutted squid. Do not forget to bring a roll of paper towels and the plastic."

It is 2 o'clock on a Thursday afternoon. Already in the Dungeon room, I have turned on the music and slipped into his favorite fish-net dress.

Once upon a time, he entered the space as a twenty-two-year-old guy. Now a grown man, he is still coming back, and he is more addicted to his fetish than ever.

The door squeaks as he enters. "Hello, Mistress!"

I take two bags from his hands and place them on the counter. Sorting out the various foods, I open the packages so we are ready to play.

"Slave. Prepare the floor areas and bondage table with a layer of plastic. Take this refrigerated pasta to the bathroom and run hot water over the noodles. Bring them back to me when they are nice and warm. Then take off all your clothes and put on this diaper."

Walking over to me: "Yes, Mistress!"

I lounge back on the chaise and rest while he scurries around the room.

The preparations are set. "Bring me the pasta and come here. Hold your diaper open."

I lift the thin strands of dough and tease his lips. "Open wide! Wider!"

His mouth, wide like a trout, is ready to gulp down the tendrils of taste. Only the food is not meant to be eaten, so I drop the linguine straight into the diaper. Handful after handful, I fill up the diaper with the pasta and command him to get down on his knees.

Adjusting my position on the chaise: "Put this pillow under the plastic to protect your knees and slip off my stilettos to gently rub my feet!"

I enjoy a ten-minute foot massage before commencing with the food play. The metal bowl is big enough for both of my feet. Slowly, I drop the remaining linguine into the bowl.

Instructing him: "Get the rest of the ingredients and place them down on the floor beside you. Bring the paper towels and tear off ten sheets for me to use."

Obeying: "Of course, Mistress!"

Crack! With a gentle tap, I open the concealed sunrise within the egg. Dribbling the silky fluid between my toes, I watch as he becomes hypnotized by the act. The slippery egg begins to lubricate the linguine that is now gliding in and out of my ten petals.

Tap! Tap! "Pull open your diaper. It is egg time! Let us get your little linguine all slippery and wet. See, here is the thing: if you had a bigger cock, I would prefer to be doing other things to you. Unfortunately, your wiener is pathetic and tiny. So, no, there is not anything else I want to do with this useless stem. Put your hand inside the diaper and mix it all up!"

I grab the pizza dough and begin to knead the pillowy satisfaction with my hands. My long fingers pressing together as the dough squishes between my fingers drives him crazy. I shape the dough into a substantial cock and have him hold out his hand.

Placing the dough dick onto the palm of his hand: "I would love to help push the shame that follows you everywhere down the garbage disposal, but I don't think I can really help you on this one. I want you to see and feel the difference between a puny penis and an ample cock. Open that diaper and have a look inside. What do you see? You see nothing, because there is nothing to see! I couldn't fuck you even if I wanted to!"

I take the dough dick from his hand and drop it into the diaper. "Now that is a substantial cock! Feel it! With a cock like that, I would not be able to resist. Lucky for me, my man has a substantial cock and brings me endless pleasure: something you will never be able to do for any woman. Now hand me the pudding!"

Peeling back the foil from the six pudding containers, the sweet smell spreads throughout the room. I scoop the pudding into the bowl and begin to mix up the ingredients with my feet. I crack six more eggs over my feet and take out more pizza dough. I throw it into the bowl and step down onto the dough that feels like soft terrain beneath my soles.

Infusing his fantasies, I command him to put his hands into the bowl. "Rub me, slave. Massage my feet and calves with the dough. Press it onto me. Crack an egg and open it over each of my knees. Watch the juicy slime slide down my legs."

Excited: "Oh God, Mistress! Yes! Thank you, Mistress!"

The time for satisfying his fetishistic needs is coming to an end. "Stop touching me and stand up!"

With fifteen minutes left in our one-hour visit, I direct him to lie down on the plastic-covered bondage table. I pull his diaper down to his knees. I restrain his wrists and ankles to the corners of the table.

Carrying over the last ingredient: "It is time to truly punish you for having such a small penis. I went easy on you during the last forty-five minutes. But not now! Can you smell the subtle aroma, Mr. Disappointment?"

Squirming: "No, Mistress. Please, I beg you. No!"

Laughing: "You can beg all you want. That is not going to stop me. It is not my fault you came here unprepared and offered up an itty-bitty dick."

The gutted sea creature slips right out of the package, and I almost lose my grip. I move towards his miniature dick figure and dangle the squid's pearlescent body over his ball sack. I lower the tentacles towards his flesh, stopping to ask a few questions.

Asking: "Shall I drag these slimy tentacles all over your body? Or should I try to stuff your little dick inside the body of this squid? Hmmm, maybe I should make you leave with this inkfish inside your pants. What do you think?"

Desperate, he cries out: "None of the above! Please! No!"

Too bad for him, I am not asking him for permission, and I lower the squid once again.

Abruptly stopping: "I have decided! I want you to take the squid home with you and cook up a nice linguine and squid pasta for dinner. You will stop on your way home to pick up two glazed donuts for dessert. Take this extra diaper to wear during dinner, and when you sit down to eat your meal, get your cock hard and try your best to insert that tiny thing through the donut holes. After you finish all your dinner, you may enjoy the two donuts!"

Confused: "You want me to eat the donuts out of the diaper after I eat all of the linguine?"

Making myself very clear: "No, I want you to celebrate your yummy cravings and use the two donuts to masturbate yourself."

I take the squid and nicely wrap it back up into its package. I take off his restraints, command him to get off the table, and tell him to clean up the mess. Our time is over, and it is time for him to get dressed and leave.

Standing at the door laughing: "Order up! And I want pictures of your food porn. Bye-bye!"

REFLECTION: RAINA MARKS

Chew on that. No! Not a linguini and squid dinner! And the donuts… I actually can visualize this entire scene. This woman's imagination is full of ideas, but this guy? He is dead serious about his food.

Immediately, my thoughts go to how society loves to giggle at whipped cream and strawberries in the bedroom. It's cute, it's fun, and it's what most of us are used to seeing. However, if a man admits he gets off on spaghetti or scrambled eggs, he's suddenly a freak. I feel like the rules aren't about logic, they're about who gets to decide what's normal.

Almost two hours have passed, and Raina checks her phone once again, seeing that she still hasn't heard from her husband.

Yes, the doubt is creeping in and out of my mind. Probably because I'm now full of so many questions. I kind of feel like I have taken my relationship for granted, and I now understand that the two of us have dropped the ball. Hello to being awake!

It's around 2 AM back east, and it's unlike him not to send me a good-night text. Maybe he fell asleep! Maybe a lot of things. Now, I'm questioning a "Sunday night meeting with an associate."

Feeling a certain type of desperation herself, Raina sinks into her nest of downiness and settles into the living room couch. Her mind has taken over, and her insecurities have blossomed into a bouquet of doubts.

Looking down the hallway at the door to his office, she feels the temptation creep back into her mind.

Do I dare? Raina, stop! You've already played the snoop game once with yourself today. And you respected his privacy by not looking. Don't be that woman. Don't do it!

Peering into her phone. *Should I text him? Or test him?*

Contemplating. *Decisions, decisions. I choose test!*

CHAPTER 29

I ASKED MEN THE FOLLOWING QUESTION

What would be the main tip you would give your partner or potential partner to make you feel comfortable enough to confess your desires, needs, fantasies, and sexual secrets?

I heard:

#1 "I don't give a fuck! I would be straightforward and honest with a woman. They need to know who I am and what I want. Take it or leave it! After all, how am I going to be pleased and fulfilled if I can't be honest? The same goes for her. We are either going to be compatible or we won't be. And this isn't something we should find out a year into the relationship."

#2 "I don't have any tips. Ever since I was a young man, I have been direct and told the woman that I have specific desires that I enjoy. I ask her how she feels about my fantasies and see if she wants to play with me. It's important to just ask a woman."

#3 "Patience. A lot of patience. I need to know that a woman is open-minded before I can share my desires. Especially my deepest secrets. I also need to know my privacy is going to be respected, and this is where feeling safe enough to share gets tough. We all know most relationships end. I don't know how much I am willing to share when the likely outcome is an ex knowing all my secrets."

#4 "I am quite shy, so I don't think there is anything a woman could do to make me feel comfortable. Maybe over time, I could open myself up more, but I think it would take a Dominant woman to take charge. I mean, I will go along with things if she leads."

#5 "If I met a woman with whom I was interested in having a potential relationship, I would first ask her about what her sexual needs are. If she weren't that sexually experienced or seemed vanilla, I would doubt that it was safe to share my kinky sides with her. I might experiment by asking her questions, but I wouldn't be fully transparent with her about who I am sexually. I don't think I would take the risk out of fear that she would not be accepting of what I wanted. I have no way of knowing if my kink would destroy the potential relationship, so I wouldn't take the risk of sharing. I would be willing to pursue the relationship anyway and just keep hiding my secrets. I have done this several times in long-term relationships. But honestly, then I would end up cheating on her. I would satisfy myself somewhere else."

#6 "I would want her to confess her secrets first! This would make me feel more comfortable opening myself up to her."

#7 "The relationship would need to be strong, with a great foundation. Otherwise, I don't think the relationship would be able to sustain the truth."

#8 "I would hope the relationship would be established enough to discuss such topics. If it's a new relationship or a less-than-stable relationship, then it might not be time for these discussions."

#9 "The other person would need to open themselves up honestly. They would have to share their insecurities, fears, and what they want to have a real connection. They would need to be open and understanding."

#10 "The more comfortable I feel around the person, the more willing I am to open up to them. We would need to take the necessary time in the relationship to get comfortable enough to confess to each other."

#11 "I would like the other person to share the same level of interest and intimacy with me first. They must leave their inhibitions behind. They would need to be open and honest. The relationship should be a give-and-take!"

#12 "I am a Christian. I have never been asked a question like this before in my life. I hope one day I will have an open relationship to be able to discover this."

#13 "People need to always be truthful and honest, no matter what. Talks need to be honest. Women want to hear they are safe and heard. Let them know that they are so we can connect and bond."

#14 "Share theirs! I feel more open when other people share themselves first."

#15 "There needs to be an open environment that allows you to safely talk and share your thoughts. Otherwise, it makes it difficult to open up about your vulnerabilities."

#16 "Honesty is the most important thing when establishing any kind of relationship. If I don't tell the truth, what kind of relationship am I going to have?"

#17 "Just be honest!"

#18 "I wait for the woman to tell me what she wants. I need to see how open she is before I surprise her with what I like to do. I don't want to scare her away!"

#19 "I feel like things will naturally progress once enough time passes. Then it becomes much easier to test the waters and open up about what I want. Especially after I learn what she wants."

#20 "If I see that the other person is judgmental, I'm not going to tell them who I am. If I see that they are open-minded and willing to listen to me, I am more inclined to be honest about who I am."

#21 "I'm just flat-out honest. Hopefully I don't freak her out, and she's willing to give me a try!"

#22 "I won't be with a woman I'm not comfortable sharing everything. If I see she is unwilling to have a deep conversation about what she wants, then I know the relationship won't go anywhere."

#23 "I think people need to be more honest in general. I repeatedly find out things that should have been shared with me at the beginning of the relationship. I think I would be more comfortable if I knew I was getting full transparency from the other person."

#24 "I'm not sure I know everything I want. I'm still exploring myself. I think I need someone who can explore with me to help me figure these things out."

#25 "If a woman is 100% honest with me and I see this through her actions, then I feel less awkward about sharing what I need and like. If I can tell her actions don't match her words in the sex department, then I pull back and start to distance myself."

#26 "I am a serious man. I look for the same in my partners. If it feels like a game, then I won't engage with the person any further. There is no need for my full transparency in the beginning. She needs to be serious about my time and the relationship, before I disclose myself."

#69 *(Because this man stated he would only answer my question if he could be #69!)* "I'm a very private person. I am averse to risk. For the last few years of my marriage and for the 14 years after it ended, I was under a lot of stress, so this has solidified my approach to being more cautious with relationships. It takes time before I trust someone. What I require from someone I date is reliability, stability, loyalty, extreme trust, and a natural penchant for being cautious and private. Once those characteristics are proven, the girl also needs to be very sexually open. I need her to be an energetic and vibrant young woman, at least in spirit, rather than someone who has hung up her naughty ways and chosen to be a dull, boring, and matronly mom type or old woman. After all these boxes are checked, and she and I are experiencing a collaborative relationship, she will have earned the right to hear me share more about myself. Basically, there are a lot of stupid fucking people out there who do stupid fucking things, male and female, and I don't participate with that. But that doesn't mean I can't be dirty as fuck!" "Wait, don't go yet; I have a joke for you: How does a Dominatrix communicate with her submissive? *Dommunication!*"

REFLECTION: RAINA MARKS

Straight from the horse's mouth. I wonder how many of these men truly live by what they say? I also wonder if any of these 27 men have cheated on their partners?

I guess we all have some extra tools to use now. Helps us see a little more clearly and have a better understanding of what to look for and ask.

Is it hot in here? No, it's not hot in here; that's my blood pressure rising because I STILL HAVEN'T RECEIVED A TEXT FROM MY HUSBAND!

Flipping through to the end of the book. *I am finishing this book tonight. I'm almost done. Just a few chapters left. He'd better text me soon. I'm not going to be able to sleep if he doesn't!*

Restless. *What is wrong with me? I know I am in my head from reading this book, but I also need to remember that my husband has never given me a reason to distrust him. I think this goes beyond our relationship and might not have anything to do with him at all.*

Driving herself absolutely crazy. *What is this feeling? Am I weirded out since I've just assumed my husband is totally satisfied: like, emotionally, sexually, all of it? Have I been coasting on comfort and convenience, taking our relationship for granted?*

Or am I just spiraling in insecurity? The truth is, it's probably a messy mix of both. I'm in that internal chaos that hits hard when a mirror gets held up to your reality and you realize: maybe I don't have it all figured out.

There's a strange relief in that honesty, though. A lightbulb moment flickers on, and suddenly, she's not drowning; she's curious, motivated, and empowered.

Okay, this is my opportunity to lean in: to talk to him, and get the answers and reassurance I've been quietly needing.

And just like that, her bouquet of feelings turns into action. *Understanding what you need is one thing, but choosing to go get it? That's everything.*

Pushing send: *"Are you awake?"*

CHAPTER 30

FANTASY SESSION STORY
BREATHLESSLY NOOSE

This chapter presents a fantasy session story involving consenting adults only. All scenarios are fictionalized composites inspired by themes from my professional practice, and identifying details have been altered to protect privacy. The story explores adult BDSM dynamics, trust, and power exchange within a safe, consensual, and controlled environment.

Character Development: *This client has been married for over 30 years and has three children. With Europe being his home base, he frequents the States often. He has a stable marriage and loves his family. Through open communication, he has an agreement with his wife, who accepts his kinky desires outside the marriage.*

A seasoned player is an understatement!

I have learned the hard way, been tricked, and been taught lessons I never saw coming. "But not today, Houdini, not today!"

I am deciding whether to use the stool or the chair. It is all about the height. However, there is no need to make it comfortable for him. He once said to me, "You are way too easy on me, Mistress!" and now I have no mercy on him.

Pondering to myself: *What do I need? Two carrying bags for all this equipment. The stool. The chair is already upstairs. My black fishnet catsuit and tank boots. And my strength! A lot of mental and physical strength. Standing at 6'2 and 265 lbs., he does not make my job easy. He is a lot to bind up!*

I was a new Domme when we first met. It was my first taste of playing with a seasoned BDSM player. He has played with dozens of Dominatrices over the years and has put them all to the test. I will never forget the first few times I played with him. I was humbled beyond belief. Only now, 20 sessions later, I am ready to go; my days of humiliation are far behind me, and it is game time!

Step by step, I make my way to my favorite playroom to get ready. I have played so many times in this specific room that the black entry door has taken on a personality in my mind and is now called Sir Egress. The room is spacious, and I have a familiarity with these black and red painted walls that is comforting. The red accents highlight the blackness of the room and bring out my seductive aura. We have imprinted on each other, and it will forever be my favorite sanctuary of play.

Most of today's activities will take place at the suspension bar located in the middle of the room. The room always smells the same: the smell of cheap candles mixed with disinfectant spray and whatever perfume the last Mistress was wearing. Finding this unacceptable, I whip out a bottle of my own perfume and scent the air with smooth vanilla bean, amber, Sichuan pepper, and vetiver notes.

My mind rattles on. *My hangman's knot came out perfectly! I love this electric blue rope!*

It took me a while to learn how to skillfully put someone into inescapable bondage. Now that I have mastered this skill, there is no way he is getting out.

It is time to prepare the play equipment. I place all the equipment on the black leather bondage table. I organize the rope, mouth ball gag, blindfold, wrist and ankle restraints. Then the chain, locks and keys, handcuffs and key, riding crop, wood and leather paddles, stretch wrap, whipping rod, feather tickler, clothespins, ball stretcher, cock ring, zip ties, leather straps, carabiners, safety knife, safety scissors, and a stool.

Leaning over the table, I carefully look. *Am I missing anything? Nothing but this slut! He had better hurry up and get here. I am ready to go!*

Five minutes pass by, and my eyes are met by a disembodied big forest green duffel bag being squeezed through Sir Egress.

Out of breath, he expels: "All I need is ten minutes to get dressed. I booked us a three-hour session, so we have plenty of time to play. You look amazing. I have missed you so much. Okay, I am getting ready now!"

Having a love for cross-dressing, I am always amazed at the detailing in his outstanding outfits. Adorned in a deep purple colored tutu, a tight black top, purple lace gloves, black stockings, black high heels, and a beautiful long red wig, this sissy is not holding back. No one transforms himself into a slutty sissy girl quite like he does.

He has now become "she," and I take a moment to be complimentary to my little slut. "Jana, it is you, and you look stunning! Now, get on your knees, slut!"

Bashfully smiling: "Thank you, Mistress!"

There is no hesitation in her movement. I grab the stool, noose, and blindfold before making my way over to the dirty little bitch. After placing the blindfold over her eyes, I remove the suspension bar and attach the noose to its cable.

Ordering her: "Get up! On your feet. Now!"

I place my safety knife and safety scissors near the play scene. I move the stool beneath the noose and guide her body to the stool.

"Spread your legs. Now wider!" She complies, and I make my next move.

I grab the thin rope, ball stretcher, cock ring, and ball gag off the bondage table. I pull up her tutu and tuck it inside the waistband. Pushing the white panties to the side, I release the cock and balls. It is an average-sized cock that will be receiving this rubber cock ring. Pulling the fleshy illusion out and away from his—now her—body, I slip the black ring over her cock and balls and nestle it closely to her body. Next is the ball stretcher. Down with the lemon drops I pull, before securing the leather stretcher around the top part of her testicles. I fluff her pretty tutu back into place and move on.

Moaning escapes her mouth, and I know what is coming next. Only I am going to put a stop to it. "There we go, all nice and secure. Now it is time to secure your mouth and shut you up!"

Teasing her lips with the ball gag: "Open wide! I know you are a little slut and dream of having a nice big cock shutting up your mouth, but this is the only thing you are getting in this mouth today."

Crying out: "Please, Mistress!"

I place the red ball gag into her mouth and secure the black strap around the back of her head. I lock the strap of the ball gag into place with a small padlock and make her swallow the key. *That's a joke! I put the key back in its baggie for safekeeping.* Unfortunately, I continue to hear her grunting sounds, but not for long.

Still blindfolded, I back her body right up to the stool. "Slip off your heels. Reach down and feel for the stool."

She has secured her feet onto the stool. "Put out both of your hands." I place the noose into her hands. "You know what to do, slut."

Jana secures the noose around her neck. With the noose in place, I pull the rope and lock it into place. Slowly, I turn the crank on the suspension bar. Turn by turn, I watch the willowy rope strand become tighter and tighter. My wicked howl takes a seat next to me like an evil sidekick ready to cry out once more.

I'm not sure this situation warrants laughter, but here it goes again. "Now put your hands up!" Balancing on the stool, she firmly slips her fingers between the rope of the noose and her neck and holds on for literal dear life.

Cautiously watching: "Here we go, sissy slut."

I watch as her firmly planted feet begin to rise off the stool. My fingers grip the handle of the crank. Steadily, I turn the metal crank and watch the wheel revolve in an ever-changing motion that could seal her fate. Again, I turn the crank. The balls of her feet are the only part of her body still touching the stool seat. With a solid grip, her white knuckles desperately grab at the tight noose.

Laughing: "Looks like your ten little piggy friends are struggling. Hold on!"

Rope vs. crank, and I make one more turn of the crank. The tension of the rope tightens as her tippy toes dance like an unbalanced drunk after a long night out.

Hand pausing on the manual controller, I decide to go for it. "I think you can handle one more turn of the crank, tramp!" And before I finish my sentence, the wheel is cranked, and the sounds of worry scream out through her muffled ball gag.

"Let us see how much you can take, little girl!" For her, thirty seconds is going to seem like an eternity. She begins to wobble and squeal. For safety reasons, I pull the crank back to stabilize her feet.

Almost flat-footed, she regains her composure, and I watch her stance. "That is a long enough break. Back up you go, Tippy Toes Tina!"

I swiftly turn the crank and lock it in to place. I walk over to her and hold her waist. I pull up her tutu and begin to swat her cock and balls with my leather paddle. "What a crybaby you are!"

Securing her with my hands, I focus, as she manages her balancing act. I let her struggle for twenty more seconds. I know she can take it, so I push the limits.

"You know what time it is, Jana." I stand back at the suspension bar crank. In three seconds, I release the crank for one turn; two, another turn of the crank, and one. It is in this moment that I watch her tippy-toes stretch up from the wooden slab as she hangs there, barely touching the stool. Her hands, red like fire, clutch the inside rope area of the noose and her neck. As she holds all her weight, I wait for a few more seconds.

"Down you go!" I release the safety lock, hold the crank, and have her securely back down onto the stool. Carefully, I guide her down to the floor. "Take a moment to give me five deep breaths and regain your composure, slut."

Oh, but it is not over. I am not done with her yet.

I pull off the blindfold, remove the noose from around her neck, and take the ball gag out of her mouth. I place a heavy bondage collar around her neck and command her to lie down on the floor, face up.

Riding crop in hand, I command her to expose her "pussy" to me. She loves the idea of her cock being called a beautiful and tight pussy. Her sweet tutu looks pretty fluffed up on her belly, and it is time for more punishment.

With everything exposed to me: "There is your tight pussy, you little slut—*whack!*" The crop contacts the shaft area of her cock-pussy, and I land another crisp smack! Only twenty more smacks of the crop to go. "Thank me for taking your breath away!"

Squealing: "Thank you, Mistress, thank you! Thank you!"

Whack! Whack! Whack! "Pull down your tutu and cover yourself up. Act like a lady, not a slutty sissy girl. Oh, I forgot! You love being a slut! You must be punished for being so slutty!"

Bondage time. "Trust me, you won't be escaping me today."

I place a thick yoga mat on the ground. Three separate bondage straps are spread apart and placed on the mat. One strap is placed just below shoulder level, another at the waist, and the third at the ankle area. I command my sissy girl to lie down on her back. I make sure to maneuver the straps to fit exactly where I need them to secure her body.

First, I put the leather wrist and ankle restraints on her and place the padlocks through their lockable top straps. I attach the carabiners to the insides of the wrist and ankle restraints, positioning them together. Next, I put the handcuffs on her just below the leather wrist restraints. The key goes down my bra for safekeeping.

I secure two three-foot-long pieces of heavy chain to my bondage extravaganza. Each chain is attached separately around each ankle and padlocked to the leather restraints. The remaining length of both chains is strung up over her chest area and secured to the bondage neck collar. Her wrists are locked into the chain.

Now it is time for the heavy-duty zip ties. I put one around each ankle and zip-tie them together. I do the same thing around her wrists and slip the zip tie through the chain. I pull the bondage straps up and over the three parts of her body and belt her in. I use the stretch wrap to finish off her ankles. Once again, I place the blindfold over her eyes and the ball gag back into her mouth.

My laughter bursts out: "You are not getting out, slut! I told you: escape from me once, my bad, but never again. Now squirm!"

I pull up a chair. I set my timer for thirty minutes. It is time to relax and enjoy the show. I am confident in my work and do not see any weak areas that would allow her to escape.

Watching: "The struggle is real, I see. You are fucked, slut, and I just might leave you here for the rest of the night. Maybe I should leave you here for someone else to find. I would be curious to see what they would do with you."

She has managed to roll herself over. "Perfect! Now it is time to punish you for your dirty ways. I am sorry, but I don't understand all that noise coming out of your mouth!"

Back up with the tutu and smack down with the wood paddle I go. "I think I heard the word "ouch" come out of your mouth. I am glad it hurts!"

I hear more mumbling and make out one word. "You think it is funny to call me a bitch? You bratty little whore. The next ten swats will not be as nice as the first ones. This is your doing. Screw the paddle! I need something more intense."

I pull the whipping cane off the table. "I am supposed to be relaxing. I will teach you to never call me a bitch again!"

Taking the stretch wrap, I spin it around her head and seal her mouth. "This will shut you up!"

I spend my time giving her a series of whippings. Her bottom becomes red with my pleasure, and it is her own pain that will teach her a lesson.

Flailing about, she tries to miss my cane. "Looks like you are in need of corporal punishment to change your bad attitude!"

She is still unable to escape, and I roll her onto her back. I have pulled her panties to the side and extracted her ball sack. I snag the clothespins off the table and pour them onto the floor.

Pinching the clothespins all over her testicles: "Say you are sorry for calling me a bitch. Say it!"

Mumbling, she tries to get out the words: "I am sorry, Mistress. I am sorry!"

Pressing her into the floor: "Louder, slut! Or I will pinch this pussy closed with more than just clothespins!"

Screaming, she whimpers out: "I AM SORRY, MISTRESS!"

"Good," I calmly remark.

I get up and check my clock. Our time together is almost over. I pull off the clothespins from her testicles and release her right hand from the bondage restraints. I take off the stretch wrap from around her mouth and prepare her to suck cock.

I remove the blindfold and ball gag. "Open your hand."

I squirt a generous amount of white lotion into the palm of her hand. "Look down at your hand. See that big load of cum? That is from this morning when I jerked off my boyfriend. I should make you lick it up. Maybe I will bring my boyfriend in here and make you suck his big cock. What do you want to do with this cum, sissy slut?"

Looking at her hand: "I want to use it, Mistress! Please! May I use it? I promise I will be a good girl!"

Contemplating: "Do a better job at begging me. Convince me that your pussy is throbbing and wet."

Her face begins to soften, and the whining serenades me like a screeching insect at midnight. "Pleeeeease, Mistress, my pussy is so wet and throbbing! I am really, really horny and I want to be fucked! I am a dirty-sissy-whore that just wants to orgasm! Please, Mistress, please!"

"Enough!" I stop her squawking, and she proceeds with her business.

Like melted whipped cream, her pleasure cascades slowly down her cock-pussy. Satisfaction unbinds the stressors of life outside these walls, and "she" is back to a "he."

I undo his other hand and give him all the padlock keys. "Go for it! Get out!" And just like that, the little slut is out of the bondage.

Three hours flew by and our time is over. "It is time for you to change and leave." Before I know it, with his duffel bag packed, he is ready to go back into the real world.

Escorting him to the door: "See you soon, Jana! Next time, can you wear pink?"

REFLECTION: RAINA MARKS

Do flies get tired? That story wore me out! I should've flown away before this one even started. Holy crap, that was intense. Who does this for fun?

Raina wasn't sure if she was exhausted from the emotional whiplash or from trying to picture how something so extreme could be someone's idea of pleasure.

I can't even begin to imagine what his wife would think if she really knew the details of her husband's kinky session. I mean, accepting of his kink or not… this? This was dangerously crazy. And still, somehow, not cheating?

Exactly. What now?

CHAPTER 31

"I READ YOUR BOOK! SO, WHAT NOW?"

You have swallowed the truth about why men cheat on their partners with me. Now it is time to digest it. No matter where you stand, aware, unaware, betrayed, or holding the secret, this is about truth, choice, and change.

Generally speaking, brutal honesty is rare. People avoid, sugarcoat, perform, or say whatever keeps the peace. Silence and surface answers are not transparency. You have to listen deeply, express more, and ask harder. Often, the real answers, the ones that matter, can be buried under layers of fear, shame, and the stories we tell ourselves to get by.

The most important relationship you will ever have is the one with yourself. You cannot accept others if you cannot accept yourself. You cannot be honest with others if you are lying to yourself.

If you are hiding from your own truth, what chance does your relationship have?

Unspoken truths build walls between us. Behind those walls, resentment will most likely take hold and trust cannot surface. We are left asking ourselves: Can I trust my partner? Can I trust myself? Most of the time, the answer feels iffy, not from either of you being untrustworthy, but from neither of you being fully real.

We all perform. Every day, we play roles at work, with friends, and with partners. But behind closed doors, alone, the illusion breaks. No one is watching. No one is judging. You are free to be exactly who you are. Some people embrace that freedom and accept their desires and choices. Others sit alone and tear themselves apart for wanting what they want and for doing what they do. In my opinion, many people are not being completely honest and transparent. Not with themselves, and certainly not with their partners.

People can keep playing the secretive games, maintain the status quo, or they can prepare themselves for something real. Everyone faces choices: to stay in comfort zones, even when those are built on illusion or avoidance, or to take the risk of embracing truth and growth.

I walk through neighborhoods and wonder what goes on behind closed doors. Typically, I do not think about what two people are doing as a couple within the walls of their home. Instead, I wonder what they are doing as individuals when they are left alone inside their private domain.

Consider this moment: a husband, alone for hours before his wife gets home. What is he really doing? Working? Watching television? Indulging in porn? Booking a session with a Dominatrix? Talking to other women? Eating the chips his wife forbids him to eat?

Let's say he is booking that appointment with a Dominatrix. He knows what he is doing. He is clear on his needs and intentions. He has rationalized it: *I deserve this. It is not hurting anyone. I will keep it secret, and everything stays normal.*

But what if he told his wife? Would she divorce him? Shame him?

Never trust him again? Or would she surprise him by asking questions, finding a solution, or maybe even accepting what he wants? What would you do?

Begin with honesty. Communicate. Actively listen. Ask yourself questions. Ask your partner questions. What are you hiding from? What am I hiding from? Who am I when no one is watching? What do I really want and need? What is the truth I am afraid to face?

Uncovering your truth is not easy and asking for his is not either. It can feel like a mountain of fear standing between you and the freedom to say what you want, need, and feel. Vulnerability is not typically comfortable. It is exposing and can feel paralyzing.

People are judgmental, and society labels certain desires "unacceptable." That little voice in your head whispers: *You are wrong. You are weird. You will be rejected.* You shut down, hide, or offer the world a curated version of yourself. This doesn't stem from being a bad person; it comes from the weight of judgment feeling heavier than the lie. But here is the problem: when you deny your truth to fit in, you don't just hide… you disconnect.

This, I believe, is a big part of why people cheat. This is why they run from real conversations. Honesty takes courage. Open, transparent communication is the only thing that can change the trajectory. It won't be perfect, and it might hurt, but it is the only way to build a relationship rooted in trust instead of performance.

Once more, these words come back to me.

I also believe that a significant reason why men cheat is that some are simply manipulative assholes. They selfishly take advantage of others, wanting the best of all worlds while refusing to be held accountable for the fallout they leave behind. You must discern which man is standing in front of you: the one who hides because he fears your judgment, or the one who hides because he enjoys the game.

Each of us is built in our own unique way. We carry different wounds, beliefs, and ways of expressing ourselves. Listen. Really listen. Not to respond, but to understand. When someone shares something hard, do not look away. Meet them there; be present, patient, and kind. Give yourself the same grace. Even when truths are hard to say, hard to hear, or hard to live with, they remain true.

Breaking free from fear, shame, and insecurity is not easy. But it is necessary. Being authentic might ruffle feathers and challenge comfort zones. It might go against what is "acceptable." But living in chains that were not made for you? That is worse than standing in your truth: loud, raw, and unfiltered.

It starts with you. Get to know yourself. Be brutally honest. Get real. What is your truth? And what are you going to do about it?

Start the Conversations

- Ask questions.
- Share secrets.
- Step outside your comfort zone and take a risk.
- Be vulnerable.
- Be honest with others.
- Treat people like stories. Pretend the person in front of you is a book. Read the whole book, not just a few chapters.

Build Better Connections

- Ask yourself the same questions you want to ask others.
- Figure out your dealbreakers.
- Be open to feedback.
- Try to understand others' perspectives.

Say What You Mean

- Mean what you say.
- Provide clear and concise responses.
- Stop performing and start telling the truth.
- No filters. No performances. Silence and half-truths will only build walls.

Open Up and Take the Chance

- Find the courage to have hard, deep conversations.
- There is always an opportunity to try, and that chance starts now.
- Create a safe space for effective communication.
- Think of the aftermath of your actions. This might stop you from making bad choices.

Know Your Limits

- What are your boundaries?
- Do not settle. Do not overly tolerate.
- Take care of yourself first!

Connect the Dots

- Listen actively and look for patterns.
- Trust your intuition.
- If you doubt it, question it.

Expand Your Thinking

- Step outside the box.
- Be curious about each other's differences.
- Be there for the discomforts of real connection.
- Be Free. Be Real. Be Authentic.

The Moment of Truth: For the Woman Choosing to Move Forward with a New Partner

You have asked the real questions, the ones most people shy away from, the ones that make others uncomfortable because they fear what the answers might reveal. You have had honest conversations about sex, BDSM, Kink, Fetish, fantasies, desires, and more. Through it all, you have stayed true to who you are as an individual, including your values, your boundaries, your quirks, and your needs.

Now, with everything laid bare, you face the crucial decision: do you want to move forward with this person or not? This is the moment where clarity takes over. Not the haze of fantasy, not the allure of potential, but the unfiltered truth. Understanding what someone wants is only the first step. The real question is whether you are willing and able to meet them there and if doing so aligns with your own needs, boundaries, and vision for your future. The truth is your compass, and your choice is your power.

For the Woman Who Wants to Know More About Her Man: Unlock the Conversations

What if you are not starting fresh? What if you are standing in front of the man you are already with, wondering how to have the conversations you have never had? You do not necessarily want to control him; you want to know him. All of him.

Sit him down and ask questions. Connect. Share your thoughts and needs as well. Ask the questions that matter, the ones that get past the surface. Ask about what he wants. What he fantasizes about. What he might be ashamed of. What he is afraid to say since he does not know how you will respond. Ask with softness, but do not hold back. You are not being "too much." You are being honest, intentional, and present.

Watch how he responds, not just with words, but with energy. Does he open up? Or does he shut down? That will tell you a lot. This is not about catching him off guard or finding something "wrong." You want to make room for something real. This is about intimacy, the kind that requires courage.

The truth is: if you do not ask and share, the two of you might keep hiding or might never uncover the truth. This is not necessarily out of malice, but out of habit or fear. That fear will quietly build distance between you.

So no, you are not crazy for wanting to know more. You are just brave enough to find out. You are not here to settle for safe versions of intimacy. You are here for the real thing.

For the Suspicious Woman: Before You Ask, Be Ready to Hear Anything

Whether it is about cheating, desires, kink, secrets, or fantasies, ask only if you are prepared to face the full truth. Honestly, this holds true no matter what the conversation is about.

The conversation is just a door. You get to decide if you walk through it into healing, clarity, or closure. You might decide to slam it shut and reclaim your power in silence. Recognize that you have the right to protect your peace, maintain your boundaries, and walk away without needing to explain, defend, or justify yourself.

Before you go asking him, "Is there someone else?" Before you sit across from him, trying to have the conversation that might shatter your chest wide open, please ground yourself. In reality, the truth does not always show up naked. Sometimes it shows up in latex. Sometimes it does not even involve sex, just secrets, desire, and the kind of emotional intimacy he never gave to you.

You might hear specific details about his secrets, kinks, or fantasies. You might find out he cheated, is having an affair, or has been in contact with a person for hire. You may find out he is paying someone like me to play out a fantasy where he is not judged, not challenged, or required to be the man you recognize. You might hear that what he needs is not even physical; it is psychological. Or he might avoid every question you ask with intent and defense.

This honesty could be difficult for you to hear, and maybe you will want to shut down. You might want to scream, cry, beg, or leave. Maybe you will. It is okay to break down, but do not break down alone. Get support. Do not isolate yourself.

This honesty might also spark new levels of excitement. It could awaken parts of you that have been numb, stir your curiosity, or even turn you on. Both responses, grief or thrill, are valid. Truth is not betrayal; hiding it is.

Kinks do not ruin relationships; lies, secrets, and emotional dishonesty do. The betrayal is not that he has a desire. The betrayal is that he denied you the right to choose whether you could meet him there or not.

Before You Talk: A Checklist

- I have cleared my head with no distractions and no noise.
- Feel what you are feeling without judgment. This is your truth. Claim it. Name your fears and your hopes.
- Remind yourself: Do not beg. Do not explain yourself to death. Do not get loud to prove your pain.
- Get clear on what you know, what you need, and what you will no longer accept. I know exactly what I need to ask.
- I have set my boundaries and I am ready to enforce them. Know what you will accept and what you will not. If the answer breaks you, how will you handle the rush of feelings? If he lies, will you call it?
- Prepare for any truth, good or bad. The conversation might not go how you want. He might confess. He might deny. He might attack. Be ready to hear things that hurt, confuse, or shock you.
- Your power lies in your ability to listen without losing yourself.
- Have your exit strategy. I have a safe place to go if I need to leave. Have a friend on standby, a safe space to breathe, and

a plan to protect your heart. Your emotional and physical safety is non-negotiable.

- I have told at least one trusted person where I will be and what is happening.
- I have reminded myself: I am worthy of honesty and respect.
- I am open to listening while still staying grounded in myself.
- I have practiced breathing through the shock, anger, or pain.
- I am ready to say enough if the truth is not what I deserve.
- I understand that asking for the truth means I cannot expect things to stay the same.
- Prepare and create a safe space to have these conversations.
- "I have decided what *enough* looks like for today." I do not have to solve the whole marriage in one talk. I can just aim for *one* truth today.

Journal This:

- Define love.
- How am I feeling?
- What are my questions? Identify the key questions that matter most. Think about how different answers might impact your choices.
- What are my emotional non-negotiables?
- What does safety actually look like in my body, not just in theory?
- What version of myself did I abandon to keep this relationship alive?
- What do I need from him to feel whole again, and what do I need from myself?
- If he has lied or cheated, do I want out of this relationship?
- What is my plan if walking away becomes the right choice?
- "I will not interrogate!" Make a list of ideas that work for you to stay in control. This protects you from spiraling into defensiveness or confusion. If he deflects, minimizes,

or gets defensive, stay grounded in your original purpose: clarity, not chaos. What does staying grounded look like to you?

- Take a moment before speaking and think: If he says yes, what steps can I take to protect myself emotionally, financially, and practically?
- Also consider: If he says no, what would help you trust or verify that answer? Write out ways he can verify that answer.
- Think ten steps ahead. Be prepared.

Remind Yourself: You Are Enough

- No matter what comes out of his mouth, your worth is not tied to his honesty or his lies. You are whole. You are fierce. You deserve a truth that honors you.
- Give yourself permission to hurt, to question, and still choose to love.
- Self-respect, not sacrifice.

The Truth Bomb—Now What?

Maybe it was "traditional" cheating, or maybe it was with a Professional Dominatrix. Maybe it was not "sex," but it was still betrayal. Maybe it was a kink you never saw coming or a version of him you do not recognize and do not want to.

If he cheated, emotionally or otherwise, it was not just about you. It might have been about a part of himself he could not share. Maybe he needed to feel like someone else for a while, free from expectations, judgment, or the weight of being seen a certain way. Maybe he did not have the tools or courage to bring that truth into the relationship, so he went elsewhere with it. This doesn't stem from a lack of caring, but from not knowing how to hold both parts of himself in front of you. He did not want permission, and in some way, he never meant for you to find out. This was not out of malice, but to avoid facing the consequences.

But now you know. Now that you do, you need to tell yourself the truth first: *I might not be what he needs. And he might not be what I deserve.* Or: *This is a workable situation, and I will move forward with him as openly as possible.*

You are not weak for being shocked. You are not naive for not knowing or for hoping it was not true. You are damn powerful if you can hear the truth and face it. Now here you are, sitting in the aftermath. The silence. The ache. The part where everything is real and nothing feels right.

Detach from the fantasy. Let go of the version of him you built in your mind: the loyal partner, the honest man, the one who would never choose to hurt you like this. That version may have felt real, but it was built on hope, not fact. Clinging to it keeps you tied to someone who does not exist in the way you believed.

Please Consider:

- Know the difference between being open and being erased. Being curious about someone's desires does not mean losing yourself. This is not about judging kinks. Were you offered the truth, ever given a chance to consent, or fed a lie while decisions were made behind your back?
- Stand in your center. If the truth guts you, makes you nauseous, enraged, or devastated, that is your nervous system ringing the alarm. It is intuition speaking. Just because someone else is comfortable with a certain reality does not mean you have to be. You are allowed to say: This is too much. This is not mine to hold.
- Do not spiritualize, sexualize, or justify betrayal. "This is just what men do." "It is my fault for not being enough." "I should have been more adventurous." "Maybe it is his trauma; I should be understanding." These are escape routes

designed to avoid pain and they will not heal you. Betrayal is betrayal, no matter how evolved or empathetic you try to be.

- You do not need to become a Dominatrix, porn star, therapist, mind-reader, or the other woman to keep your man. You do not have to decode him to be worthy. You can hold both things at once: "Your kink is valid. But your betrayal is not." And: "Your truth matters. But so does mine." This is about self-respect, not judgment.

- You get to walk away, even if he did not hit you, scream at you, or cheat in the "traditional" sense. Emotional betrayal, secrecy, and manipulation count. If your boundaries were violated or your consent bypassed, that is real. Emotional erosion is just as damaging as physical harm, sometimes more.

- You do not owe anyone a performance of healing. You do not have to "rise above" in a way that makes others comfortable. Healing does not have to look graceful; it looks like crying on the floor, blocking his number, unfollowing his social media, screaming in your car. That is healing too.

- This is not your failure. It is his exposure. The truth did not break anything; it revealed what was already fractured. What is being asked of you now is to choose yourself in the aftermath. Over and over. Even when it hurts. Especially when it hurts.

- There is nothing wrong with wanting safety, transparency, and mutual respect. These are not "vanilla" values; they are basic human needs. Wanting to feel safe, seen, and secure is not close-minded; it is intelligent. It is emotionally literate. It is healthy.

- Let the ending teach you, but do not let it define you. Yes, this changed you. Yes, it cracked you open. But you are not what he did. You are what you choose next. You are the boundaries you draw, the self you return to, the truth you finally honor. You are your own rescue.

- Or, if you are willing, you can fuel your new reality with positivity, openness, compromise, and negotiation. That is also your choice.

Ask yourself and be brutally honest:

- Can I respect him after this?
- Do I feel emotionally safe anymore?
- Would I be compromising myself to stay?
- Can I trust him to be honest going forward, or am I now in a permanent guessing game?
- Can I build something real from a foundation that cracked beneath me?
- Am I only staying because I can't afford to leave or pay to be on my own? (If your answer is yes, please figure it out. Dependency is a prison. Map your exit, gather your resources, and reclaim your financial breath so that staying becomes a choice, not a sentence.)

Whatever your answer, you do not need to explain it to anyone. Not to him, and not to anyone else.

Do not mistake "willingness to stay" for healing. Some women stay because they feel stuck, scared, or helpless. Some stay because they feel their commitment of love demands it. But staying without change is self-abandonment. If he is not willing to do the work— therapy, transparency, accountability—you are not in a relationship. You are in an emotional hostage situation. Staying is only brave if you are not betraying yourself.

If you leave, leave with power, not shame. If your gut says, *I cannot unsee this. I cannot come back from this,* trust it. You are not crazy. You are not dramatic. You are finally awake. And if you stay? Stay with both eyes open and a list of non-negotiables that are not up for debate.

Now that you know, do not unhear the words. You do not have to be perfect in your pain. You do not have to forgive on demand or understand it all right now. Go forward, whether with him, without him, or deep into your own healing. Do not go silently. "I will not betray myself to keep you comfortable in your lies." You will know what is next when you are ready. It is not that you have it all figured out, but that you trusted yourself enough to feel it. And that is enough.

For the Woman Choosing to Stay After the Truth Breaks Her Open

You know. The truth is out. The betrayal is no longer hidden in shadows or brushed off as "just a mistake." He cheated with a Professional Dominatrix, another woman, or his own secrets. Maybe it was not cheating in the way most people define it, or maybe it was. Whichever it was, it was a betrayal of trust, desire, and emotional intimacy. And yet, here you are, still considering staying.

Why?

Some part of you believes there is still something left to save. Your love does not evaporate just because of betrayal. Your mind, open, wise, and resilient, is willing to see if this breakdown could become the start of a new truth. Just know: Staying is not a reward for his lies. It is a choice you make only if he is willing to earn it. This is not about being "cool" with what he did. This is not about swallowing your pain to keep the peace. This is about raw, unfiltered accountability. If you stay, it is not because you are desperate. It is that you are demanding a new foundation, one built on transparency, not secrets.

Here is what that looks like:

- You can stay and still keep your self-respect. But only if he is doing the work: therapy, transparency, accountability. No excuses.

- You can forgive, but forgiveness is not a free pass. It is a process, and it requires him to show up, every damn day, with nothing left to hide.
- You can compromise, but you will not contort your soul to fit into someone else's kink, someone else's lies, or someone else's comfort. Your boundaries are not negotiable.
- You are not here to approve of his lies. You are here for the full story, on the table, with nothing left in the shadows.
- You want to understand what he was seeking that he did not know how to ask you for. But understanding is not the same as tolerating. If he cannot answer your questions, if he cannot face the disaster he caused, then staying is just another form of self-betrayal.
- You are negotiating for your power, not his pleasure. If he wants to stand by your side, he will have to earn it, not with apologies, but with action.

Words to add to your new rulebook:

- No more emotional crumbs. No more watered-down truths. No more "I was afraid to tell you."
- No more escaping into fantasy to avoid emotional accountability. If he wants you, he gets all of you: your pain, your questions, and your conditions.
- No more "I do not know how to tell you." He is a grown man. He will figure it out.
- If he is not willing to face himself, to take accountability, or to show up with humility and transparency, then you are not in a relationship.
- If he is not willing to burn down the lies and rebuild with you, then staying is just another way of abandoning yourself.

Ask yourself:

- Is he doing the work, or just waiting for me to "get over it"?
- Is he giving me real transparency, or just performing remorse until things blow over?
- Are we rebuilding something stronger, or are we just patching up the same broken structure?

Love can survive betrayal. But only if the betrayer is willing to fight for it. If he is not, then the choice is already made. If you choose to stay, it will not be for the man who lied. It will be for the man who is willing to tell the truth and love you out loud in every shade of it.

Your decision to stay is not a weakness. It is warriorship. You are not surrendering. You are choosing from your whole and awakened self. This chapter does not tell you what to do. It gives you back the tools, the sword, and the match. What you burn, rebuild, or walk away from is up to you. You get to decide what you do next. But do not forget: no man, no kink, and no fantasy is ever worth trading your truth for silence.

My Reflection: I Didn't Write This Book to Defend Him or Destroy Him

I wrote this book so you can understand him. Not knowing, or pretending not to see it, will not protect you. You need to understand the layers of the *potential Cheater* and *Cheater's* betrayal, or you will never be able to protect yourself from it.

Ultimately, this understanding is not just for your survival; it is for his transformation. It is for him to see himself in these pages, to confront the choices he has made, and to learn. He must learn what to do and what not to do. Only when he faces the truth can he begin to change. Only when you both see clearly can you decide what comes next.

Too many women sit in silence, spinning in confusion, and hiding under betrayals they cannot even name. Some do not even realize a Dominatrix could be part of their story. Just because you think your man would never be that guy does not mean he is not already on that path or already "my guy."

Women are often expected to swallow the pain, to be "understanding," and to rise above what should never have happened. That expectation is not compassion; it is conditioning. It is designed to protect the ones who caused the harm.

Please understand this: I know the world tends to tell women to be soft, forgiving, and silent, especially when we have been hurt. Asking a woman to be understanding in the face of betrayal is just another way to shield the man from consequences. Her frustration is not a threat; it is the moment the truth finally rises to the surface.

Whether you stay or you go, do not fear the silence of a quiet house. That silence is far more peaceful than the noise of a thousand lies. If you walk away, you aren't "losing" him; you are gaining yourself. You are trading a scripted performance for an unwritten future. And in that future, you are the one holding the pen.

Love can still exist inside betrayal. From the ashes, if both parties are brave enough and honest enough, something deeper can be born. Self-love can also take shape. Once the light is on, you have a choice: keep going in a potential or existing relationship, walk away, or rebuild something new. This time, you will be making that choice fully awake.

REFLECTION: RAINA MARKS

Results are in.

Nothing!

Disappointed.

He didn't call or text back.

I keep telling myself. Remember, Raina, you have put all these new doubts into your head. He hasn't done anything for you to question him. He thinks today is like any other day.

Maybe this silence between us is exactly what I needed, a moment to pause and listen to my own thoughts. Maybe this is less about him and more about me figuring out what I want, for me. And from him.

I owe it to both of us to be honest—like really honest—with who I am, what I need, and what I can no longer keep shoving under the rug. General "talking" won't cut it anymore. I need to strip it down and say the words that make me nervous. That's the only way this relationship is going to stretch into something more open and transparent.

And honestly? Maybe he's been avoiding certain conversations because he knows I've only been giving him the safe, edited version of myself. That wouldn't be unfair. It's true! I do hold back. I swallow my thoughts until they dissolve. But I've got this feeling he sees more of me than I realize. Maybe he's just waiting for me to catch up to myself or doesn't want to be pushy.

Realizing. *My leather collection? I am the one completely obsessed with leather, not him. It's me. I've been the leather lover all along and I know this. I told him so! I just didn't overthink it all the details.*

It started way back in high school, when the hottest guy in my class walked in smelling like cologne-soaked confidence, zipped up in a leather jacket that could melt a girl on sight. I used to steal it off his back just so I could wear it for the rest of class and imagine making out with him right there on the desk. Leather did something to me; it flipped a switch. And it never flipped back.

Early in our relationship, I told my husband about my love for leather. I asked him to wear cologne-drenched jackets for me, and he did. He still does. He must have figured it out. My man has been silently feeding my kink with every leathery gift he's ever wrapped up for me.

Mr. Marks, you sneaky, sexy genius. Well, played!

Raina hugs the book to her chest and takes a deep breath. *One more thing. I need to trust my gut. My intuition isn't whispering, it's screaming. And it's saying: My husband is not a cheater. I believe that with every ounce of who I am.*

Thank God, I avoided the temptation to snoop. If I had gone through his office drawers, I would have broken a level of trust. Something I would have regretted.

CHAPTER 32

POWER OF KNOWLEDGE: TRUTH, TRAUMA, & TURNING POINTS

*T*his account is based on my personal experiences and memories. Names, identifying details, and some events have been changed to protect privacy.

The year was 2007. For one last time, I lifted my boulder of a suitcase and slipped it into the trunk of my car. My journey as a Professional Dominatrix was far from over. Still, as a mother, volunteer, and businesswoman, I had other callings to attend to, build, and nurture. The years behind me had set the stage for the years to come, a life where Dominating, modeling, and producing fetish films would continue and evolve into a full scope of mainstream production work.

As the trunk closed, I paused to reflect on my journey and the countless hours I had spent with men from all over the globe. Being a Dominatrix has been one of my many callings, a mission grounded in connection, intention, and a desire to leave a meaningful mark on those around me.

My heart does not just beat; it leads. It is driven by something much bigger than me: a deep, undeniable need to help, to guide, to give, and to show up for people in ways that actually matter. Whether I am mentoring, motivating, or simply holding space for someone to be raw and real, this purpose is not a phase. It is part of every layer of my life, and it always will be.

One of my greatest gifts has been the ability to stay receptive to a person's views, desires, ideas, and honesty. It is not always easy to be present without judgment, but when it is done, I witness powerful transformations. They reveal the parts of themselves they usually hide from the world. In those moments, I am reminded of the importance of creating safe and accepting environments where no one has to pretend. The truth is, we are all just trying to be understood. We want to feel like we matter. We want to be seen, heard, and accepted for exactly who we are.

Remaining open does not mean I agree with everything I hear. It means I am listening. I am learning. I am choosing curiosity over control and empathy over ego. That openness has shaped how I connect with others, not just in my professional life, but in my personal relationships as well.

Being able to honor someone's truth, even when it is different from mine, is a privilege. Through that exchange, both of us are changed for the better. I have come to realize that people like me are gateways. We provide the entry point into the truth and a haven where people can safely lay down their secrets and fantasies without shame, fear, or judgment. Sometimes all it takes is an open ear, a little kindness, and a moment of compassion. It is the ability to sit still with someone and say, "I see you!"

I looked up into my rearview mirror as I drove away. I could see the Dungeon begin to fade in the distance. Looking ahead, I smiled with the eternal knowing that I was only getting started. The stories I could tell. The insights and lessons I could share. *One day, one day!*

In that moment, one particular event from my past stood out—a harrowing experience that would leave an indelible mark on my soul. Little did I know that a seemingly ordinary day back in the mid-seventies would take a dark turn, forever altering the course of my life. Simultaneously, it granted me some of the most significant lessons that would guide my journey.

1977

Kidnapped by my father and taken back east, I was thrust into a nightmare that would test the limits of my overall strength and resilience.

The unfortunate events that happened when I was a seven and eight years old, both in the moment and over future reflection, have shown me the innermost depths of the sexually eager man.

I am jolted by the fact that many voracious men seem to operate the same way, always on the hunt to satisfy their carnal cravings. I have found there is a common momentum among many of them. Once aroused, they become powered by their sexual endeavors. The neurological system inside their brains becomes fixated, a laser-focused fixation that overrides logic and consequence. It's like a thought they can't turn off, an obsession that consumes their attention and pulls them deeper into desire, need, and fantasy. Everything else fades into the background and reality begins to blur as their mind anchors itself to that singular craving. The Cock: Ejaculation and satisfaction!

Having experienced sexual abuse for the first time at the age of seven years old, I remember examining my perpetrator's rituals. My juvenile brain probed into my abuser's psyche, and over the course of several months, I began to turn the tables on him. He was no longer in control. I was! He was simple. His innermost depths weren't so deep after all, and I knew it.

What was purely sexual for him was about to be engulfed in an entangled web of what women are beautifully woven from: emotion, intellect, intuition, embodiment, and power.

Since this young man lived under the same roof as me, his under-the-bed den that hosted his sexual feasts would not be the only hideout of my existence. I knew I had no way to physically escape him, but this meant that he could not escape me either. I was everywhere! This creep was no longer able to simply feed on his sexual endeavors and be done with me. Soon, he had to attend to a young girl who found a way to drive him mentally insane.

I began to question his actions. I questioned where he was going, what he was doing, and with whom he was doing it. I followed him to social events, and I suffocated his brain with my simulated emotional and logical dependence. Once I discovered his disdain for my behaviors, I applied intense pressure. The more emotional I became, the more distance I put between us. The more logical I became, the clearer and more consistent my patterns were.

My persistence aroused something different inside of him, but this time it was something non-sexual. He was getting increasingly angrier with me, and his sexual appetite for my youthful meat began to dissipate. My emotional needs were not what he had signed up for, and he was not prepared for my emotional demands. I became a problem for him!

My sexual abuser, who in the beginning verbally threatened me to cover up his actions, was now beginning to fear that his threats would make their way out of my mouth and into the ears of an adult. He realized that I was not a powerless victim and that I was becoming a vigilant liability.

I vividly recall a moment I experienced with this young man long after we began our emotional dance. We were swimming in the lake. He was submerged in the water, swimming around my legs. I looked down into the murky silence and had two thoughts. *One: I could wrap my legs around your neck and kill you. But I will not, because instead, two: I now have you right where I want you, and you will never sexually abuse me again.*

As his head rose above the water, I looked down into his piercing eyes. With a serious smirk, I nodded—a silent pact with my own power—and turned to walk back onto the shore. In that moment, it was as if my youthful innocence was gone, and I remember feeling like a grown woman. No, I would never be the same.

I was no longer just a young girl, but an 8-year-old girl with an older inner companion. "Little Me," my inner child, would meet "Adult Me" very early on in life. I came to understand that my innocence was not actually gone; it was being protected by an older, fiercer guardian because it had to be. From that moment on, "Adult Me" and "Little Me" continued their journey. While the memories did not disappear, I never felt my sexual assaulter's hands on me again.

The story back east continues, and all began to fade into another dimension a few months later.

All was calm until the ghostly shadows attached themselves to the school bus that winter day. Stepping up onto the entry stairs of the mustard-colored transporter, I felt an unfamiliar hand grab the back of my neck. With confusion, I wondered if it could be him, my sexual abuser, the one who stole a virgin's delicate bud.

It was not him. The question remained: who?

My echoes screamed in the dust as I was being dragged through the dirt. Gone. I was kidnapped for a second time, taken away from one nightmare to another. I was back with my mother, with whom I experienced physical, mental, and emotional abuse. Unfortunately, back in the Golden State, I would soon be targeted again by other sexually abusive men and their desperate needs.

After years of continuous sexual assaults by no fewer than a dozen horny thieves, I began to understand "man" more and more. Something deep inside me was realizing how "sexual men" and my "perpetrators of sexual abuse" functioned. It was obvious to me that I needed to be six steps ahead of these sexual beasts. I became more calculated, patient, knowledgeable, and curious.

In my teenage years, I learned how to "lean in—to get out" and escape my sexual assaulters. I leaned in through manipulation and control. I got out through trickery. Leading them to believe they had me, I used my internal tease and denial techniques to gain my footing and then ran like hell.

As a young woman, I found my center and leaned into the study of control, refining my explorative choreography with men. I explored and groomed my natural Dominance, and men quickly became "church mice" scattering around for me to catch and release.

In the crucible of my youth, I was forged not with the gentle hands of love, but with the harsh, unyielding grip of abuse. Emotional, mental, physical, and sexual trials, *though brutal*, did not break me. Instead, they ignited within me a resilience as unyielding as the stars and as profound as the deepest oceans. Emerging from the shadows of my trauma, I found not just survival but a strength that transcended my suffering.

In my journey as a Dominatrix, I wield this strength with purpose and intention. My past has granted me a unique insight into the human psyche, allowing me to better understand those who seek my services. Through this work, I offer more than just Dominance in the Dungeon. I provide a confessional where my clients can find insight, comfort, care, and protection.

Through the alchemy of my own healing, I have transmuted pain into power. I extend this metamorphosis to those who enter my realm, guiding them towards their own transparency, honesty, liberation, and wholeness. I contribute to the openness of humanity in a safe and nurturing way.

My evolution from victim to victor has equipped me with the empathy and fortitude to help others navigate their own paths to healing and satisfaction. I have proven that even the darkest days can give way to the most radiant tunnels of light. My path through the shadows of abuse has illuminated the clear boundaries that distinguish non-consensual violence from the consensual, respectful, and negotiated power exchange of BDSM play.

I understand my calling as to why—and how—I became a Professional Dominatrix. With age comes perspective, and I have earned mine through every twist, turn, and trench life has given me. I was not handed this role; I uncovered it.

That "one day" I once thought of is finally here! The day I get to share with you the valuable insights I have gathered from countless encounters with men from around the world. **Cheaters or not!**

Whether in a professional or personal capacity, I will always be a Dominatrix at heart with a deep and meaningful purpose. Some things in life arrive without our choosing and without a clear explanation. But one thing is certain: nothing comes to us without purpose.

My life has been a poetic tale of beauty, chaos, and thievery. Yet, some things cannot be stolen or brutally glorified: the resilience, experience, and knowledge I have gained along the way. I have come to believe that knowledge is power, and what we know and understand should be shared with others. My ears are open. Are yours?

If I could tell my twenty-year-old self something, it would be this: I said it earlier in this book, and I will say it again.

"The most important relationship you will ever have is the one you have with yourself."

Find a way to be your own best friend. Being your own best friend means showing up for yourself with the same respect, loyalty, care, and honesty you would give someone you love. This is not about isolation or shutting people out. What matters is building a solid inner foundation so your worth is not dependent on anyone else's approval or presence.

It's not always easy, but when you have your own back, you stop taking less than you need and start demanding what you truly deserve. Do not settle for less than your worth. **Ever.**

I am a woman of empowerment and transformation. I reclaimed my own narrative, and I have found authority in what I have lived. Through years of study—books, bodies, truth, and both personal and professional experience—I have gained my most vital survival tool of all: *KNOWLEDGE.*

I am.
The Professional Dominatrix.
The Real Deal!
What is your fantasy?

REFLECTION: RAINA MARKS—WHEN THE BOOK CLOSES, THE REAL TALK BEGINS

With the weight of the book tilting heavily in her lap, Raina Marks flexes her fingers: acknowledging the subtle reminder of time spent in thought. Most of the pages now sit on the left, signaling she was nearing the end—not just of the book, but of something else too. An irreversible change had begun.

This book has stirred something in me. Something real.

She didn't marry her husband to play it safe or drift into some autopilot version of love. She married him because she wanted it all: a partnership built on honesty, fueled by passion, and committed to growth.

Raina stood up, made her way to the bedroom, and sat at the edge of the bed with a heavy kind of stillness. *It's on us. We have to be willing to ask the hard questions, the awkward ones, the ones that might make us feel uncomfortable. Those are the conversations that should bring us closer, not further apart.*

She glanced down at the book still in her hands. The cover now felt less like a curiosity and more like a window. *I want to be the woman who explores my man's fantasies, not the one left out of them. I want to feel safe sharing mine too!*

She wasn't delusional. She knew the potential for cheating was real, anywhere and at any time, in any relationship. *No one is immune. Ignoring that truth doesn't protect you from it. Only honesty and transparency do.*

How am I ever going to know what he really needs if we don't talk about it? And how will he know what I want if I keep pretending I'm fine?

The thoughts repeated in her head: *What if he judges me? What if I judge him? What if it ruins the way we see each other? What if I'm too much? Or not enough?*

But then came the louder question: *What if I never speak up at all and eventually lose him to someone else who isn't afraid to?*

That thought settled deep in her gut. No. She wouldn't let silence be the reason their relationship fell apart, especially now that she knew better. *I see just how crucial it is to communicate: not casually, but completely. If cheating can be avoided through honesty and transparency, why the hell wouldn't we go there?*

Placing it perfectly on the nightstand, she angled it just right. The dim light caught the cover, casting a gleam over the bold title. It wasn't just a book anymore. It was a silent invitation. A message. A challenge. And Mr. Marks wouldn't miss it.

The next morning rose with quiet ease. Sunlight streamed through the curtains, casting soft shadows across the floor, but Raina's mind raced. Her body moved through routine, coffee, shower, and emails, but her thoughts were far from ordinary. She found herself flipping mental pages: words she'd read the day before had planted a seed of curiosity, slight discomfort, and desire. Now, it all looped on repeat in her head.

By midday, she'd tackled the remaining poolside mess and a few chores in the kitchen. With the countertops wiped down and the dishes put away, she stood in the center of the kitchen for a moment, looking around like she'd forgotten what came next.

The silence in the house felt thick, like it was holding its breath.

Buzz. A curious housefly skimmed past her cheek and landed on the window ledge. Her eyes narrowed. "Not today," she muttered, reaching for the flyswatter. Raina stalked across the room, hunting down the fly that seemed to mock her with its freedom.

I see you're unbothered and full of chaotic joy, she thought, watching the fly dart through the air.

Before reading the book, Raina might not have noticed its unrestrained flight: a wild, untamed movement that once felt so distant from her own tightly wound thoughts. But today felt different. She didn't feel trapped; she didn't feel powerless. The tension she hadn't even known she was carrying had started to release. She was exhilarated by the idea of honest freedom, moving with intention, and reflecting with courage.

There it was: wings still, perched on the edge of the fruit bowl. She crept closer, one slow step, then another. Just as she raised her arm to strike, she heard a thud and rustle from the front room.

"Mr. Marks, is that you?" she called out.

A loud "Hey you!" boomed back, casual and warm: his signature sound that always brought her comfort.

Grinning, Raina ran into the living room. Without hesitation, she playfully swatted her husband's ass with the flyswatter and smiled like a woman on a mission. "Welcome home, babe!"

She leaned in with a spark in her eyes: "Asher… we need to talk!"

This isn't the end of their story. It is the start of their complete honesty.

I spy *Effective Communication* in their near future...

CHAPTER 33

BONUS CHAPTER— INTERACTIVE FANTASY SESSION: SENSUALLY SAVAGED

This chapter presents a fantasy session story involving consenting adults only. All scenarios are fictionalized composites inspired by themes from my professional practice, and identifying details have been altered to protect privacy. The story explores adult BDSM dynamics, trust, and power exchange within a safe, consensual, and controlled environment.

Character Development: *You, the reader! Or, the choice is yours!*

Character Development: *A Professional Dominatrix. She is Dominant, creative, imaginative, passionate, sensual, and wickedly charged. She has been and will always be… ME!*

Find a quiet moment and insert your earbuds for this interactive session. The following story is a true testament to my Dominant endeavors. Every scene I conduct has the following pieces of myself.

Open up your favorite music platform—whether it's YouTube, Spotify, Tidal, Apple Music, or even Alexa. Search for the songs listed below and either queue them up into a playlist or play them one by one as you read.

When a song is still playing and you reach the next one, pause your reading until it finishes. Then start the next track and continue.

You'll see "**Start Track**" at the beginning of each section—that's your cue to hit play!

Now turn up the music and join me!

Playlist

Track 1:
"Fundamentum" – *Lesiem*
Track 2:
"Running Up That Hill" – *Placebo*
Track 3:
"I'll Make You Love Me" – *Kat Leon*
Track 4:
"Angel" – *Massive Attack*
Track 5:
"King" – *Amanati*

Silence your phone. Put up the "Do Not Disturb" sign. Relax, breathe, and join me on this journey where sensual art meets reality… inside of my mind. And now yours!

Let us begin!

Disrupting the energy, the Dungeon room becomes still. I have entered. And soon, you will too!

Start Track 1 and *Slowly* Begin to Read
Track 1:
"Fundamentum" – *Lesiem*

The preparations are made, and I will now await your arrival.

You begin to hear the music as you approach my lair. Covering your chest with your hand, you press against your heart. The vibrations press back against your chest as you feel the energy fill up your soul.

Pushing open the door, you become instantly captivated.

The room is dark. A single candle captures my presence, and you stand firmly at the threshold.

Before you, I sit on my mahogany throne. My face is draped with cascading dark lace; my fingers tracing the black velvet armrest. Powerfully and mysteriously drawing you into me.

Nothing is moving but the rise and fall of your torso. Finding it hard to breathe, you reach inwardly to gasp for air.

Penetrating my interest, I focus on your behaviors and calculate my plan.

Slowly, I rise to my feet. Overlapping my sable cloak, the lace falls to the floor, creating a veil of hidden enchantment.

Allured by my magnetism, you take several steps forward, only to be ceased by the gesture of my hand that tells you to stop.

Anticipation fills the space. Feeling the moment, our distance pulsates, and with every vital drum, it is time for me to advance. I move forward.

Enthralling you with the idea of me, my intoxicating blends of sensuality and enigmatic ways begin to stimulate your senses.

My undeniable essence invites you into the forbidden, and I am about to make you mine.

Steadily, I circle you, moving in more closely with every turn.

I find you appealing: a vision that makes me yearn for more of you.

I dare you to tremble!

Face to face, you feel my stare rip through your existence. Our intensity grows in the profound soundlessness that encompasses US.

Gently, my hand serenades your face with vitality before I gently close your eyelids with my finger.

Waiting. Contemplating. Watching you.

You have become my prey. Vulnerable. Susceptible. Soon to be exposed.

You feel the weight fall upon you. Your face is now disguised with my lace veil, hiding undisclosed secrets for me to discover.

Shhhhh! "Open your eyes!"

Wearing nothing but a black, backless, satin gown, you gaze through the lace, tracing the intricacy of my frame.

You catch a glimpse of the side of my face but become lost in the eroticism of my dance. Communing intimately with the subtle sounds of ether's embrace, I find magic in the buildup, and my spirit is fueled!

And you are in trouble!

Undulating with tremors, I serenely drift towards you. My eyes terrorize your mind. Your submission provokes and tantalizes my needs to sensually ravish every inch of your flesh.

With your wrists in my hands, I push you gently, yet strongly, and guide you up against the wall. Holding you there breathless and unsure, I pause.

My arm securely rests upon your upper chest, and I graze my

fingers across your filigreed lips. Delicately outlining their subtleties, I lean in closely to warm your expression with my breath.

It takes one bite. And I pull the veil. Slowly. Carefully.

Secured between my teeth, I move backward. Step by step, I invade the space behind me, never losing eye contact with you.

Revealing your beauty, the lace hits the ground, draping a path for my return. To you!

Feeling my chest press into your body, I gradually lift your arms above your head. Resting my cheek into yours, you begin to quiver. Our body temperatures begin to rise, and our heat is now speaking a language of determination and ache.

Bodily secretions privately display what your groin is telling you: *I want more!*

Swiftly, I lower your arms and spin you around. Now, with my back up against the wall, I pull you into me. Holding your wrists behind your back with one hand, I gently grab your throat with my other.

Whispering: "I see you biting your lip. I take this as an invitation to utterly fuck you up. Look at me! Do not you dare move! Move, and I will make you pay the price for disobeying me."

Choked up, you surge into a motionless state.

Pulling your wrists forward, I guide your fingertips down both sides of my neck. Imprinting your DNA upon me before I give you more of mine.

Letting go of your wrists, I watch as your limp limbs fall to your sides, confirming the significance of your weakening exhibit.

Taking your hand, I place a single kiss atop your vibrating flesh and wickedly charm your psyche with my laugh.

Your life is no longer your own and rests solely in the sphere of my mind's eye.

Stating: "Do you trust me?" Pause! Pause! Pause ....!

Finish listening to Track 1 before starting the next track!

Start Track 2 and Slowly Begin to Read
Track 2:
"Running Up That Hill" – *Placebo*

The black leather bondage table highlights the flesh that beholds you: the flesh that shells every spec of your being into a perfect combination of curiosity and submission.

The perfect canvas for me to create my sensual obliteration and artistic reflections upon.

Fully clothed, you rest atop the leathery slab that will soon become the very device for me to bind and entrap you.

Studying every inch of you, I grace the area with my intent to gently touch you. Only your clothing is a barrier that must be removed.

Slowly. Precisely. With insistence.

The sounds of my voice quietly echo. I sing lustful hymns from the sounds that are rumbling the walls.

Pacing, I touch parts of your body. Measuredly searching for your skin. Sliding my spellbinding talons under your shirt to send arcane messages into your cells.

It is time to communicate! It is time for you to feel more of me!

The weight of my body gradually lowers onto yours. Making an impact, I hold my position. Your heartbeat serenades me back, and together we are harmonizing the most beautiful composition.

Refraining from luring your mouth into mine, I lift myself up and hover over you. Straddling your thighs, I mount my position and initiate my scheme.

Pursuing your nudity, I watch your shirt fly with ambition. I grab your hands and place them on my hips.

Circling my hips, I deliberately grind into your thighs. Passionately staring into you.

Leaning back down into your face: "Can you feel me?"

The rope dangles off the side of the bondage table. Grabbing two pieces of the silky twine, I individually tie up your wrists.

Poetically, my body moves, tethering your wrists with the rope around my waist. Bound to me. Holding you in the tender embrace of my willingness.

I reach for the button on your pants: the key to unlocking the lower parts of your uncontrollable urges. "I bet you are eager to show me. Hungry for me to explore. To touch. No, not yet!"

The ropes swing, a near miss to your head, and I am off the table. Abruptly making my move, securely binding your wrists to the kinky slab.

Crack! Off goes my whip. "You are here to please me; it is not the other way around!"

With a maleficent guffaw: "Now, where was I?"

You feel my hand slide into your waistline, separating the woven coverage from your skin. "If only!" *Whack!* The crop hits the table, awakening you to the possibilities.

With a loud thud, your shoes hit the floor.

Aggressively, I tug at your pants, spreading your denim legs. Smacking your inner thighs with my hands. The sting sends shivers down your spine, and I promise you I will be gentle.

Haaaa! "Tell me you want me inside! Tell me you want me to enrapture what it is you are hiding from me!" *Shhhh!* "Do not speak! I already know the answers!"

Overwhelming your senses with the desperation to feel more, I tease your groin with my leather crop. "I cannot wait to give it to you! Only, I have not quite decided what it is you will be receiving. Time will tell!"

Slipping the blindfold over your eyes, your mind falls deeply into a world of anticipation. Penetrating through your ability to control what was once so easy for you to do.

Powerless. Helpless.

My mind privately toys with my instincts: *Let us make you wait. And Wonder. While I delay and prepare.*

Taking my time, the sounds of shuffling, clanking, and motivation take you over.

Thinking from within: *Will you submit to my Dominance? The decision is no longer yours. Welcome, my submissive one!*

Finish listening to Track 2 before starting the next track!

Start Track 3 and Slowly Begin to Read
Track 3:
"I'll Make You Love Me" – *Kat Leon*

One button! Undone! And I am inside!
Feed my appetite! Cure my cravings! **Or else!**
With one swift pull... off they go!
Pause!

Blading your flesh with my long red nails, I trail their tips along the outside of your creamy bare legs, gradually making my appearance on your chest.

Pleasure and Pain.

Deeply piercing my nails into your nipples, I give you just enough pain to arouse your sensations. I express my kindness by offering you an additional experience with my feather tickler.

Alternating between the two vices, I make sure you get a better understanding of who I am. "Does it hurt? Does it feel nice?"

"Your face tells me maybe it does not hurt enough. Or maybe you are reacting to the pleasures of my tickler. Nothing I cannot fix! Show me it hurts when I stab my nail into your nipple. And do not disappoint me!"

Satisfied, I eat off your angst and continue to subtly and provocatively distress you.

Probing around your groin area with my pinwheel, it is time to unnerve your nerves. But first, I am going to make you give me more of what I asked for: painful expressions to satisfy my sadistic nature.

Spinning over your fleshy temples, the pinwheel incrementally glides over your already sensitive nipples.

Taking the pressure I am applying: "It hurts, right? I know it does!" *Sigh*

Your groin is preparing for disruption, throbbing for my attention. Around and around I go, pinning the area with my wheel of unsettling discomfort.

Offering you a tender giggle: "But it hurts so good!"

The ropes at the bottom of the table tempt me, and I agree to accommodate. Spreading your legs widely, I bind your ankles through the O-rings that are screwed into the bondage table.

With villainous laughter: "There is no escaping now. No one is going to help you get out. Continue to please me, and I will think about eventually letting you go. But not until …!"

Pulling up your blindfold, my eyes once again engage with yours. "Bound down and mine! I can do anything I want to you!"

Tapping your groin with my feather tickler, I taunt at your burning needs. It takes one soft moan out of your mouth, and… there it is.

Whack! I give you one firm hit and walk away.

With feline grace, I prowl back up onto the table like a predator stalking your inner desires.

Situating myself across your body, I premeditate my next move. Visually penetrating your windows to the soul, I fold into you and slowly pull back down your blindfold.

My soft touches of passionate play intrigue you, prompting and provoking your irrepressible instincts to push your body into mine. I can feel you. Hear you. And I, too, will imagine what it feels like to have you!

You are raring with arousal. Desirous. Yearning. Ready.

With secretive intent: "I could dry fuck you so good. Press my wet pussy into you and treat you like a pleasure toy. Or I could just fuck you! But I will not!"

Letting my words sink in, I suspend my movement and wait before ripping the blindfold off your eyes.

After throwing the blindfold away from me, I give you a sweet example. As our eyes link together, I slowly suck on my finger between my lips. Deeply stroking my finger in and out of my mouth, I watch you, and it is obvious that you would like a taste.

Quickly, I release the rope from your wrists and turn my body around to release the rope from your ankles.

I lay myself down on you, my back up against your chest. Grabbing your arms, I wrap them around the front of my chest and tuck my legs around the outer parts of yours. Holding you securely under me, I squeeze you and feel your heart crashing into my back.

Singing the echoing tunes that assist me from my speaker, I instantly jump off the table and grab you.

Pulling you onto your feet, I push you back up against the wall. "Touch me! I want you to! I dare you!"

Hesitation commands your obedience, and I stand in front of you, wondering what you will do!

Finish listening to Track 3 before starting the next track!

Start Track 4 and Slowly Begin to Read
Track 4:
"Angel" – *Massive Attack*

Waiting. "Still thinking? Time is up! Let's go!"

After slipping off your undergarments, I guide you backward by the neck. Lining you up, I command you to take a seat as the leather bondage swing behind you accommodates your fall. Hitched to the chains are two stirrups for me to slip your legs into. Placing your wrists into the suspension cuffs, I attach them to the hanging chains by the sides of your head. I slip on two ankle restraints and lock your ankles into the stirrups.

Walking around the room, I begin to blow out all but two candles.

I am now fully encompassed inside my underground chambers of Dominant euphoria, and it is time to turn up the heat: heated passion of naughtiness and potential danger.

Pedestalled in front of you, I take in the sight of you. Your legs spread, showing me your private vulnerabilities. Shifting your body, I know you are nervous, maybe even self-conscious. However, this still does not deter my absence of mercy for you.

Instead, you stimulate me to bask in your precious exposures.

"Is it time for a little push?" With my body between yours, my hands grab the chains. I generously give you a full view of my femininely clad breasts.

Focusing on your neck—the one I grabbed firmly—I bend in to nuzzle my face against yours. My hair falls onto your naked chest as I breathe myself into your body.

Our eyes lock. "This is going to pain you?"

I hold your gaze and trace my fingers lightly down your chest. Pulling a riding crop out from my boot, I swing up and around. Taking a step back, I strike your inner thigh hard and firmly.

I walk away, glancing back at you. Taking my vampire gloves off the bondage table, I creep back over to you and adorn my hands with my spiky assistants.

Your body, smooth and enticing, invites me in to scrape your silken surfaces. Delicately, I touch your skin. Sensations of prickly pain carefully pierce the top layer of your flesh, and I remind you that I do not have to be so nice.

I love the way you sound when you become enthralled in our moments together: the way you look at me, your desperation, your silent words that beg me to give you more of what I can offer you.

Pulling and swinging my hide flogger from off the wall, I lay into you. A collision of the softest leather tresses transfixes your flawless skin. Continuously marking my territory with my implement, I take over every inch of your body, and you are lost in pleasure: the pleasure I am giving you.

The leather falls of my flogger, smelling like the temples of India, imprint inside the cortex of your brain. Harmonizing with you, I continue to indulge on what you are submitting. "Enjoy it while you can!" *Haaaaaaaaaaaaaaaa!*

Turning to my left, I blow out one of the two remaining lit candles.

Changing my focus, my eyes glance to a side table. Lifting a small silver tray, I examine the instruments I have prepared.

The blade is sharp. My lighter is full of fluid and ready to ignite.

The room, dimmed by my choice, offers hints of light that bounce off the south-facing wall.

Carrying the tray, I make my way over to the last lit candle. Slipping the candle out of the holder, I pace in silent steps back towards you.

Holding the candle in my hand, I lean into you and blow. Complete darkness overwhelms the chamber as my wicked laughter forces its way deeply into your psyche.

Suggesting: "Do not move! I need you to barely breathe. I do not want to severely harm you!"

Taking the Zippo lighter off the tray, I invoke its fiery flame. Providing me with just enough light, I remove the sharp knife from the silvery plate and extend the blade.

"*Mmm…* yesss! What have you gotten yourself into?"

Out goes the lighter, and we are once again prisoners of the dark.

I place the blindfold comfortably back over your eyes. Without your awareness, I relight the candle to my left.

Dragging the blade of the knife down the inside of your arm, I scrape its tip against your skin to give you an idea of what I am doing. "Remember, I told you not to move!"

Given that you are remaining perfectly still, I drag the blade up towards your throat.

Letting you know I am there: knife in hand.

Whispering: "What if I didn't stop? What if I take this sharp blade and show you what I am really made of? Let me remind you, this is not a game for me."

Your body begins to quiver, and I hold my stance for one more minute. Blowing the candle back out, I reignite my lighter and tear off your blindfold. With heavy breath, you gaze about, glossy-eyed and weak.

Lighting my candle with the lighter: "I just want to give you a little bit more pain!" I set the lighter to the side and hold the candle above your chest. Slowly, I tilt its beautiful glow, and within an instant, one drop of wax hits your skin. Only I do not stop and continue to mark your flesh with red droplets of waxy torment.

Setting the candle back into its holder, I grab the knife and begin to pick away at the pieces of wax. "Lucky for you, I am a perfectionist! I will not stop until I have removed every drop of wax!"

Redirecting: "It is time to get you out of this swing. Come with me, I have something I want to show you!"

Finish listening to Track 4 before starting the next track!

Start Track 5 and Slowly Begin to Read
Track 5:
"King" – Amanati

Questioning: "Are you comfortable inside my cage? I understand it is a tight fit, but do not worry; I will have you out in no time at all."

Like a silent huntress, I pace around the cage, watching you while I conjure up my plan of attack. You look helpless and beautifully trapped inside my cage of haunting recollections: like all the others, waiting for me to pounce!

Rattling the bars with my paddle: "It is you I want to participate in my activities of fiendish pleasures!"

Unlatching the door, I command you to temporarily wait.

Back in my throne, I summon you with my finger. "Crawl. Come to me!"

Upon your presence at my feet, I inform you that you will now be worshipping your Mistress. "Kiss my hand. Now, slowly remove my boots and place them to your left side."

My legs are bare before you and welcome your touch. "I told you to touch me. Now, do it! Gently! Show me how you worship me. Thank me for my efforts. I am working hard for you today."

Massaging the tiredness out of my legs, I stare down at you. Several minutes pass. "That is enough! Stop touching me!"

I push you down onto your back. Falling atop my faux fur rug, I descend, and you are now trapped beneath me. I pin your hands over your head and bite into your neck. Sending chills throughout your body, you begin to playfully laugh.

Asking you: "What is so funny? I did not give you permission to giggle!" Promptly… you stop.

Towering over you, I place my foot on your chest. "Expand yourself. Spread those legs and arms straight out for me."

After swatting the inner parts of your thighs back and forth with my paddle, I start to tease your groin. "I know that you are wet. I don't have to touch you to know this fact."

Instructing: "Roll over and give me your bottom. Raise your bottom up for me. Do not make me work for it! Make it very easy for me to reach you!"

With your bottom raised: "I think you have earned 25 swats. Start counting!"

The sweet tempo of your voice hits every note with grace and appreciation.

Ordering you: "Now that you have received my 25 swats, show me my work. I want to see the hue of redness I have gifted you."

Pleased, I reach out my hand to you. "Grab my hand and come with me." Taking you back to the bondage table, I command you to lie face up.

Tenderly and deliberately, I touch you, calming you back down into a state of divine elation.

Rhythmically with the music, I tend to your inner and outer needs as you conform to my touch. You are submissive to my hands and controlled by my influential Dominance. Together, we are responsive to each other's intimate demands: the giver and receiver of sensual affections.

Commanding you: "Close your eyes and do not open them until you have my permission."

After placing a white sheet over your body, I take my hands and hover them over your face.

Transcending the physical, I send energetic vibrations into you. Pulsating energy, I circulate my aura of energy and light into your being.

Making my way down to your chest area, I continue with an intuitive understanding that you need my sacred and healing touch to conclude our time together.

Slowly, I move over your body, yielding to our final moments with each other and begin to think: *You have beguiled me with your trust and unveiling exposures. I thank you, for my soul is fulfilled with gratitude.*

The scene closes to end and I bid you farewell. "Thank you for entrusting me with your mind, body, and spirit. It has been my pleasure! Until we meet again! You may open your eyes. I will send someone in to release you."

CHAPTER 34

THE DUNGEON DICTIONARY

Ethical practices require all participants to prioritize consensual and mutual respect in the worlds of BDSM, Kink, and Fetish. Having a foundation that encourages trust creates an environment that enables effective communication. It is important to value one another's feelings and opinions. Respecting boundaries is essential for all players to feel safe, seen, and heard. If all measures are taken, there will be space for mutual fulfillment.

In the world of alternative sexuality, we use a specific language. This glossary reflects the various realms of erotic exploration—inclusive of all gender identities, expressions, and relationship dynamics—extending beyond traditional labels or specific BDSM practices.

As defined by standard usage, some of these words are familiar to the outside world, yet they take on a deeper weight within these pages. Others belong strictly to the shadows and sanctuaries of the scene.

Active listening

The practice of fully listening with intention and presence. One must focus on, understand, and respond to someone who is speaking, rather than just hearing their words. It involves paying attention, noticing both verbal and nonverbal cues, and giving feedback that shows you truly understand and are engaged.

Aftercare

The intentional time following a BDSM scene for participants to recover, reconnect, and process the experience. It supports emotional and physical well-being and reinforces trust. Common practices include cuddling, reassurance, hydration, scene discussion, and quiet rest.

Autogynephilia

A male's propensity to be sexually aroused by the thought of himself as a female.

Autonepiophilia

Commonly known as "Adult Baby" play. This involves participants engaging in age-play scenarios (sexual or non-sexual) that incorporate diapers, nursery themes, and caretaking dynamics.

Ball-busting (BB)

The act of inflicting sensation, pain, or constriction to the male genitals. This is a requested BDSM activity where clients may seek kicks, slaps, or punches to the scrotum for erotic fulfillment.

B&D, B/D, BD

Bondage and discipline.

BDSM

Consensual erotic practices involving bondage, discipline, Dominance/submission, and sadism/masochism. It can include physical restraint, role-play, sensation play, or giving and receiving pain for pleasure. BDSM relies on negotiation, communication, and consent, and can be sexual or non-sexual, offering intimacy, self-exploration, and connection through structured roles and experiences.

Body Worship

A consensual act of kissing, massaging, licking, or touching another person's body, often with reverence or adoration. Common areas include feet, hands, legs, buttocks, or genitals. Body worship can be sensual, sexual, or symbolic, reflecting power, devotion, and admiration. In D/s, it is often part of the power structure.

Bondage

A consensual BDSM practice involving the physical restraint of a partner using ropes, cuffs, straps, chains, or other tools. Bondage can provide immobilization, sensory control, power exchange, or aesthetic pleasure, enhancing the connection between Dominant and submissive.

Bottom

The participant in a BDSM scene who receives the action or sensation from their partner. A bottom may be tied, spanked, Dominated, or otherwise acted upon. While often submissive, the role is defined by receiving rather than giving control. Consent, communication, and negotiated limits are essential.

Boundaries

Personal limits defining what a person is comfortable with physically, emotionally, and psychologically. In BDSM, boundaries are fundamental; they must be clearly communicated, respected, and honored to ensure consent and safety.

Chastity Cage/Belt

Rules and limitations are placed on the man by placing a chastity cage around his penis and testicles. The cage is locked in place. Controlling a man's sexual pleasures may reduce anxiety and stress. Devices are used for orgasm denial or other sexual activities. (Note: Female chastity devices are equally utilized for long-term denial and control.)

Cheating

The act of being dishonest in a committed relationship to gain self-gratification. Cheating can involve emotional, kinky, or sexual engagement with someone outside the relationship without the knowledge or consent of one's partner. It is a breach of trust that disregards agreed-upon boundaries and undermines the integrity of the relationship.

Compassion

The awareness of another's suffering paired with the desire to ease it.

Consensual Non-Consent (CNC)

A form of negotiated power exchange in BDSM in which all participants explicitly agree in advance to role-play scenarios that *appear* non-consensual, while remaining fully consensual at every level. This consent is established through prior discussion, clearly defined boundaries, agreed-upon signals or safeties, and an understanding that consent can be withdrawn. What may look like a loss of control is, in reality, carefully structured trust, communication, and mutual responsibility.

Cock and Ball Torture (CBT)

The act of inflicting pain and constriction directly to the male genitals.

Consent

The foundation of all safe, sane, consensual activity. The informed, voluntary, and intentional agreement by an individual to engage in a specific activity, given with full understanding of the nature, risks, and potential consequences of that activity, without coercion, manipulation, or undue influence. Consent is ongoing and can be withdrawn at any time.

Individually, each player should have a clear understanding of their fetishes, kinks, and fantasies. When coming together to explore one's fantasies and desires, all participants must remain vigilant and aware of potential dangers.

Contrapolar Stimulation

Providing a play participant with moments of both pleasure and pain through exploration. "It hurts so good!"

Corporal Punishment (CP)

A consensual form of physical punishment that deliberately inflicts pain on the participant for psychological and physiological reasons.

Cuckolds (Cucks) and Cuckqueans

Participants who gain emotional, erotic, or psychological pleasure from knowing or watching their partner engage sexually or intimately with someone else. This dynamic may involve power exchange, teasing, or erotic humiliation. Roles are flexible and negotiated, and activities can include observation, storytelling, photos, or verbal recounting. These acts are all consensual.

Desires

Strong longings or cravings for a person, object, experience, or outcome. In intimacy and kink, desires drive fantasies, preferences, and behaviors. When explored safely and consensually, they can deepen connection and personal fulfillment.

Dominant

A participant who leads and guides a consensual BDSM or power exchange dynamic. The Dominant sets boundaries, directs the scene, and provides structure while respecting the submissive's limits and well-being. Leadership combines authority, responsibility, and emotional awareness.

Dominatrix/Dominatrice/Domme/Domina/Ma'am

A person who takes the Dominant role in BDSM, guiding and controlling a submissive partner. They lead scenes using physical, psychological, or emotional techniques, always within negotiated boundaries. Confidence, skill, and respect for limits are essential, as their authority is exercised through consent and trust.

D/s Relations

Relationships based on Dominance/submission, where one partner (Dominant) takes control and the other (submissive) willingly surrenders it. D/s can occur in casual play or long-term dynamics and may involve physical acts, psychological games, rules, or rituals. Boundaries and intensity are negotiated, and trust, communication, and consent are essential. D/s roles may exist only during scenes or extend into daily life, shaping routines, decisions, and interactions.

Drop

Physical or emotional exhaustion after a BDSM play scene.

Dungeon

In BDSM, a Dungeon refers to a dedicated space or room designed specifically for BDSM activities. It is often equipped with various tools, furniture, and accessories that support different aspects of BDSM play. The Dungeon is typically a safe and controlled environment where participants can explore power dynamics, physical sensations, and psychological experiences related to BDSM in a consensual and structured manner.

Dungeon Monitor (DM)

This person supervises and oversees interactions between participants at a BDSM event or Dungeon. The monitor will make sure that all the ethical practices are being respected and will distribute essentials (towels, equipment, etc.) to all participants as needed.

Edge Play

BDSM activities that involve heightened physical or psychological risk, requiring negotiation, experience, and consent. Edge play can be intense and potentially dangerous, so participants must fully understand the risks. Examples include fire play, breath play, cutting, piercing, extreme power exchange, and other high-risk activities. Safety, training, and trust are essential.

Effective Communication

Sharing information clearly to ensure all participants understand each other. In BDSM, it's essential before, during, and after play to establish trust, safety, and consent.

- Before Play: Discuss boundaries, limits, desires, and expectations.
- During Play: Use agreed-upon cues, signals, or safe words to maintain consent and adjust the scene as needed.
- After Play: Check in for emotional well-being, provide aftercare, and review the scene to strengthen trust and understanding.

Clear, honest communication ensures all participants feel safe, respected, and fulfilled.

Emotional Compartmentalization

When someone locks away their feelings and desires, showing only fragments of themselves to the world. It keeps honesty at a distance and intimacy just out of reach. My clients aren't cut off from their emotions, they can express them with me, and they're not necessarily suppressing them either. They've just learned where it feels safe to be honest.

Emotional Suppression

The conscious act of pushing down or avoiding the expression of emotions, especially difficult or uncomfortable ones like anger, sadness, fear, or even vulnerability.

Empathy

The ability to understand and feel what someone else is experiencing.

Enthusiasm

An active, positive energy toward something or someone. It's a visible interest, eagerness, and emotional presence that says, "I care, I'm engaged, and I want to be here."

Erotic

Relating to sexual desire, arousal, or attraction.

Erotica

Writing, art, or media created to evoke sexual desire or arousal.

Exhibitionism/Voyeurism

Pleasure from being watched or watching others.

Fantasies

Imaginative scenarios or desires a participant enjoys envisioning, often involving power exchange, role-play, or experiences outside everyday life. Fantasies allow safe exploration of deeper needs, different personas, or boundary-pushing scenarios. Clear communication ensures the line between imagination and reality is respected.

Female Dominant

A female who assumes the Dominant role in BDSM activities, exercising control and authority over a submissive partner. A Female Dominant often establishes control structures and enforces rules or boundaries within the BDSM scene. Her role may be psychological, physical, or both, depending on the interaction of roles. Examples of titles include: Dominatrix, Mistress, Domme, Domina, Dominatrice, Goddess, Queen, Lady, Miss, Ms., Governess, Ma'am, Madam, Boss, Femme Fatale, and others.

Femme Fatale

A mysterious, seductive woman who captivates and commands others through charm, beauty, and wit. In BDSM or power exchange, she uses her presence and intelligence to Dominate, blending sensuality with control. Her allure lies in maintaining authority while leaving others captivated, combining desire with a dangerous edge.

Fetish/Fetishist

A sexual fixation or strong attraction to a specific object, body part, material, or activity. For a fetishist, arousal and gratification are closely tied to this focus, which may include feet, leather, latex, uniforms, or bondage equipment. Fetishes vary widely and are typically expressed consensually, often within BDSM, kink, or other erotic practices. Open communication ensures mutual understanding and comfort.

Fetish Wear

Clothing or attire worn in BDSM or kink that reflects specific fetishes, desires, or fantasies. Often made from leather, latex, PVC, or other materials, fetish wear enhances roleplay, power dynamics, arousal, or humiliation. Examples include corsets, harnesses, stockings, uniforms, collars, leashes, and high heels. Its use is always consensual and designed to heighten the erotic experience for all participants.

Financial Domination (Findom)

A consensual financial fetish where the "pay pig" or "money servant" willingly gives control of their money or gifts to the Dominant individual (FinDomme).

Forced feminization

A consensual role-play dynamic in which one partner is required to adopt feminine clothing, behaviors, or roles as part of a negotiated power exchange.

Frisson

That sudden, electric rush that tingles through your body. It's a moment where emotion, sensation, and meaning collide, sending a shiver down your spine. It's brief, intense, and unforgettable, reminding you that you're alive in a way words sometimes can't fully capture.

Furry

A person who enjoys dressing as or embodying anthropomorphic animals, often using "fursuits" to create characters with unique personalities. Furries may role-play, express identity, or engage in playful escapism. While some incorporate BDSM, kink, or sexual roleplay, many participate for creativity, self-expression, and community. Not all furry activities are sexual.

Gender Play and Age Play

Participants will role-play as a person of the opposite sex or a person of a specific age during a scene.

Gentle Femdom (GFD)

A nurturing, "Mommy-style" Dominance. It focuses on praise, care, and "loving authority" rather than harsh punishment.

Gimps

Participants who like to dress head-to-toe in latex or leather.

Hard Limits

A participant expresses what BDSM activities they will not do. Hard limits are non-negotiable boundaries that a participant refuses to engage in, regardless of the situation. If a hard limit is crossed, the playtime experience will immediately end.

Hard Power

Relies on the physical manifestation of authority. It is the sting of the flogger, the cold bite of steel, and the undeniable restriction of restraints. It is power that can be measured in sweat, heartbeats, and red marks. Hard power isn't about cruelty; it's about immediacy. For the man who is stuck in a loop of high-stakes emails and board meetings, hard power is a gift. It is the only thing loud enough to drown out the noise of his life.

Honesty

Telling the truth and acting with sincerity, free from deceit or misrepresentation.

Humiliation Play/Degradation

Erotic pleasure derived from verbal or psychological submission.

Impact Play

Impact play is an umbrella term for all things sexual involving hitting or being hit with an object in a safe and consensual way. Impacting a participant's body with implements such as whips, riding crops, floggers, paddles, hands, and other accessories. Different levels of pain may be inflicted throughout the experience.

Implements/Tools

Tools or devices used on a consenting participant during a BDSM play scene. Examples include: whips, riding crops, paddles, pinwheels, nipple clamps, floggers, rope, chains, vampire gloves, restraints, and more.

Integrity

Integrity is doing what you said you would do, even when no one is watching and especially when it would be easier not to. It's the alignment between your words, your actions, and your values. Integrity shows up in consistency, accountability, and the willingness to hold boundaries, even when desire, money, or pressure push in another direction.

Kink-Informed

A professional (like a therapist or a coach) who doesn't judge BDSM and understands its psychological benefits.

Kink/ Kinky Sex

Kinky sex refers to sexual activities that deviate from traditional or "vanilla" practices. It involves exploring unconventional desires, fantasies, or fetishes, often incorporating elements of BDSM, power dynamics, role-playing, and various forms of sensation play. Kinky sex can include activities such as bondage, impact play, Dominance/ submission, voyeurism, exhibitionism, and more.

"Kink" Slang

The word "Kink" has become a general slang word. If someone says, *"Rainy days are my kink,"* they don't mean it's sexual. The slang is used as a very specific, intense preference that defines their "vibe."

Kinksters

Individuals who enjoy exploring BDSM, fetishes, and alternative sexual practices. They participate in consensual play, including Dominance, submission, bondage, discipline, and other kinks. Kinksters connect in clubs, events, or online communities, embracing their desires in a playful, adventurous, and non-judgmental way, whether occasionally or as part of their sexual identity.

Knowledge

Understanding or awareness gained through experience, learning, or discovery. It includes facts, skills, and insights, whether practical or theoretical. Knowledge is power!

Leather/Latex/PVC

Materials often used for clothing, fetish, or sensory stimulation.

Lifestyler in BDSM

Individuals or partners who integrate BDSM into their daily lives, not just as occasional play. They often embody roles—Dominant, submissive, switch, etc.—beyond the bedroom, applying this relational interplay to routines, relationships, and communication. Some create lifestyle contracts to define boundaries, responsibilities, and rituals, building trust, structure, and deeper connection. Being a lifestyler is about living the values of power exchange, discipline, and emotional intimacy, not just play.

Limits in BDSM

Specific activities or behaviors a participant is unwilling or hesitant to engage in during BDSM play.

- Soft limits: Hesitations that may be explored with trust or negotiation.
- Hard limits: Non-negotiable boundaries that are never crossed.

Open communication about limits is essential for safety, consent, and well-being. Claiming to have no limits should be approached with caution, as self-awareness and mental health are vital in BDSM.

Macrophilia

When someone has an attraction to extreme differences in size, often tied to the pull of a much larger body and the emotions that come with it. For many, it doesn't have to be about sex at all, but about how size makes them feel. A person may feel safe, overpowered, surrendered, or intentionally small.

Male Dominant/Master/Dom/Sir (in BDSM role)

A male who takes the leading role in a BDSM dynamic or scene. He directs activities, sets boundaries, and guides the emotional and physical experiences of his submissive partner, always within the bounds of consent, trust, and mutual understanding.

Masochist

A person who derives sexual or non-sexual pleasure from experiencing pain, humiliation, or discomfort. This can include physical acts like spanking, flogging, or bondage, as well as emotional or psychological experiences. In BDSM, masochism is explored consensually, with negotiated boundaries and safe words to ensure a safe and enjoyable experience.

Medical play/Needle play

Erotic play involving medical scenarios or body piercing.

Mind-Fucking (The Aradia Method)

Like stoking a fire, I wickedly *fuck* with the mind. A psychological rollercoaster where playful games instill uncertainty and desperation. It is the art of being "so close, yet so far." I lean in closely with intention and then take it all away; teasing, tormenting, and denying until they are ravenous for a piece of me I may or may not never truly give. In my BDSM world, mind-fucking is essentially the manipulation of the "Power Exchange" at a psychological level. Think of it as a loop between anticipation, denial, and so much more.

Munches

Informal social gatherings or meetups where individuals within the BDSM, Kink, or alternative lifestyle communities come together to socialize and connect with others who share similar interests. These events typically take place in neutral, public spaces, such as restaurants, cafes, or bars, rather than in private BDSM or Dungeon settings. The goal is to foster a comfortable, low-pressure environment where people can talk about their shared interests in kink or BDSM without the need for engaging in play or any physical activities.

Negotiation

The discussion between participants about limits, boundaries, desires, and expectations before a scene or play, ensuring consent and safety. The foundation of all safe, sane, consensual activity.

Neural Play & Biofeedback

The intersection of technology and submission. By monitoring real-time data like heart rate, breathing, and stress levels, the Dominatrix can precisely calibrate the intensity of a scene. It is "science-based" surrender and measures a man's response before he even knows it himself.

Neuro-Spicy Kink (Slang)

While "Neuro-Spicy" is a colloquialism popularized within online neurodivergent circles, the practice it describes—using BDSM for sensory regulation—is a well-recognized phenomenon among those with Autism and ADHD.

Nipple Torture (NT)

Physical pleasure and/or pain applied to the nipples of a play participant through various techniques and devices.

Non-judgmental

Accepting or listening to someone without criticizing, blaming, or making negative assumptions about them.

Open-Minded

Willing to consider, accept, and explore new ideas, experiences, or perspectives without judgment. In BDSM or relationships, it means being receptive to others' desires, kinks, and preferences, fostering understanding, empathy, and personal growth.

Pets (in BDSM context)

Participants in pet play adopt animal roles, with one as the "pet" and the other as the "handler." Pets may wear animal-themed attire, mimic behaviors, follow commands, or participate in activities like crawling, wearing collars, or being trained. Pet play is consensual, emphasizing power exchange, trust, vulnerability, and emotional bonding between pet and handler.

Play Partners

Participants who partake in BDSM, kink play, or fetish play.

Play/Playtime

Participants come together for an amount of time and engage in BDSM/Kink/Fetish activity sessions.

Polyamory/Open relationships

Non-monogamous relational structures often overlapping with kink.

Post-Sexual Play

Sessions that strip away the traditional sexual script to focus entirely on psychological care, Dominance, or "minding." It is the sanctuary found after the physical urge is gone and where the client is cared for, controlled, or disciplined without the distraction of a sexual goal.

Power Play/Exchange

A consensual BDSM dynamic where control is negotiated and exchanged, typically between a Dominant (top) and submissive (bottom). The Dominant guides or exerts authority, while the submissive willingly yields, exploring physical, psychological, and emotional power structures. Roles, rules, and limits are negotiated beforehand, with consent, communication, and trust ensuring a safe and satis-fying experience for both participants.

Protocol/Ritual

Structured rules, behaviors, or ceremonies for submissives.

RACK: Risk-Aware Consensual Kink

Playing with breath, sharp objects, needle play, cutting, extreme medical play, and other activities are inherently dangerous, and potential risks cannot be eliminated. All participants must be fully educated and trained about such practices and the risks they are about to take during the BDSM playtime.

Role-Play

Role-play involves participants acting out a wide range of con-sensual scenes and fantasies. These often center around power dy-namics, with one person assuming a Dominant role and the other taking on a submissive role. Through role-play, individuals can tem-porarily step away from their everyday identities and responsibili-ties, allowing them to safely explore different aspects of themselves in a structured, imaginative, and nonjudgmental environment.

Sadist

A person who derives emotional or sexual gratification from inflicting pain, discomfort, or humiliation on a consenting partner. In BDSM, this is always consensual, negotiated, and safe, often in-volving safe words, aftercare, and clear boundaries. Sadists typically pair with masochists to explore power, sensation, and emotional with mutual respect.

Safe, Sane, and Consensual (SSC)

A guiding principle in BDSM ensuring all participants are of sound mind, give voluntary consent, and engage in activities within negotiated safety limits. SSC emphasizes physical and emotional safety, mental well-being, clear communication, and the right to withdraw consent at any time, distinguishing consensual play from abuse.

Safe Word

A safe word is a pre-agreed code word or signal used by participants in BDSM or kink play to slow down, adjust, or immediately stop an activity. It is an essential part of safe, sane, and consensual play. Safe words ensure that everyone involved feels empowered to maintain their physical and emotional safety during a scene. The words must be respected without question, and players should always check in afterward during aftercare to ensure well-being and emotional support.

Common systems include: "Green" – Everything is okay, continue. "Yellow" – Slow down or check in; something may be uncomfortable. "Red" – Stop immediately; the scene is over.

S&M, S/M, SM

Stands for Sadism and Masochism, the consensual practice of inflicting or receiving pain, humiliation, or control for sexual or emotional pleasure. Sadists enjoy giving, masochists enjoy receiving, and all activities are negotiated with clear boundaries, consent, and communication. S&M often overlaps with power exchange, Dominance, and submission.

Scene

The setting or event where BDSM activities occur. A scene includes the physical space, roles, and activities of participants, with intensity, style, and duration defined by negotiation and agreed-upon boundaries.

Seasoned Player

An experienced participant in BDSM who understands the dynamics, safety, consent, and nuances of kinky play. Seasoned players are skilled in communication, boundaries, and aftercare, can adapt to different partners or scenes, and often guide or mentor newcomers to ensure safe and enjoyable experiences.

Sensory Play

Broad term for engaging sight, sound, touch, taste, or smell.

Service Submission

Serving a partner as an act of devotion.

Session

A designated period for BDSM or kinky play, structured around exploring power dynamics, role-play, or specific desires. Sessions vary in length, intensity, and focus, and are negotiated in advance to establish boundaries, limits, and expectations. Aftercare often follows to help participants transition safely and comfortably.

Soft Limits

After trust is built within the BDSM relationship, participants may be willing to partake in certain activities they might not have otherwise wanted to try. Soft limits are activities that a participant may be hesitant about but could potentially be open to with the right circumstances, trust, or negotiation.

Soft Power

The art of psychological gravity. It is the authority that doesn't need to shout to be heard or strike to be felt. These interactions operate from a quieter place and focus on tone, the precision of a gaze, and the usage of trust to guide a person's mind into complete surrender.

Slave

A consensual role in D/s or M/s relationships where a participant willingly gives a high degree of control to a Dominant during playtime. Often part of long-term or 24/7 dynamics, this role is negotiated with clear boundaries, trust, and mutual consent, and can be deeply affirming and meaningful for the participant.

Somatic Kink

The practice of using physical sensation to bridge the gap between the mind and the body. Rather than focusing on a sexual "peak," it uses the nervous system to release stored stress and trauma. It is the art of "feeling" in a world that forces us to go numb.

Sound Frequency

The rate at which sound waves vibrate, measured in hertz. In the Dungeon, frequency is the pitch of power. High frequencies, like the sharp *crack* of a whip or a stinging slap, trigger an immediate, jolting "fight or flight" response in the body. Low frequencies, like a deep, resonant command or the thud of a heavy paddle, vibrate deep in the chest, grounding the submissive and demanding a different kind of surrender.

Sound Waves

The invisible energy that travels from my hand to your body. Measured in Hertz (Hz), these oscillations determine how a sensation is processed. A single, sharp cycle creates a "sting," while a rhythmic, low-cycle vibration creates a "throb." Understanding sound waves allows a Dominant to orchestrate a scene like a symphony, moving the submissive between sharp peaks of pain and deep valleys of relief.

Squick

The uncomfortable feeling you may get when you see or hear about kinky activities.

Sub-Drop/Dom-Drop

The emotional "crash" some people feel 24–48 hours after a high-intensity session.

Submission

The act of consciously yielding control to a Dominant, either temporarily during a scene or as part of an ongoing relationship.

Submission can be physical, emotional, or psychological, depending on the dynamic.

Submissive/Bottom/Sub

A participant who willingly gives up control to a Dominant. Submissives may surrender physically, emotionally, or psychologically, enjoying guidance and direction during scenes or relationships. Their role can be temporary or part of a long-term dynamic.

Switch

A participant who enjoys both Dominant and submissive roles. Switches can alternate roles within a scene or across different sessions, adding flexibility and variety to BDSM play.

Taboo Fantasies

Erotic thoughts or imagined scenarios that explore socially, morally, or culturally forbidden themes. In BDSM, these fantasies are explored consensually, ethically, and with clear boundaries, often reflecting curiosity, power, or emotional exploration.

Temperature Play

Using hot or cold stimuli (ice, wax, metal) for sensation.

The Craft

The art and skill of creating safe, meaningful, and transformative BDSM experiences. It combines physical techniques, emotional intelligence, psychological insight, and ethical awareness, ensuring scenes are intentional, consensual, and deeply engaging for all participants.

Tickling/Erotic Tickling

Stimulating sensations for play or control.

Top/Dominant

A Top is the one who gives stimulation, direction, or sensation. This could include physical actions (like spanking or bondage), psychological control (like verbal Domination), or orchestrating a scene (like a power exchange role-play). A Dominant goes a step further, taking on longer-term authority in a consensual power exchange relationship, where they may guide or control aspects of the submissive's behavior, routines, or mindset, based on agreed-upon terms.

Topping from the Bottom

When a submissive tries to direct or control the actions of the Dominant during a scene, undermining the agreed-upon power dynamic. While sometimes consensual, doing so without agreement disrupts the flow and authority of the Dominant.

Transparency

Openly sharing information, motives, and processes, making actions and decisions clear and accessible to others.

Tribute/Donation

Monetary compensation is gifted to the Professional Dominatrix/ Pro Domme/Dominatrix for services rendered. Gifts and other pricey goods are accepted and appreciated as well.

Vanilla Person / Vanilla Sex

A person who does not engage in BDSM, kink, or fetish practices. Vanilla sex refers to intimate experiences that are non-kinky, without power dynamics, role-play, or unconventional practices. While "vanilla" describes the baseline, it is not a term of judgment; it is simply the starting point from which the kinky journey departs.

Virtual Reality (VR) Scenes

Digital immersion designed to test boundaries in a safe, simulated environment. VR allows the mind to enter the Dungeon while the physical body remains behind, creating a bridge between fantasy and the physical world. A Dominant can assign a participant an **Avatar** to serve as a psychological shield, allowing them to shed their "public face" completely. This technology enables global Dominance; a Dominant can maintain a **"Sovereign" presence** over a client in Tokyo from a studio in New York without ever physically touching them.

Vulnerabilities

The courageous willingness to show emotions and parts of the self openly, even at the risk of being judged. In the context of the Dungeon, vulnerability is a form of profound strength, it is the raw material required for connection, healing, and authentic self-discovery.

Wax Play

A form of sensation play involving the dripping of low-temperature candle wax onto the body. It combines thermal sensation with the psychological thrill of "marking" the body temporarily.

WIITWD

An acronym for **"What It Is That We Do."** A broad, community-based term used to encompass the entire spectrum of alternative sexuality, BDSM, and kink culture without needing to list every specific practice.

REFERENCES

1. **American Psychiatric Association.** (2013). *Diagnostic and statistical manual of mental disorders* (5ᵗʰ ed.). American Psychiatric Publishing.

2. **Ariely, D., & Loewenstein, G.** (2006). The heat of the moment: The effect of sexual arousal on sexual decision making. *Journal of Behavioral Decision Making,* 19(2), 87-98.

3. **Beauregard, M., & Paquette, V.** (2006). Neural correlates of conscious self-regulation of emotion. *Journal of Neuroscience,* 26(38), 9882-9887.

4. **Berridge, K. C., & Robinson, T. E.** (1998). What is the role of dopamine in reward: hedonic impact, reward learning, or incentive salience? *Brain Research Reviews,* 28(3), 309-369.

5. **Cutlip, S. M., & Center, A. H.** (1952). *Effective Public Relations: Pathways to Public Favor.* Prentice-Hall.

6. **Daley, J.** (2016, June 20). What happens in the brain when music causes chills? *Smithsonian Magazine.* https://www.smithsonianmag.com

7. **Faccio, E., Castro, E., & Pazzaglia, F.** (2021). Rejection sensitivity in BDSM practitioners: Evidence for emotional resilience. *Journal of Sexual Medicine,* 18(5), 876-885.

8. **Georgiadis, J. R., & Kringelbach, M. L.** (2012). The human sexual response cycle: Brain imaging evidence linking sex to other pleasures. *Progress in Neurobiology,* 98(1), 49–81.

9. Merriam-Webster. (n.d.). Merriam-Webster.com dictionary. Retrieved June-December, 2025, from https://www.merriam-webster.com

10. **Moser, C., & Kleinplatz, P. J.** (2006). DSM and the paraphilias: An argument for removal. *Journal of Psychology & Human Sexuality, 18*(3-4), 91-109.

11. **Oxford University Press.** (n.d.). Oxford Languages. https://languages.oup.com

12. **Pfaus, J. G.** (2009). Paths of desire: The neural science of sexual motivation. *Progress in Neurobiology, 88*(1), 144-159.

13. **Sachs, M. E., Ellis, R. J., Schlaug, G., & Loui, P.** (2016). Brain connectivity reflects human aesthetic responses to music. *Social and Affective Neuroscience.* doi:10.1093/scan/nsw009

14. **Sescousse, G., Caldú, X., Segura, B., & Dreher, J.-C.** (2013). Processing of primary and secondary rewards: A quantitative meta-analysis and review of human functional neuroimaging studies. *Neuroscience & Biobehavioral Reviews, 37*(4), 681-696.

15. **South Denver Psychotherapy.** (n.d.). *Emotional vs. Physical Cheating: What's the Difference?* South Denver Therapy.

16. **WebMD.** (n.d.). *15 signs your husband may be cheating.* Retrieved June 28, 2025, from https://www.webmd.com

17. **Westmaas, R.** (2019, August 1). What getting chills from music says about your brain. *Discovery.*

18. **Wismeijer, A. A. J., & van Assen, M. A. L. M.** (2013). Psychological characteristics of BDSM practitioners. *Journal of Sexual Medicine, 10*(8), 1943-1952.

Editorial Note

Portions of this book were edited with the assistance of AI tools:

- **Mistral AI.** (2026). *Le Chat.* https://mistral.ai
- **OpenAI.** (2026). *ChatGPT.* https://chat.openai.com
- **Google.** (2026). *Gemini.* https://gemini.google.com

This work was authored by Aradia Rain and refined with the assistance of AI technology to ensure the clarity and precision of the message. All core content, ideas, and final narratives remain the author's own; AI was utilized solely as a tool for editing, phrasing, and structural refinement.

ACKNOWLEDGMENTS

This book exists because of the courage, honesty, and relentless discipline required to bring it to life.

To everyone who invited me into their worlds behind closed doors: Thank you for your trust, your stories, and your vulnerability. Though you remain unnamed and unseen, your experiences live in the heart of these pages. Our time together was as much a lesson in healing as it was an exploration of the beautiful complexity of being human.

To those who offered editorial guidance and feedback—both human and AI-assisted: Thank you for helping me translate raw ideas into a clear, meaningful message. The way you honored my experiences and provided the perspective to help move this project forward made all the difference. I deeply appreciate the focus and energy you provided to stand by me throughout this process.

To the community of kinksters, educators, and advocates: Thank you for your tireless work in normalizing informed consent, emotional intelligence, and embodied sexuality. Your work matters more than most realize; this book is an echo of that mission.

And finally, to the reader: Whether you came here for insight, affirmation, curiosity, or catharsis, I see you. May these words cut through the noise, remind you of your power, and guide you toward your own truth.

ABOUT THE AUTHOR

Aradia Rain is a Professional Dominatrix, film actress, and Certified Life Coach with over two decades of lived experience. Beyond the dungeon, she is a business owner and mother, who serves as a volunteer "Human Book" with the Human Library Organization, where she uses personal storytelling to dismantle stigmas and challenge societal prejudices.

Based in one of the country's busiest metropolitan hubs, Aradia has built a career navigating the hidden truths of the male psyche: their fantasies, power plays, and emotional contradictions. Her work is forged in more than just a commanding presence; it is built on radical honesty, fierce compassion, and a deep understanding of the human condition.

Whether in the dungeon, on the page, or in conversation, she is committed to eroding shame and encouraging others to own their truths without apology.

This is her debut book—but not her final word.

Connect with Aradia Rain

Inquiries: iamaradiarain@gmail.com
Socials:
Instagram: aradiarain
X:AradiaRain
Tik Tok: aradia.rain
Facebook: Aradia Rain

"The truth is only the beginning. Let's keep the conversation going."